Jasmine Cookbook

Over 35 recipes to design and develop Jasmine tests to produce world-class JavaScript applications

Munish Sethi

PUBLISHING

BIRMINGHAM - MUMBAI

Jasmine Cookbook

First published: April 2015

Production reference: 1200415

Published by Packt Publishing Ltd.
Livery Place
35 Livery Street
Birmingham B3 2PB, UK.

ISBN 978-1-78439-716-6

www.packtpub.com

Credits

Author

Munish Sethi

Reviewer

Devin Weaver

Commissioning Editor

Amarabha Banerjee

Acquisition Editor

Larissa Pinto

Content Development Editor

Ajinkya Paranjape

Technical Editor

Vivek Pala

Copy Editors

Pranjali Chury

Kriti Sharma

Project Coordinator

Harshal Ved

Proofreaders

Martin Diver

Elinor Perry-Smith

Paul Hindle

Indexer

Mariammal Chettiyar

Production Coordinator

Nitesh Thakur

Cover Work

Nitesh Thakur

About the Author

Munish Sethi is a postgraduate in computer science and MBA in IT from SCDL.
He has 18 years of industry experience and has a sound knowledge of test automation,
test- and behavior-driven development, white box testing, big data testing, review techniques,
test estimation, and requirement analysis. Currently, he is working with Impetus Infotech
Pvt. Ltd. where he plays the role of test craftsman and automation architect. With his diverse
experience, he helps engineering teams with deliveries and also with designing test solutions
and formulating test strategies for his clients. He has also designed and implemented many
automation frameworks (such as modular, hybrid, data-driven, keyword-driven, and page-object
models) using Jasmine/Protractor, QTP, Selenium Web driver, Junit, TestNG, SOAPUI, Sikuli, Test
Complete, and so on. He's very keen to explore new and upcoming tools and technologies.

He has worked with both product- and services-based organizations. Munish's Twitter
handle is `@munishksethi`.

First of all, I would like to thank Lord Krishna for inspiring me at every
movement. You have given me the power to believe in my passion and
pursue my dreams. I could have never done this without the faith I have in
you, the Almighty.

I would like to take this opportunity to thank the team at Packt Publishing
for all of their outstanding work in helping to bring this book to fruition.
They were very supportive and their processes are designed to improve the
quality of the book. I have thoroughly enjoyed working with them throughout
the entire process, and appreciate their candid feedback, which ultimately
raised the standard of my work. I would like to give a big thank you to the
reviewer, Devin Weaver, whose constructive criticisms and observations
have also served to raise the standard of the final product.

I would also like to say thanks to Rakesh Gupta, AVP of Engineering, Impetus,
for his continuous support and for encouraging me to write this book.

Finally, I would like to say thanks to my wife, Sweeni Sethi, and my kids,
Pranjali and Punya, for their never-ending support, which keeps me going.

I would like to thank my mother, Sudesh Sethi, and father, Jagdish Lal Sethi,
for giving me constant morale throughout my life.

About the Reviewer

Devin Weaver is a software developer by day and a software hobbyist and mentor by night. His interest in programming started with his first Commodore 64, where he learned BASIC from the manual. Since then he has studied many languages, and JavaScript is among his favorites. He is dedicated towards his family. He continues to learn and strives to achieve a level of quality above the rest.

I would like to thank my life partner, Maddy Pendleton-Weaver, for her unwavering confidence in me, and her love. I thank my mother, Marcia Ball, for her continued support and encouragement of my interests.

www.PacktPub.com

Support files, eBooks, discount offers, and more

For support files and downloads related to your book, please visit www.PacktPub.com.

Did you know that Packt offers eBook versions of every book published, with PDF and ePub files available? You can upgrade to the eBook version at www.PacktPub.com and as a print book customer, you are entitled to a discount on the eBook copy. Get in touch with us at service@packtpub.com for more details.

At www.PacktPub.com, you can also read a collection of free technical articles, sign up for a range of free newsletters and receive exclusive discounts and offers on Packt books and eBooks.

https://www2.packtpub.com/books/subscription/packtlib

Do you need instant solutions to your IT questions? PacktLib is Packt's online digital book library. Here, you can search, access, and read Packt's entire library of books.

Why Subscribe?

- ▶ Fully searchable across every book published by Packt
- ▶ Copy and paste, print, and bookmark content
- ▶ On demand and accessible via a web browser

Free Access for Packt account holders

If you have an account with Packt at www.PacktPub.com, you can use this to access PacktLib today and view nine entirely free books. Simply use your login credentials for immediate access.

Table of Contents

Preface

Today, application quality is a major concern among organizations. Lack of quality not only affects one's credibility but is also detrimental for end users and business operations. It is very important to develop applications by applying best practices and effective processes, and exercising the entire code base before deploying it on the production.

Jasmine is an open source Behavior-Driven Development (BDD) framework for testing JavaScript applications. It encourages good testing practices and application development using a BDD approach. Jasmine provides a rich set of libraries to design and develop tests for JavaScript (or JavaScript-enabled platform) applications. The entire application code can be exercised to ensure the quality and correctness of functional behavior. Jasmine also provides the mechanism to define custom functions and spies to test end-to-end (E2E) scenarios.

This book is written to get you up and running with Jasmine faster than any other book. Each chapter focuses on a specific aspect of Jasmine and is broken down into easy-to-follow recipes. While most chapters make use of previous skills that you'll have learnt from earlier the text, you don't necessarily need to read each chapter in order. Each recipe begins with the explicit steps that you need to accomplish the goal of the recipe, followed by an explanation as well as some other ideas you may wish to explore on your own.

Lastly, let's focus on building high-quality apps with Jasmine to minimize defect leakage in production. All you need is this book, a computer with Jasmine, and a constructive mind.

What this book covers

Chapter 1, Getting Started with Jasmine Framework, introduces the basics of Jasmine, demonstrates its usage, and explains how unit tests will be designed for JavaScript. This also discusses the role of matchers for writing Jasmine specs.

Chapter 2, Jasmine with TDD and BDD Processes, describes how Jasmine tests will be designed along with application code using TDD and BDD processes, and also explains how to write Jasmine specs for new and existing code by applying TDD and BDD processes.

Chapter 3, Customizing Matchers and Jasmine Functions, elaborates Jasmine functions and the need of custom matchers and their usage. This also examines the concept of pending specs and designing Jasmine specs for exceptions.

Chapter 4, Designing Specs from Requirement, explains how meaningful specs can be designed by determining test requirements.

Chapter 5, Jasmine Spies, illustrates the concept of mocking and how to create Jasmine tests for methods or objects which are dependent on other methods or objects. This also demonstrates how to develop custom or user-defined mock functions.

Chapter 6, Jasmine with AJAX, jQuery, and Fixtures, elaborates how to design and develop a Jasmine spec for AJAX calls, jQuery, and asynchronous operations. This also examines the data-driven approach and how to design Jasmine specs with fixtures to manipulate DOM.

Chapter 7, Code Coverage with Jasmine Tests, covers how to configure code coverage tools and generate coverage reports using karma and istanbul, and it also explores how to increase code coverage for the existing or legacy code.

Chapter 8, Jasmine with Other Tools, describes how to implement Jasmine specs for AngularJS, CoffeeScript, and Node.js.

Chapter 9, Developing JavaScript Apps Using Jasmine - A Real-time Scenario, elaborates a real-time scenario to develop JavaScript applications using Jasmine and explains how to design specs with HTML using BDD approach, and also examines how to develop specs for a Change Request and validate the output of a method, object, or unit using the data-driven approach.

What you need for this book

Jasmine should be pre-installed on your computer before starting with *Jasmine Cookbook*. We'll be working with Jasmine 2.x. You can download the Jasmine from `https://github. com/pivotal/jasmine/releases`. We will be using Notepad++ or WebStorm/NetBeans IDE to design the Jasmine specs and the Firefox, Chrome, or Internet Explorer browser to run the specs. You will need to have access to a reasonably modern computer, with a reasonably modern operating system. For Windows users, Windows XP, 7 or newer should do fine. I'd recommend at least 2 gigabytes of RAM. Mac OS X and Linux users should also be OK, as long they have a similar or superior amount of RAM.

Who this book is for

If you are a competent JavaScript developer who wants to design and implement tests using Jasmine in order to minimize bugs in the production environment, then this book is ideal for you. Some familiarity with unit testing and code coverage concepts such as branch coverage along with basic knowledge of Node.js, AngularJS, and CoffeeScript is required.

Sections

In this book, you will find several headings that appear frequently (Getting ready, How to do it, How it works, There's more, and See also).

To give clear instructions on how to complete a recipe, we use these sections as follows:

Getting ready

This section tells you what to expect in the recipe, and describes how to set up any software or any preliminary settings required for the recipe.

How to do it...

This section contains the steps required to follow the recipe.

How it works...

This section usually consists of a detailed explanation of what happened in the previous section.

There's more...

This section consists of additional information about the recipe in order to make the reader more knowledgeable about the recipe.

See also

This section provides helpful links to other useful information for the recipe.

Conventions

In this book, you will find a number of text styles that distinguish between different kinds of information. Here are some examples of these styles and an explanation of their meaning.

Code words in text, database table names, folder names, filenames, file extensions, pathnames, dummy URLs, user input, and Twitter handles are shown as follows: "Run spec file `TDS_spec.js` with the Jasmine runner (that is, `SpecRunner.html`)."

A block of code is set as follows:

```
describe("Employees of <XYZ> Company:",function(){
  //Scenario -1
  describe("Tax deducted for Indian Employees, ", function(){
    it("Currency should be used INR", function(){
    });
  });
});
```

When we wish to draw your attention to a particular part of a code block, the relevant lines or items are set in bold:

```
describe("Employees of <XYZ> Company:",function(){
  describe("Tax/TDS Currency", function(){
    //Scenario -1
    it("Currency should be used INR", function(){
      var myCurrency = new Currency("INDIA");
      expect(myCurrency.currency).toBe("INR");
    });
```

Any command-line input or output is written as follows:

```
npm --version
npm install karma-cli
```

New terms and **important words** are shown in bold. Words that you see on the screen, for example, in menus or dialog boxes, appear in the text like this: "Here, notice that the error message is changed to **Currency is undefined**. Earlier, it was **myCurrency is undefined**."

Warnings or important notes appear in a box like this.

Tips and tricks appear like this.

Reader feedback

Feedback from our readers is always welcome. Let us know what you think about this book—what you liked or disliked. Reader feedback is important for us as it helps us develop titles that you will really get the most out of.

To send us general feedback, simply e-mail feedback@packtpub.com, and mention the book's title in the subject of your message.

If there is a topic that you have expertise in and you are interested in either writing or contributing to a book, see our author guide at www.packtpub.com/authors.

Customer support

Now that you are the proud owner of a Packt book, we have a number of things to help you to get the most from your purchase.

Downloading the example code

You can download the example code files from your account at http://www.packtpub.com for all the Packt Publishing books you have purchased. If you purchased this book elsewhere, you can visit http://www.packtpub.com/support and register to have the files e-mailed directly to you.

Errata

Although we have taken every care to ensure the accuracy of our content, mistakes do happen. If you find a mistake in one of our books—maybe a mistake in the text or the code—we would be grateful if you could report this to us. By doing so, you can save other readers from frustration and help us improve subsequent versions of this book. If you find any errata, please report them by visiting http://www.packtpub.com/submit-errata, selecting your book, clicking on the **Errata Submission Form** link, and entering the details of your errata. Once your errata are verified, your submission will be accepted and the errata will be uploaded to our website or added to any list of existing errata under the Errata section of that title.

To view the previously submitted errata, go to https://www.packtpub.com/books/content/support and enter the name of the book in the search field. The required information will appear under the **Errata** section.

Piracy

Piracy of copyrighted material on the Internet is an ongoing problem across all media. At Packt, we take the protection of our copyright and licenses very seriously. If you come across any illegal copies of our works in any form on the Internet, please provide us with the location address or website name immediately so that we can pursue a remedy.

Please contact us at `copyright@packtpub.com` with a link to the suspected pirated material.

We appreciate your help in protecting our authors and our ability to bring you valuable content.

Questions

If you have a problem with any aspect of this book, you can contact us at `questions@packtpub.com`, and we will do our best to address the problem.

1

Getting Started with Jasmine Framework

In this chapter, we will cover:

- ▶ Writing your first Jaşmine test
- ▶ Adding specs to your Jasmine test
- ▶ Adding expectations and matchers to the test
- ▶ Applying different matchers to the Jasmine test
- ▶ Applying setup and teardown functions to the Jasmine test
- ▶ Using the "this" keyword

Introduction

Nowadays, JavaScript has become the de facto programming language to build and empower frontend/web applications. We can use JavaScript to develop simple or complex applications. However, applications in production are often vulnerable to bugs caused by design inconsistencies, logical implementation errors, and similar issues. For this reason, it is usually difficult to predict how applications will behave in real-time environments, which leads to unexpected behavior, non-availability of applications, or outages for short or long durations. This generates lack of confidence and dissatisfaction among application users. Also, high cost is often associated with fixing the production bugs. Therefore, there is a need to develop applications that are of a high quality and that offer high availability.

Jasmine plays a vital role to establish effective development process by applying efficient testing processes. Jasmine is an excellent framework for testing JavaScript code both in browser and on the server side. We well use version 2.0.1 of Jasmine in this book. In this chapter, we will cover how tests can be written for JavaScript code using the Jasmine framework. You will also learn how various Jasmine matchers play a pivotal role for writing the tests.

Writing your first Jasmine test

To write our first Jasmine test, we will use a program that will calculate the factorial of a given number.

"As a user, I want to validate/evaluate factorial functionality so that I can get the exact factorial value for a given number."

Let's consider some scenarios in the current context:

▶ **Scenario-1**: Factorial value should be evaluated for a given positive number
▶ **Scenario-2**: A 'null' value should be returned for negative numbers

Getting ready

To start writing Jasmine tests, you need to download Jasmine from the official website. Download the **Jasmine Standalone** release (that is, **jasmine-standalone-2.x.x.zip**) from the following website:

```
https://github.com/pivotal/jasmine/releases
```

How to do it...

To start a Jasmine test, perform the following steps:

1. First, you need to create a spec file under the `/spec` folder. Create the `Factorial_spec.js` file and code the following lines:

    ```
    describe("Factorial", function() {

    });
    ```

2. Next, add the following code to `Factorial_spec.js`:

    ```
    describe("Factorial", function() {
        it("should get factorial of given number", function() {

        });
    });
    ```

3. Further, add another `it` block to your Jasmine test and use the following code:

```
describe("Factorial", function() {
    it("should get factorial of given number", function() {

    });
    it("should return null value for passing negative number or
less/more than one argument", function() {

    });
});
```

4. To implement the factorial functionality, we need JavaScript code. So, create a `Factorial.js` file and put it under the `/src` folder:

```
function factorial(num)
{
    if (num==1 && factorial.arguments.length == 1) {
        return 1;
    }
    else if (num >1 && factorial.arguments.length == 1) {
        return num*factorial(num-1);
    }
    else {
        return null;   /* Validate if parameter is passed as negative
number or less/more than one parameter */
    }
}
```

5. Now, to test the `Factorial` functionality, we will implement it in the Jasmine test using the following code:

```
describe("Factorial", function() {
    it("should get factorial of given number", function() {
    expect(factorial(3)).toEqual(6);
    });
    it("should return null value for passing negative number or
less/more than one arguments", function() {
    expect(factorial(-3)).toEqual(null);
    });
});
```

In the preceding code snapshot, notice that we implemented both scenarios with the help of assertions using expectations and matchers.

An expectation in Jasmine is an assertion that is either true or false.

Jasmine provides the `expect` function to test the code. It accepts a value called the actual. Furthermore, it is chained with the matcher function, which accepts the expected value. In current context, the matcher function is `toEqual`.

To learn more about expectation and matchers, refer to the recipes *Adding expectations and matchers to the test* and *Applying different matchers to the Jasmine test* in this chapter.

6. To run Jasmine's spec for both scenarios, we need to add the reference of the JavaScript file (that is, `Factorial.js`) and spec file (that is, `Factorial_spec.js`) to the test runner (that is, `SpecRunner.html` file). Use the following code:

```
<!-- include source files here... -->
  <script type="text/javascript" src="src/Factorial.js"></script>

<!-- include spec files here... -->
  <script type="text/javascript" src="spec/Factorial_spec.js"></
script>
```

In your test runner (that is, `SpecRunner.html`), you can see the reference to different source files (that is, `Player.js` and `Sonj.js`) and spec files (that is, `SpecHelper.js` and `PlayerSpec.js`). These files are shipped along with the Jasmine standalone release. Here, you need to remove the references to these files and add the reference to your source file (that is, `Factorial.js`) and spec file (that is, `Factorial_spec.js`).

7. Now, execute the test suite by opening the Jasmine runner (that is `SpecRunner.html`) in a browser, and you will see something similar to the following screenshot, which will let you know that the tests have run successfully:

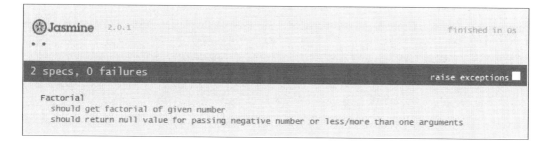

The `SpecRunner.html` file acts as a test runner for Jasmine tests. We can also call it the Jasmine runner. Indeed, from now onwards, throughout this book, we will refer to the `SpecRunner.html` file as the Jasmine runner.

How it works...

Let's take a look at what we did in this recipe.

In step 1, we defined the test suite using the `describe` function. It is a global Jasmine function and accepts the following two parameters:

- `String`: Usually, we mention this parameter as the name of the test suite corresponding to the functionality that is currently being tested. A test suite represents a specific functionality or component of our application. In our case, it is `Factorial`.
- `Function`: This is a block of code that implements the suite. You can create *n* suites corresponding to functionality/application components, as needed.

In step 2, we defined the condition of scenario 1 by implementing the `it` block inside the `describe` block. It's also a global Jasmine function that accepts two parameters, that is, a `string` and a `function`:

- `String`: This is the title of the spec. In our case, we created the spec as *should get factorial of given number* for scenario 1.
- `Function`: Here, we write Jasmine code (test code or the actual 'spec'), corresponding to the spec title to test the JavaScript code.

In step 3, we defined another condition for scenario 2 by adding a second spec using an additional `it` block. You can define as many specs within a test suite as your test requires.

In step 4, to test the JavaScript code, we created the `Factorial.js` file and wrote code for factorial functionality. We defined the conditions for scenario 1 and scenario 2 in the factorial function.

In step 5, we passed a value to the `expect` (that is, the expectation) function, which needs to be tested; this value is called the actual value. Furthermore, the `expect` function is chained to the matcher function, which takes the expected value. On the basis of actual versus expected value, it reports to Jasmine that the spec has either passed or failed.

In step 6, to test and execute the JavaScript code, we included the reference of the JavaScript file (`Factorial.js`) and the corresponding spec file (`Factorial_spec.js`) in the `SpecRunner.html` file.

See also

▶ To understand more about specs and how to apply expectations and matchers, refer to the recipes *Adding specs to your Jasmine test* and *Adding expectations and matchers to the test*.

 Jasmine is a **Behavior-Driven Development** (**BDD**) framework. However, for now, we are not following the BDD process to write Jasmine tests as it is outside the scope of this recipe. In *Chapter 2, Jasmine with TDD and BDD Processes*, we will discuss in detail how Jasmine test and application code is developed alongside using **Test-Driven Development** (**TDD**) and BDD process.

Adding specs to your Jasmine test

To write specs for a given requirement, let's consider the following example of <ABC> company.

<ABC> is a product-based company that develops cutting edge software/products for sales and inventory control systems. Currently, they have one base product that offers all the standard features required of a sales and inventory system (for example, generating sales invoice, sales return/issue, vendor analysis, billing management, budgeting, finance, stock update, and so on). They also customize base products as per customers' specific needs. Recently, the <ABC> company has provided software to a spare parts company and the customer is performing acceptance testing for the inventory system.

"As a Store Administrator, I want to update stock on every new transaction so that I can get the balance/stock in hand for further usage."

Let's consider some scenarios in the current context, that is, updating inventory stock in the event of any new transaction:

▶ **Scenario-1**: Inventory Stock should be updated on account of item(s) sale or issue of item(s)

▶ **Scenario-2**: Inventory stock should be updated on return of any item(s)

▶ **Scenario-3**: Inventory stocks should be updated on receiving/procuring new item(s)

How to do it...

To write specs to a Jasmine test, perform the following steps:

1. First, you need to create a spec file under the /spec folder. Create the InventoryStock_spec.js file and code the following lines:

```
describe("Inventory Stock", function() {
//Scenario - 1

});
```

2. Next, use the following code to define specs:

```
describe("Inventory Stock", function() {
//Scenario - 1
    it("Inventory Stock should be updated on sale/issue of an
item", function() {

    });
  });
```

3. Now, to run the spec defined in the previous step, we need to add the reference of the spec file (that is, InventoryStock_spec.js) to the Jasmine runner (that is, SpecRunner.html file):

```
<!-- include spec files here... -->
  <script type="text/javascript" src="spec/InventoryStock_spec.
js"></script>
```

4. To execute the test suite, open the Jasmine runner in a browser and you will see the spec results, as shown in the following screenshot:

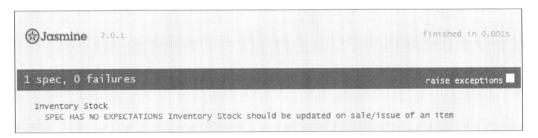

You can see two things from the execution results:

- ❑ The spec is prefixed with **SPEC HAS NO EXPECTATION**.
- ❑ The spec passes even if we do not specify any expectation within the `it` block. In Jasmine, we need to implement an assertion to make the spec pass or fail. An assertion is a comparison between two values/expression that results in a Boolean value. A spec will only be considered passed if the assertion returns the Boolean value as `true`.

5. Next, use the following code to optimize step 2:

```
describe("Inventory Stock", function() {
    //Scenario - 1
it("Inventory Stock should be updated on sale of item", function()
{

    });
it("Inventory Stock should be updated on issue of an item within
organization", function() {

    });
});
```

In the preceding code snapshot, you can notice that we further divided the spec into two specs where the first spec represents a sale and the other spec is for the issuing of an item. Now, both the specs represent unique behavior.

It is highly recommended to refactor the requirement up to granular level. This will help you to analyze test execution results. Moreover, you (and other stakeholders) can easily identify root causes and map precisely the failed specs with application code.

6. Next, let's use the following test code to implement the specs functionality:

```
describe("Inventory Stock", function() {
    //Scenario - 1
it("Inventory Stock should be updated on sale of item", function()
{
            var stockinhand_item1=11;
            var item1 = 1;
            var transaction = 'SALE';
            expect(stockinhand_item1-item1).toEqual(10);
        });
```

```
it("Inventory Stock should be updated on issue of an item within
organization", function() {
        var stockinhand_item1=11;
        var item1 = 1;
        var transaction = 'ISSUE';
        expect(stockinhand_item1-item1).toEqual(10);
    });
});
```

7. Now when you run the spec file, you will see that both the specs pass for scenario 1, as shown in the following screenshot:

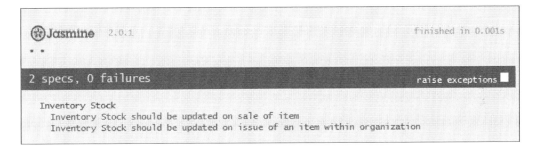

8. Now, use the following code to define and implement the specs for scenario 2 and scenario 3:

```
describe("Inventory Stock", function() {
  //Scenario - 1
  it("Inventory Stock should be updated on sale of item",
function() {
        var stockinhand_item1=11;
        var item1 = 1;
        var transaction = 'SALE';
        expect(stockinhand_item1-item1).toEqual(10);
    });
    it("Inventory Stock should be updated on issue of an item
within organization", function() {
        var stockinhand_item1=11;
        var item1 = 1;
        var transaction = 'ISSUE';
        expect(stockinhand_item1-item1).toEqual(10);
    });
    //Scenario - 2
    it("Inventory Stock should be updated on return of any item",
function() {
```

```
        var stockinhand_item1=11;
        var item1 = 1;
        var transaction = 'SALE RETURN';
        expect(stockinhand_item1+item1).toEqual(12);
    });
    //Scenario - 3
    it("Inventory Stock should be updated on receiving or
procuring new item", function() {
        var stockinhand_item1=11;
        var item1 = 1;
        var transaction = 'PROCUREMENT';
        expect(stockinhand_item1+item1).toEqual(12);
    });
});
```

9. Finally, run the spec file (`InventoryStock_spec.js`) using the Jasmine runner. You will see the test execution results, as shown in the following screenshot indicating the success of all four specs:

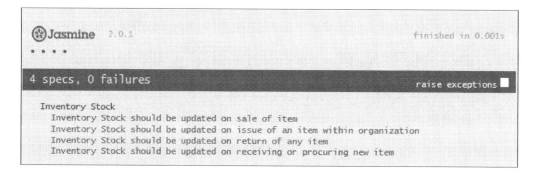

How it works...

Let's understand what we did throughout this recipe.

In step 1, we created a spec file and defined the name of the test suite corresponding to the functionality, which is currently being tested. In the present scenario, we named it as **Inventory Stock**.

In steps 2 to 4, we created the spec to define scenario 1 and executed the scenario using the Jasmine runner. In this scenario, we defined specs to validate whether the stock is being updated (or not) on account of the sale of an item or the issue of an item to a person/ department within the organization.

In step 5, we further refactored the specs of scenario 1 to make them more understandable and granular.

In steps 6 and 7, we implemented the test code for scenario 1 corresponding to specs.

In steps 8 and 9, following the same pattern, we implemented the test code for scenarios 2 and 3.

See also

▶ To gain a deeper understanding about how to design and write specs, refer to the recipe *Defining nested suites to write more meaningful specs* in *Chapter 2, Jasmine with TDD and BDD Processes.*

Adding expectations and matchers to the test

Inside the `it` block, you can write all the test code that is required to test the application/JavaScript code by applying assertions using expectations and matchers. Expectations are built with an `expect` function, which takes a value called **actual**. It is further chained with the matcher function(s), which takes the **expected** value. Each matcher implements a Boolean expression depending on the actual and expected value. It is responsible for reporting to Jasmine whether the expectation is true or false. Jasmine passes or fails the spec on the basis of the Boolean value returned by the matcher. In this recipe, you will learn how assertions are applied using the `toBe` matcher. You will also learn how negative assertions are applied.

To understand this recipe, assume that you are developing a bank application to track details of fixed deposit, recurring deposit, and all other financial transactions.

"As a finance administrator, I want to track all financial transactions so that I can categorize them for further assessment/processing."

Let's consider the following scenarios in the current context, that is, all financial transactions should be tracked and categorized:

▶ **Scenario-1**: Deposit should be of the **fixed Deposit (FD)** type on locking amount for a fix period

▶ **Scenario-2**: Deposit should be of the **Recurring Deposit (RD)** type for an amount deposited with regular frequency (that is, monthly, quarterly, half-yearly, yearly, and so on)

How to do it...

You need to perform the following steps to apply the `toBe` matcher on these scenarios:

1. Create the `Deposit_spec.js` file under the `/spec` folder and code the following lines:

    ```
    describe("Bank Deposit ", function() {
    //Scenario 1

    });
    ```

2. Next, use the following code to define specs for scenario 1 and scenario 2:

    ```
    describe("Bank Deposit",function(){
      //Scenario 1
      it("should be considered as FD on locking amount for a fixed
    period", function(){

      });
      //Scenario 2
      it("should be considered as RD on depositing amount on regular
    frequency", function(){

      });
    });
    ```

3. To implement scenario 1 and scenario 2, we need JavaScript code. So, create the `Deposit.js` file, put it under the `/src` folder, and use the following code:

    ```
    function Deposit(Frequency) {
      this.Type= Frequency;
    };

    Deposit.prototype.BankDeposit = function(){
      switch (this.Type) {
      case "FIX" :
            return "FD";
            break;
      case "RECURRING" :
            return "RD";
            break;
      };
    };
    ```

4. Next, use the following code to implement specs for scenario 1 and scenario 2:

```
describe("Bank Deposit",function(){
    //Scenario -1
    it("should be considered as FD on locking amount for a fix
period", function(){
        var MyDeposit = new Deposit("FIX");
        DepositType = MyDeposit.BankDeposit();
        expect(DepositType).toBe("FD");
    });
    //Scenario -2
    it("should be considered as RD on depositing amount on regular
frequency", function(){
        var MyDeposit = new Deposit("RECURRING");
        DepositType = MyDeposit.BankDeposit();
        expect(DepositType).toBe("RD");
    });
});
```

5. Now, run the spec file (`Deposit_spec.js`) using the Jasmine runner and you will see that tests pass for both the scenarios, as shown in the following screenshot:

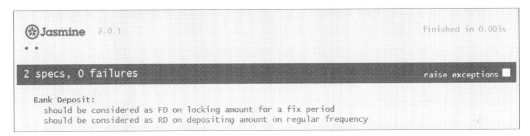

6. Now, to apply negative assertions on both of the scenarios, consider the following code:

```
describe("Bank Deposit",function(){
    //Scenario -1
    it("should be considered as FD on locking amount for a fix
period", function(){
        var MyDeposit = new Deposit("FIX");
        DepositType = MyDeposit.BankDeposit();
        expect(DepositType).toBe("FD");
    expect(DepositType).not.toBe("FD");
    });
    //Scenario -2
```

```
it("should be considered as RD on depositing amount on regular
frequency", function(){
    var MyDeposit = new Deposit("RECURRING");
    DepositType = MyDeposit.BankDeposit();
    expect(DepositType).toBe("RD");
  expect(DepositType).not.toBe("RD");
    });
});
```

In the preceding code snapshot, notice that we implemented the negative assertion by chaining the call to `expect` with a `not` before calling the matcher.

7. Now, run the spec file (`Deposit_spec.js`) using the Jasmine runner and you will see that it indicates that both the tests fail, as shown in the following screenshot:

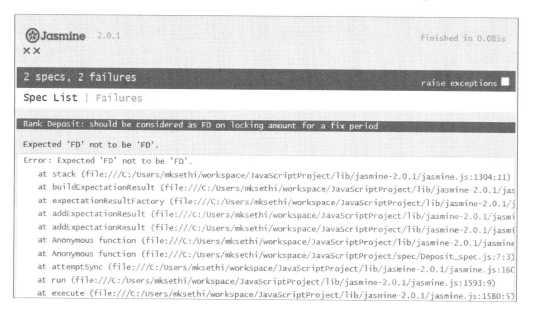

In the preceding screenshot, notice that we have provided wrong values corresponding to negative assertions.

8. Now, use the following code to pass both the tests:

```
describe("Bank Deposit",function(){
  //Scenario -1
  it("should be considered as FD on locking amount for a fix
period", function(){
    var MyDeposit = new Deposit("FIX");
    DepositType = MyDeposit.BankDeposit();
    expect(DepositType).toBe("FD");
```

```
    expect(DepositType).not.toBe("RD");
    expect(DepositType).not.toBe("Any value Other than 'FD' ");
    });
    //Scenario -2
    it("should be considered as RD on depositing amount on regular
frequency", function(){
        var MyDeposit = new Deposit("RECURRING");
        DepositType = MyDeposit.BankDeposit();
        expect(DepositType).toBe("RD");
    expect(DepositType).not.toBe("FD");
    expect(DepositType).not.toBe("Any value Other than 'RD' ");
    });
});
```

9. Finally, run the spec file (`Deposit_spec.js`) using the Jasmine runner and you will see that it indicates that both the tests pass, as shown in the following screenshot:

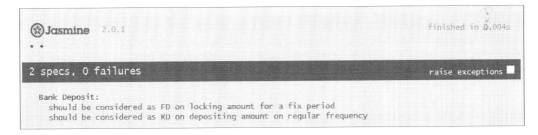

How it works...

In step 1 and step 2, we defined the name of the suite and specs for scenario 1 and scenario 2.

In step 3, JavaScript code is provided to implement Jasmine tests for both the scenarios. Here, we defined the object construction function with one parameter (that is, `frequency`) to identify the type of deposit. Also, we created a `BankDeposit()` function for the deposit object using JavaScript prototype property.

In step 4, we implemented the test code corresponding to specs within the `it` block to test the code. First, we created the object of deposit and then invoked the `BankDeposit()` function of the deposit object to get the deposit type. Finally, we implemented the assertion to compare the actual and expected value using the `toBe` matcher.

In steps 6 through 9, we implemented a negative assertion by chaining the call to `expect` with a `not` before calling the matcher. We also looked at how Jasmine tests pass/fail using the different values with negative assertion.

Applying different matchers to the Jasmine test

Jasmine provides a rich set of matchers to test JavaScript code. In this recipe, you will learn to apply various matchers in different situations.

To understand this recipe, let's assume that you are developing an application and you have to implement test code for various scenarios by applying different Jasmine matchers.

"As a developer, I want to apply different Jasmine matchers so that I can implement a test condition successfully."

Let's consider some scenarios in the preceding context, that is, where Jasmine matchers should be applied for different test conditions:

- **Scenario-1**: The `'toMatch'` matcher should be applied successfully for regular expressions

- **Scenario-2**: The `'toEqual'` matcher should be applied successfully for literals, variables, and objects

- **Scenario-3**: The `'toBe'` matcher should be applied successfully for literals, variables, and objects

- **Scenario-4**: The `'toBeDefined'` matcher should be applied successfully to compares against defined

- **Scenario-5**: The `'toBeUndefined'` matcher should be applied successfully to compares against undefined

- **Scenario-6**: The `'toBeNull'` matcher should be applied successfully to compare against null

- **Scenario-7**: The `'toBeTruthy'` matcher should be applied successfully for Boolean casting testing

- **Scenario-8**: The `'toBeFalsy'` matcher should be applied successfully for Boolean casting testing

- **Scenario-9**: The `'toContain'` matcher should be applied successfully for finding an item in an array

- **Scenario-10**: The `'toBeLessThan'` matcher should be applied successfully for mathematical comparisons

- **Scenario-11**: The `'toBeGreaterThan'` matcher should be applied successfully for mathematical comparisons

- **Scenario-12**: The `'toBeCloseTo'` matcher should be applied for precision math comparison

How to do it...

To apply different matchers to your Jasmine tests, you need to perform the following steps in the preceding scenarios:

1. Create the `JasmineMatchers_spec.js` file under the `/spec` folder and code the following lines:

   ```
   describe("Jasmine Matchers", function() {
   //Scenario - 1

   });
   ```

2. Now, use the following code to define and implement the spec for scenario 1 using the `toMatch` matcher:

   ```
   describe("Jasmine Matchers",function(){
       //Scenario -1
       it("'toMatch' matcher should be applied successfully for regular
   expressions", function() {
           var strString1 = "Packt Cookbooks are an excellent source of
   learning";
           var strPhone = "001-789-56-67";
           expect(strString1).toMatch(/Cookbooks/);
           expect(strString1).toMatch(/cookbooks/i);
           expect(strString1).not.toMatch(/Java/);
           expect(strPhone).toMatch(/\d{3}-\d{3}-\d{2}-\d{2}/);
       });
   });
   ```

> A regular expression is a sequence of characters that forms a search pattern. Search patterns can be defined based on a single character, combination of characters/strings, or more complicated patterns. To explore more about regular expressions in greater depth, visit the following website:
>
> `https://developer.mozilla.org/en-US/docs/Web/JavaScript/Guide/Regular_Expressions`

3. The next step is to run the spec file (`JasmineMatchers_spec.js`) using the Jasmine runner, and you will see that the test passes, as shown in the following screenshot:

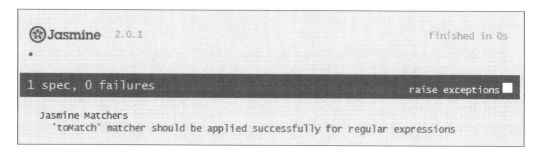

4. Now, use following code to implement scenario 2 and scenario 3:

```javascript
describe("Jasmine Matchers",function(){

    //Scenario - 2
    describe("toEqual matcher should be applied successfully",
    function(){
        it("if numbers are equal", function() {
            var intVar = 15;
            expect(intVar).toEqual(15);
        });
        it("if strings are equal", function() {
            var strVar = "Jasmine Cookbook";
            expect(strVar).toEqual("Jasmine Cookbook");
        });

        it("if objects are equal", function() {
            var MyObectj1 = {a: 12, b: 13};
            var MyObectj2 = {a: 12, b: 13};
            expect(MyObectj1).toEqual(MyObectj2);
            expect(MyObectj1.a).toEqual(MyObectj2.a);
            expect(MyObectj1.a).not.toEqual(MyObectj2.b);
        });
        it("if arrays are equal", function() {
            expect([8, 9, 10]).toEqual([8, 9, 10]);
            expect([8, 9, 10, 11]).not.toEqual([8, 9, 10]);
        });
    });

    //Scenario - 3
```

```
    it("toBe matcher should be applied successfully for literals,
variables and objects", function() {
        var MyObj = {foo: "foo"};
        var MySameObj = {foo: "foo"};
        var strVar = "Jasmine Cookbook";
        var myArr = [8, 9, 10];
    expect(MyObj).toBe(MyObj);
    expect(MySameObj).not.toBe(MyObj);
    expect(MySameObj).toEqual(MyObj);
        expect(strVar).toBe("Jasmine Cookbook");
    expect(myArr).toEqual([8, 9, 10]);
    expect(myArr).not.toBe([8, 9, 10]);
    });
});
```

In the preceding code snapshot, notice that we created two objects (that is, MyObj and MySameObj). Both look similar and equal, but they are two different objects with exactly the same attributes. Furthermore, you can observe the behavior of the toBe and toEqual matchers. Here, while comparing both the objects, the assertion value will return true with the toEqual matcher and false with the toBe matcher. Also, this is true for an array object (that is, myArr).

 The toEqual() matcher checks equivalence. On the other hand, the toBe() matcher ensures that they are the exact same objects.

5. Next, run the spec file (JasmineMatchers_spec.js) for scenario 2 and scenario 3 using the Jasmine runner. The tests should run successfully, as shown in the following screenshot:

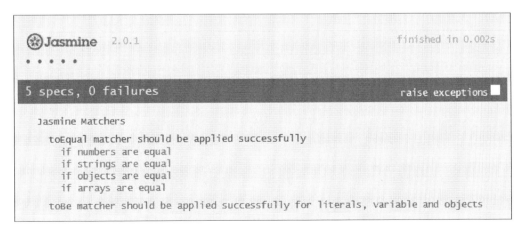

6. Use the following code to implement scenario 4:

```
describe("Jasmine Matchers",function(){
  //Scenario - 4
  it("toBeDefined should be applied successfully to compares
against defined.", function() {
        var MyObj = {
          foo: "foo"
        };
        var Myfunction = (function() {}) ();
        var strUndefined;
        expect("Jasmine Cookbooks").toBeDefined();
        expect(MyObj).toBeDefined();
        expect(MyObj.foo).toBeDefined();
        expect(Myfunction).not.toBeDefined();
        expect(strUndefined).not.toBeDefined();

    });
});
```

Undefined is a built-in JavaScript type. In JavaScript, if we declare a variable without assigning a value, its type is undefined. Also, JavaScript functions without a return statement or with empty return statements return undefined. To learn more about undefined and how it works, visit the following website:

```
https://developer.mozilla.org/en-US/docs/Web/
JavaScript/Reference/Global_Objects/undefined
```

7. Use the following code to implement scenario 5:

```
describe("Jasmine Matchers",function(){
  //Scenario - 5
  it("toBeUndefined should be applied successfully to compares
against undefined.", function() {
        var MyObj = {
              foo: "foo"
             };
        var Myfunction = (function() {}) ();
        var strUndefined;
          expect(MyObj).not.toBeUndefined();
          expect(MyObj.foo).not.toBeUndefined();
          expect(Myfunction).toBeUndefined();
          expect(strUndefined).toBeUndefined();
    });
});
```

8. Now, run the spec file (for scenario 4 and 5) with the Jasmine runner. You will see that all Jasmine tests pass for both the scenarios, as shown in the following screenshot:

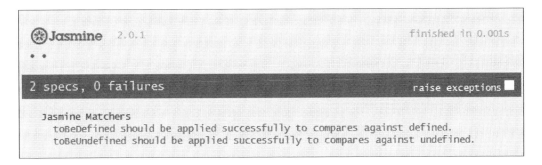

9. To implement scenario 6, use the following code:

```
describe("Jasmine Matchers",function(){
    //Scenario - 6
     it("toBeNull matcher should be applied successfully to compare
against null", function() {
         var nullValue = null;
         var valueUndefined;
         var notNull = "notNull";
         expect(null).toBeNull();
         expect(nullValue).toBeNull();
         expect(valueUndefined).not.toBeNull();
         expect(notNull).not.toBeNull();
      });
});
```

10. To see how Jasmine handles null values using the `toBeNull` matcher, run the spec file (only for scenario 6) with the Jasmine runner. You will see that the test passes, as shown in the following screenshot:

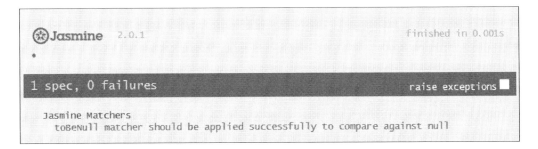

11. Use the following code to implement scenarios 7 and 8:

```
describe("Jasmine Matchers",function(){
    //Scenario - 7
        it("toBeTruthy matcher should be applied successfully for
Boolean casting testing", function() {
            var MyVar1=12, MyVar2 = "True for Non Empty Strings";
            expect(true).toBeTruthy();
            expect("Jasmine Cookbook").toBeTruthy();
            expect(MyVar1).toBeTruthy();
            expect(MyVar2).toBeTruthy();
    });
    //Scenario - 8
    it("toBeFalsy matcher should be applied successfully for
Boolean casting testing", function() {
            var MyVar1=12, MyVar2 = "True for Non Empty Strings";
            expect(false).toBeFalsy();
            expect(null).toBeFalsy();
            expect(true).not.toBeFalsy();
            expect("Jasmine Cookbook").not.toBeFalsy();
            expect(MyVar1).not.toBeFalsy();
            expect(MyVar2).not.toBeFalsy();
    });
});
```

12. Next, run the spec file (for scenarios 7 and 8) with the Jasmine runner and you will see that both the Jasmine tests pass, as shown in the following screenshot:

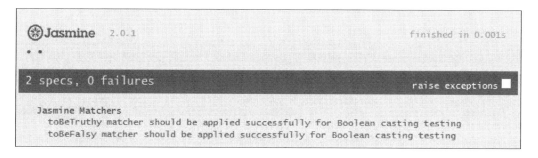

13. Use the following code to implement scenario 9:

```
describe("Jasmine Matchers",function(){
    it("toContain matcher should be applied successfully for
finding an item in an Array", function() {
        var MyArray = ["Jasmine", "Cookbook", "JavaScript"];
```

```
                 expect([1, 2, 3]).toContain(2);
                 expect([1, 2, 3]).toContain(2,3);
                 expect(MyArray).toContain("Cookbook");
                 expect([1, 2, 3]).not.toContain(4);
                 expect(MyArray).not.toContain("Java");
             });
         });
```

14. Now, run the spec file (only for scenario 9) with the Jasmine runner and you will see that all the test conditions pass for scenario 9, as shown in the following screenshot:

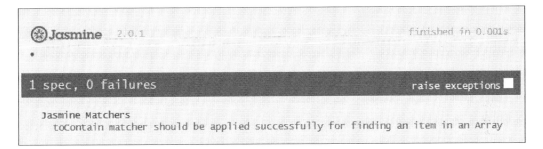

15. Use the following code to implement scenarios 10 and 11:

```
    describe("Jasmine Matchers",function(){
        //Scenario - 10
        it("toBeLessThan matcher should be applied successfully for
    mathematical comparisons", function() {
            var pi = 3.1415926, g = 9.71; num1=5, num2=9;
            expect(pi).toBeLessThan(g);
            expect(num1).toBeLessThan(num2);
            expect(g).not.toBeLessThan(pi);
            expect(num2).not.toBeLessThan(num1);
        });

        //Scenario - 11
        it("toBeGreaterThan matcher should be applied successfully for
    mathematical comparisons", function() {
            var pi = 3.1415926, g = 9.71; num1=5, num2=6;
            expect(g).toBeGreaterThan(pi);
            expect(num2).toBeGreaterThan(num1);
            expect(pi).not.toBeGreaterThan(g);
            expect(num1).not.toBeGreaterThan(num2);
        });
    });
```

16. Run the spec file (for scenarios 10 and 11) with the Jasmine runner and you will see that both the tests pass, as shown in the following screenshot:

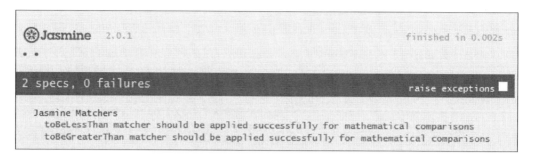

17. To implement scenario 12, use the following code:

```
describe("Jasmine Matchers",function(){
    it("toBeCloseTo matcher should be applied for precision math
comparison", function() {
        var pi = 3.1415926, e = 2.78;
        expect(pi).not.toBeCloseTo(e);
        expect(pi).toBeCloseTo(e,0);
        expect(4.334).toBeCloseTo(4.334);
        expect(4.334).toBeCloseTo(4.3345,1);
        expect(4.334).toBeCloseTo(4.3345,2);
        expect(4.334).not.toBeCloseTo(4.3,2);
        expect(4.223).not.toBeCloseTo(4.22,3);
        expect(4.223).not.toBeCloseTo(4.22,4);
    });
});
```

18. Next, run the spec file (for scenario 12) with the Jasmine runner and you will see that all the test conditions pass:

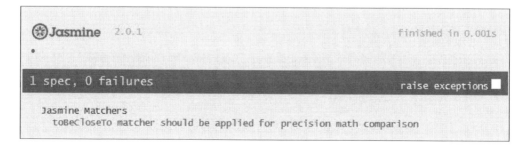

19. Finally, to run all the 12 scenarios in one go, make a single spec file with the entire test code and run it (`JasmineMatchers_spec.js`) with the Jasmine runner. You will see that all the tests pass:

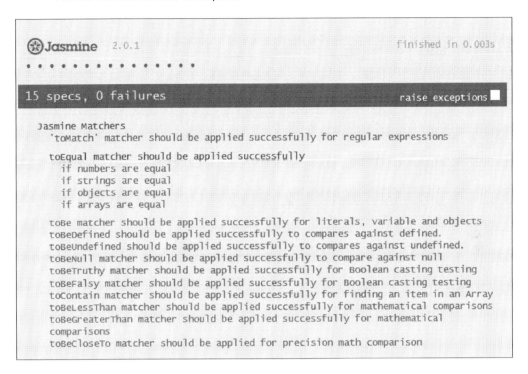

How it works...

Let's take a look at the steps of this recipe.

In steps 1 to 3, we implemented scenario 1 with the `toMatch` matcher. It checks whether something is matched for a regular expression. You can use the `toMatch` matcher to test search patterns. In our case, we implemented the test code to find out search patterns with different regular expressions.

In steps 4 and 5, we defined the specs for scenario 2 and 3, and we implemented the test code corresponding to specs using the `toEqual` and `toBe` matchers. Here, notice that `toBe` looks similar to `toEqual`, but that is not the case. The `toBe` matcher returns the value `true` if the objects are equal. For example, in our case, `MyObj` and `MySameObj` look like the same objects, but in fact both are different objects with exactly the same attribute/behavior. Therefore, the assertion will return a `true` value with the `toEqual` matcher, but a `false` value with the `toBe` matcher.

In steps 6 to 8, we implemented scenarios 4 and 5 and saw how the `toBeDefine` and `toBeUndefine` matchers are applied to test JavaScript's `Undefined` type. In step 7, we first implemented a test condition for a non-empty string and two test conditions with object variable `MyObj`. We also implemented test conditions for the `strUndefined` variable and the `MyFunction()` function by applying negative assertions. Conversely, in step 8, we implemented test conditions with the object variable `MyObj` by applying negative assertions.

In step 9, we implemented test code for scenario 6 using the `toBeNull` matcher. In step 10, we saw test conditions pass for `null` values. However, we applied negative assertions to pass test conditions for `not Null` and `Undefined` values.

In step 11, we implemented scenario 7 and scenario 8 using the `toBeTruthy` and `toBeFalsy` matchers. We use the `toBeTruthy` matcher to check whether something returns/evaluates to `true`. Similarly, we use the `toBeFalsy` matcher to check whether something returns/evaluates to false. In our case, we applied the `toBeTruthy` matcher for true value, non-empty strings and numbers other than zero. Similarly, we applied `toBeFalsy` matcher to validate false, null, and empty strings.

In step 13, we implemented the test code for scenario 9 using the `toContain` matcher. Here, we implemented test conditions to find out an element(s)/item(s) of an array using the `toContain` matcher. Similarly, we implemented test conditions to check if an element/an item does did not exist in an array by applying negative assertions.

In step 15, we implemented scenario 10 and scenario 11 to compare mathematical values using the `toBeLessThan` and `toBeGreaterThan` matchers.

In step 17, we implemented scenario 12 using the `toBeCloseTo` matcher. This matcher is used to check whether a number is close to another number, up to a given level of decimal precision. In our case, we checked whether the expected number was equal to the actual number with a given level of decimal precision.

Applying setup and teardown functions to the Jasmine test

Very often, we reuse pieces of code across different scenarios. This is due to functionality dependencies among scenarios, preconditions, or some other requirements such as initialization/declaration of application/system variables or objects. This improves code redundancy and maintainability.

Generally, to avoid code duplication (across scenarios/Jasmine specs) and increase code reusability and readability, we use setup and teardown functions. Jasmine provides two global functions (that is, `beforeEach` and `afterEach`) corresponding to setup and teardown functions. We can initialize variables and write common code and preconditions under the `beforeEach` function. Similarly, the `afterEach` function can be used to reinitialize variables or reset preconditions. The `beforeEach` function is called once before each spec is run in the `describe` block, and the `afterEach` function is called once after each spec is run. Both the functions are very useful for refactoring and optimizing the common code.

Getting ready

You will learn this recipe with the help of the second recipe in this chapter. For more information, refer to the *Adding specs to your Jasmine test* recipe. In this recipe, we implemented three scenarios for a sales and inventory control system and created a spec file (`InventoryStock_spec.js`) with the test code.

How to do it...

To apply Setup and Teardown to the Jasmine test, you need to perform the following steps:

1. First, you need to create a spec file (`InventoryStockOptimizeCode_spec.js`) under the `/spec` folder and get the following code from the spec file (`InventoryStock_spec.js`) created in the second recipe of this chapter, *Adding specs to your Jasmine test*:

```
describe("Inventory Stock", function() {
  //Scenario - 1
  it("Inventory Stock should be updated on sale of item",
function() {
        var stockinhand_item1=11;
        var item1 = 1;
    var transaction = "SALE";
    expect(stockinhand_item1-item1).toEqual(10);
  });
    it("Inventory Stock should be updated on issue of an item
within organization", function() {
        var stockinhand_item1=11;
        var item1 = 1;
    var transaction = "ISSUE";
    expect(stockinhand_item1-item1).toEqual(10);
  });
```

```
      //Scenario - 2
      it("Inventory Stock should be updated on return of any item",
   function() {
            var stockinhand_item1=11;
            var item1 = 1;
         var transaction = "SALE RETURN";
         expect(stockinhand_item1+item1).toEqual(12);
      });


      //Scenario - 3
      it("Inventory Stock should be updated on receiving or
   procuring new item", function() {
            var stockinhand_item1=11;
            var item1 = 1;
         var transaction = "PROCUREMENT";
         expect(stockinhand_item1+item1).toEqual(12);
      });
   });
```

In the preceding code snapshot, notice the code redundancy across the specs. Here, we declared and assigned value to variables in each spec separately.

2. Next, refactor the code by applying the `beforeEach` and `afterEach` function by using the following code:

```
describe("Inventory Stock", function() {
  var stockinhand_item1, item1;
  beforeEach(function() {
     stockinhand_item1=11, item1 = 1;
     console.log("beforeEach: Stock in hand for item1 before spec
execution = " + stockinhand_item1);
     });
  afterEach(function() {
     stockinhand_item1=0, item1 = 0;
     console.log("afterEach: Stock in hand for item1 once spec
executed = " + stockinhand_item1);
     });


  //Scenario - 1
  it("Inventory Stock should be updated on sale of an item",
function() {
     expect(stockinhand_item1-item1).toEqual(10);
     });
```

```
    it("Inventory Stock should be updated on issue of an item
within organization", function() {
        expect(stockinhand_item1-item1).toEqual(10);
    });

    //Scenario - 2
    it("Inventory Stock should be updated on return of an item",
function() {
        expect(stockinhand_item1+item1).toEqual(12);
    });

    //Scenario - 3
    it("Inventory Stock should be updated on receiving or
procuring new item", function() {
        expect(stockinhand_item1+item1).toEqual(12);
    });
});
```

In the preceding code snapshot, notice that we declared the common variables and assigned the corresponding values in the `beforeEach` function. Here, we have written the code just for illustrative purpose and to understand the working of `beforeEach` and `afterEach` function.

3. Finally, run the spec file (`InventoryStockOptimizeCode_spec.js`) using the Jasmine runner (that is, `SpecRunner.html`). You will see test execution results, as shown in the following screenshot, which indicates that all four specs are passing:

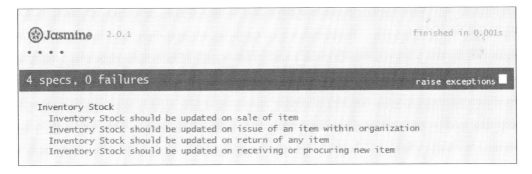

In your browser, if you go to the console window, you will see that the message defined with the `console.log()` method is printed four times, corresponding to each spec.

How it works...

In steps 1 to 3, we looked at how setup/teardown functions are applied to Jasmine tests using the `beforeEach` and `afterEach` functions. In step 2, we declared both the variables (`stockinhand_item1` and `item1`) at the top-level scope, that is, the `describe` block. Here, we refactored the test code by moving the initialization code into a `beforeEach` function. Also, we reinitialized the value of variables using the `afterEach` function.

Using the "this" keyword

In Jasmine, we can also initialize and share the variables between `beforeEach`, `it`, and `afterEach` using the `this` keyword. In this recipe, we will see how the `this` keyword can be used within the `beforeEach` or `afterEach` functions.

Getting ready

You will learn this recipe with the help of the previous recipe. For more information, refer to the previous recipe, *Applying setup and teardown functions to the Jasmine test*. In this recipe, we refactor three scenarios for a sales and inventory control system by initializing/putting together common code in the `beforeEach` and `afterEach` functions.

How to do it...

To apply the `this` keyword to your Jasmine test, you need to perform the following steps:

1. First, you need to create a spec file (`InventoryStockOptimizeCode_With_this_spec.js`) under the `/spec` folder and get the following code from the spec file (`InventoryStockOptimizeCode_spec.js`) created in the previous recipe, *Adding specs to your Jasmine test*:

```
describe("Inventory Stock", function() {
  var stockinhand_item1, item1;
  beforeEach(function() {
     stockinhand_item1=11, item1 = 1;
   });
  afterEach(function() {
     stockinhand_item1=0, item1 = 0;
   });
  //Scenario - 1
   it("Inventory Stock should be updated on sale of an item",
function() {
```

```
    expect(stockinhand_item1-item1).toEqual(10);
    });
    it("Inventory Stock should be updated on issue of an item
within organization", function() {
        expect(stockinhand_item1-item1).toEqual(10);
    });
    //Scenario - 2
    it("Inventory Stock should be updated on return of an item",
function() {
        expect(stockinhand_item1+item1).toEqual(12);
    });
    //Scenario - 3
    it("Inventory Stock should be updated on receiving or
procuring new item", function() {
        expect(stockinhand_item1+item1).toEqual(12);
    });
});
```

2. Now, apply the `this` keyword by using the following code:

```
describe("Inventory Stock", function() {
  beforeEach(function() {
      this.stockinhand_item1=11, this.item1 = 1;
      console.log("beforeEach: Stock in hand for item1 before spec
execution = " + this.stockinhand_item1);
    });
  afterEach(function() {
      this.stockinhand_item1=0, this.item1 = 0;
      console.log("afterEach: Stock in hand for item1 once spec
executed = " + this.stockinhand_item1);
    });

  //Scenario - 1
  it("Inventory Stock should be updated on sale of an item",
function() {
      this.transactionType = "SALE";
      expect(this.stockinhand_item1-this.item1).toEqual(10);
      expect(this.transactionType).toBeDefined();
    });
    it("Inventory Stock should be updated on issue of an item
within organization", function() {
        expect(this.stockinhand_item1-this.item1).toEqual(10);
      expect(this.transactionType).toBeUndefined();
    });
```

```
        //Scenario - 2
        it("Inventory Stock should be updated on return of an item",
    function() {                    expect(this.stockinhand_item1+this.
    item1).toEqual(12);
          expect(this.transactionType).toBeUndefined();
        });


        //Scenario - 3
        it("Inventory Stock should be updated on receiving or
    procuring new item", function() {
      expect(this.stockinhand_item1+this.item1).toEqual(12);
      expect(this.transactionType).toBeUndefined();
        });
    });
```

3. Finally, run the spec file (`InventoryStockOptimizeCode_With_this_spec.
   js`) using the Jasmine runner (that is, `SpecRunner.html`). You should see test
   execution results, as shown in the following screenshot, indicating that all four
   tests are passing:

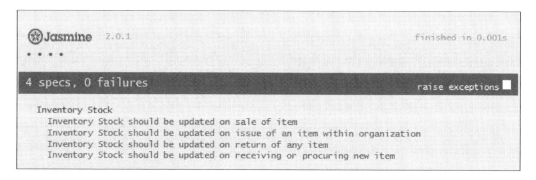

How it works...

In steps 1 to 3, we looked at how the `this` keyword is applied to a Jasmine test. In step 2, we
removed the variable declaration from the top-level scope (that is, the `describe` block) and
initialized/reinitialized the variables into the `beforeEach`/`afterEach` functions using the
`this` keyword. Also, notice that `this.transactionType` is `true` only for the spec in which
it was defined. For the other specs, the `this.transactionType` variable is considered
as undefined. In other words, the scope of the `this.transactionType` variable is limited
to the first spec only (that is, `Inventory Stock` should be updated on sale of an item).
Conversely, the `this.item1` variable is considered defined for all the specs because it is
assigned in the `beforeEach` function that runs each time.

2

Jasmine with TDD and BDD Processes

In this chapter, we will cover:

- ▶ Writing Jasmine tests using TDD and BDD processes
- ▶ Creating a Jasmine test for new code using TDD and BDD
- ▶ Designing Jasmine tests for existing code using TDD and BDD
- ▶ Defining nested suites to write more meaningful specs

Introduction

Behavior-Driven Development (**BDD**) is a software development process based on **Test-Driven Development** (**TDD**). Before we start writing Jasmine tests using TDD and BDD, let's get a briefing of how both processes work and how they play a pivotal role in software development.

TDD is a unit testing based test-first or fail-first approach where we write the test before writing the code. Thereafter, we write the minimum amount of code just to pass the test. Finally, we refactor the code to acceptable standards. This form of approach focuses on the specification of the application, thus decreasing the probability of bugs. In other words, we can say that TDD is a defect-prevention approach that focuses on internal (code) quality.

A JavaScript application can be developed using TDD by performing the following steps:

1. Write a failing unit test.

2. Make the test pass.

3. Refactor the test.

4. Repeat the steps.

5. When you cannot think of any more tests or there is no more scope for refactoring, you should be done.

The process/steps defined above can be shown as per diagram below:

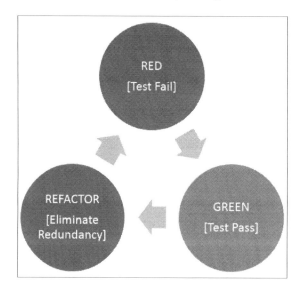

BDD is an agile development method that focuses on describing the behavior of the system from the perspective of its stakeholders. The BDD process is designed to improve the shortcomings of TDD, such as lack of specifications within TDD. Another way of looking at BDD is that it builds on TDD with more elaborate/specific choices. BDD is a communication and collaboration framework for developers, testers, product owners, and non-technical or business users. BDD enables a feedback mechanism in the early stages, which helps in improving product quality.

In BDD, tests of any unit of software should be specified in terms of the desired behavior of the unit. BDD uses a ubiquitous language from Domain-Driven Design. A ubiquitous language is a language that is shared and understood by all the stakeholders. This helps in building understanding of application/system behavior. Also, stakeholders can share their feedback in the early stages.

For more details on ubiquitous language, you can visit the following website:

```
http://en.wikipedia.org/wiki/Behavior-driven_
development#Spccification_as_a_ubiquitous_language
```

BDD writes tests from a "user story" perspective and the story's behavior is its acceptance criteria. Test scenarios or acceptance criteria are described in the following format:

- **Given**: This is the initial context
- **When**: This is when event occurs
- **Then**: Ensures some outcome

BDD can be described as shown in the following diagram:

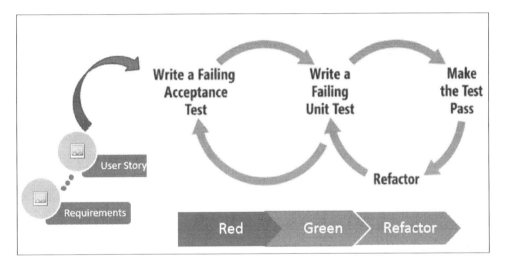

To learn more about BDD, you can visit the following web sites:

- `http://en.wikipedia.org/wiki/Behavior-driven_development`
- `http://dannorth.net/introducing-bdd/`
- `http://behaviour-driven.org/`

Jasmine has good support for developing applications in a BDD style. In this chapter, we will look at how applications are developed using TDD and BDD processes. We will also consider how to write Jasmine tests for new and existing code by applying TDD and BDD.

Writing Jasmine tests using TDD and BDD processes

To write a Jasmine test using TDD and BDD, let's assume that we are developing a payroll application for <XYZ> company. The employees of <XYZ> company work in India, UK, and the US. As per immediate need, a **Tax** (that is, Tax Deduction at Source) module needs to be developed to deduct an employee's tax in salary disbursement. There are different business rules that exist for deducting tax across different countries.

"As payroll administrator, I want to calculate an employee's tax on salary disbursement so that I can evaluate the exact tax."

Let's consider some scenarios in the context that an employee's tax should be deducted on salary disbursement:

 ▸ **Scenario-1**: Tax should be deducted in currency INR (India Rupee, Rs) for Indian employees

 ▸ **Scenario-2**: Tax should be deducted in currency GBP (British Pound, UK £) for UK employees

 ▸ **Scenario-3**: Tax should be deducted in currency USD (US Dollar, $) for US employees

 ▸ **Scenario-4**: Tax of Indian employees should be deducted by 10 percent if gross taxable income is between Rs. 250,000 and Rs. 500,000

Getting ready

Let's define all the scenarios in the **Given/When/Then** format to understand the concept from BDD perspective.

Define **scenario-1** as as follows:

 ▸ **Given**: Employees of <XYZ> Company

 ▸ **When**: Tax deducted for Indian employee

 ▸ **Then**: Currency should be used INR

Define **scenario-2** as follows:

 ▸ **Given**: Employees of <XYZ> Company

 ▸ **When**: Tax deducted for UK employee

 ▸ **Then**: Currency should be used GBP (British Pound, UK £)

Define **scenario-3** as follows:

- ▶ **Given**: Employees of <XYZ> Company
- ▶ **When**: Tax deducted for U.S employee
- ▶ **Then**: Currency should be USD (US $)

Define **scenario-4** as follows:

- ▶ **Given**: Employees of <XYZ> Company
- ▶ **When**: Tax deducted for Indian employee
- ▶ **Then**: Should be deducted 10 percent if Gross Income is between Rs. 250,000 and Rs. 500,000

How to do it...

You need to perform the following steps to write Jasmine tests using TDD and BDD processes:

1. Create a spec file `TDS_spec.js` under the `/spec` folder and code the following lines to define the spec for Scenario 1:

```
describe("Employees of <XYZ> Company:",function(){
  //Scenario -1
  describe("Tax deducted for Indian Employees, ", function(){
    it("Currency should be used INR", function(){
    });
  });
});
```

Here, observe how we translated **Given/When/Then** form of Scenario 1 into Jasmine specs. Specifically, we defined **Given** and **When** along with `describe` block. Further, we defined **Then** as an `it` block to show the outcome of the event.

2. Run spec file `TDS_spec.js` with the Jasmine runner (that is, `SpecRunner.html`). You will see that an empty spec (that is, a spec without any expectation) passes, as shown in the following screenshot:

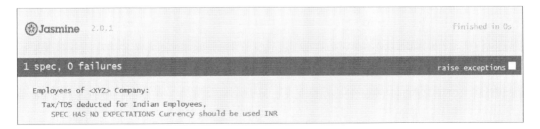

3. Let's add an expectation within the `it` block corresponding to the spec (that is, Tax/TDS currency should be INR for Indian employees of <XYZ> company) by using the following code:

```
describe("Employees of <XYZ> Company:",function(){
  //Scenario -1
  describe("Tax deducted for Indian Employees, ", function(){
    it("Currency should be used INR", function(){
      expect(myCurrency.currency).toBe("INR");
    });
  });
});
```

4. Now, run the spec file `TDS_spec.js` with the Jasmine runner and you will see that **myCurrency** is not defined:

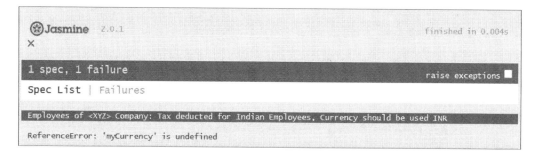

5. As indicated in step 4, let's define `myCurrency` by creating an instance of a `Currency()` object using the following code:

```
describe("Employees of <XYZ> Company:",function(){
  //Scenario -1
  describe("Tax deducted for Indian Employees, ", function(){
    it("Currency should be used INR", function(){
      var myCurrency = new Currency();
      expect(myCurrency.currency).toBe("INR");
    });
  });
});
```

6. Run the spec file with the Jasmine runner. You will see that **Currency** is not defined:

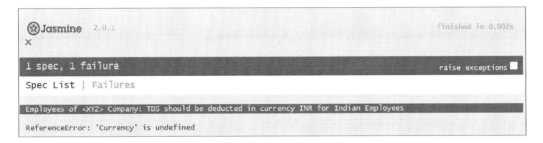

Here, notice that the error message is changed to **Currency is undefined**. Earlier, it was **myCurrency is undefined**.

7. So, let's create the `Currency.js` file under the `/src` folder and define `Currency()` using a construction function. Use the following code to define the construction function:

```
function Currency () {};
```

8. Next, add a reference of the `Currency.js` file to the Jasmine runner (that is, `SpecRunner.html`) and run the spec file. An error will be thrown as shown following screenshot, which indicates that **Expected undefined to be 'INR'**:

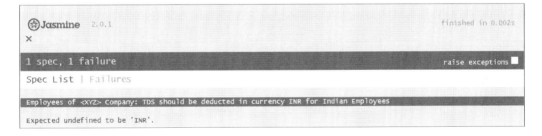

9. As indicated in the previous step, let's simply define the `Currency` attribute/property to the `Currency()` object and assign the value `INR` to it using the following code:

```
function Currency() {
    this.currency = "INR";
};
```

10. Run the spec file with the Jasmine runner and you will see that the test passes:

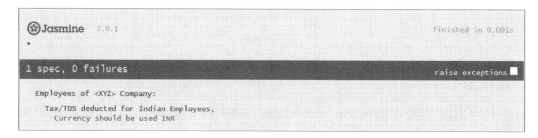

In the previous step, notice that we wrote the code just to pass the spec for scenario 1. The idea is to develop/refactor the code when it is actually needed.

In **Behavior-Driven Development** (**BDD**), you developed the code as guided by failing spec and refactor the code as needed. Typically, we follow the process:

red/green/refactor/....red/green/refactor......

11. Next, use the following code to define and implement the spec of scenario 2 and scenario 3:

```
describe("Employees of <XYZ> Company:",function(){
    //Scenario -1
    describe("Tax deducted for Indian Employees,", function(){
        it("Currency should be used INR", function(){
            var myCurrency = new Currency();
            expect(myCurrency.currency).toBe("INR");
        });
    });

    //Scenario -2
    describe("Tax deducted for United Kingdom Employees, ",
    function(){
        it("Currency should be used GBP (Pound, UK£)", function(){
            var myCurrency = new Currency();
            expect(myCurrency.currency).toBe("UK£");
        });
    });

    //Scenario -3
    describe("Tax deducted for United States Employees, ",
    function(){
```

```
it("Currency should be used USD (US$)", function(){
    var myCurrency = new Currency();
    expect(myCurrency.currency).toBe("US$");
  });
 });
});
```

12. Run the spec file with the Jasmine runner and you will see the output shown in the following screenshot:

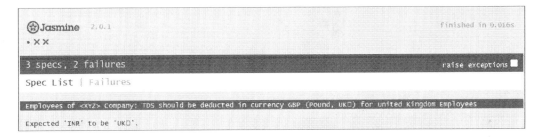

13. In order to pass the Jasmine tests for Scenario 2 and Scenario 3, let's refactor the JavaScript code defined in step 9 as follows:

```
function Currency(region) {
    this.region = region;
    switch (this.region) {
      case "INDIA" :
        this.currency = "INR";
            break;
      case "UK" :
        this.currency =   "UK£";
        break;
      case "US" :
        this.currency =   "US$";
        break;
    };
};
```

14. Next, let's update the test code for scenario 1, scenario 2, and scenario 3 as per the following:

```
describe("Employees of <XYZ> Company:",function(){
  //Scenario -1
  describe("Tax deducted for Indian Employees, ", function(){
    it("Currency should be used INR", function(){
```

```
    var myCurrency = new Currency("INDIA");
        expect(myCurrency.currency).toBe("INR");
    });
});


    //Scenario -2
    describe("Tax deducted for United Kingdom Employees, ",
function(){
        it("Currency should be used GBP (Pound, UK£)", function(){
        var myCurrency = new Currency("UK");
            expect(myCurrency.currency).toBe("UK£");
        });
    });


    //Scenario -3
    describe("Tax deducted for United States Employees, ",
function(){
        it("Currency should be used USD (US$)", function(){
        var myCurrency = new Currency("US");
            expect(myCurrency.currency).toBe("US$");
        });
    });
});
```

In the preceding code snapshot, notice that we passed an argument (name of region) with `Currency()` object.

15. Run the spec file `TDS_spec.js` with the Jasmine runner and you will see that all the tests pass:

16. Now, use the following code to implement the spec for scenario 4:

```
describe("Employees of <XYZ> Company:",function(){
  //Scenario -1
  describe("Tax deducted for Indian Employees, ", function(){
    it("Currency should be used INR", function(){
      var myCurrency = new Currency("INDIA");
      expect(myCurrency.currency).toBe("INR");
    });


    //Scenario -4
    it("Should be deducted 10% if Gross Income is between RS
250,000/- and RS 500,000/-", function(){
    var myTaxableIncome = new TaxIndiaEmp();
    //Let's assume the taxable income is RS 300,000/-
    myTaxableIncome.setIncome(300000);
    expect(myTaxableIncome.calculateTDS()).toEqual(5000);
    });
  });

  //Scenario -2
  describe("Tax deducted for United Kingdom Employees, ",
function(){
    it("Currency should be used GBP (Pound, UK£)", function(){
      var myCurrency = new Currency("UK");
      expect(myCurrency.currency).toBe("UK£");
    });
  });

  //Scenario -3
  describe("Tax deducted for United States Employees, ",
function(){
    it("Currency should be used USD (US$)", function(){
      var myCurrency = new Currency("US");
      expect(myCurrency.currency).toBe("US$");
    });
  });
});
```

In the preceding code snapshot, notice that we implemented the spec for Scenario 4 under the group **Tax deducted for Indian Employees.**

> It is highly recommended to organize specs with similar functionality into groups and subgroups. This will help you in code reviews during software development. To know more about how to organize specs into groups and subgroups, refer to the recipe *Organizing code suites into groups and subgroups as code becomes more complex* in *Chapter 4, Designing Specs from Requirement.*

17. Run the spec file with the Jasmine runner and you will see that **TaxIndiaEmp** is undefined:

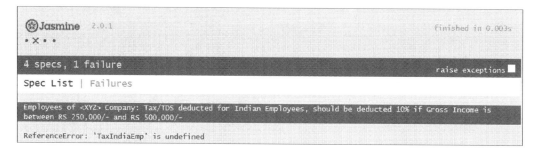

18. Next, let's create the `TaxIndiaEmp.js` file under the `/src` folder and define `TaxIndiaEmp` along with the `getter` and `setter` functions using the `construction` function. Also, add a reference of `TaxIndiaEmp.js` to the Jasmine runner. Use the following code to define the `construction` function:

```
var TaxIndiaEmp = function() {
  var grossTaxableIncome;
    //getters and setters
    this.getIncome      = function()      { return
grossTaxableIncome || 0; };
    this.setIncome      = function (grossIncome) {
grossTaxableIncome = grossIncome;};
  };
```

19. Run the spec file with the Jasmine runner and you will see that the **calculateTDS** method is not defined:

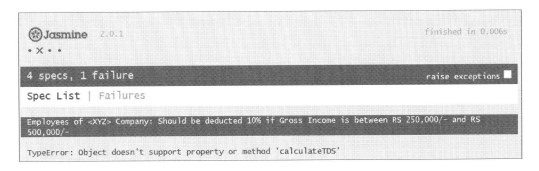

20. As guided by previous steps, let's define the `calculateTDS` method in `TaxIndiaEmp.js` using the following code:

```
var TaxIndiaEmp = function() {
  var grossTaxableIncome;
    //getters and setters
    this.getIncome      = function()       { return
grossTaxableIncome || 0; };
    this.setIncome      = function (grossIncome) {
grossTaxableIncome = grossIncome;};
};
TaxIndiaEmp.prototype.calculateTDS = function()
{
  var myTax = 0;
  if (this.getIncome() > 250000 && this.getIncome() <= 500000) {
    myTax = (this.getIncome()-250000) * 10/100;
  }
  return myTax;
};
```

21. Finally, run the spec file with the Jasmine runner and you should see that all the specs are passing:

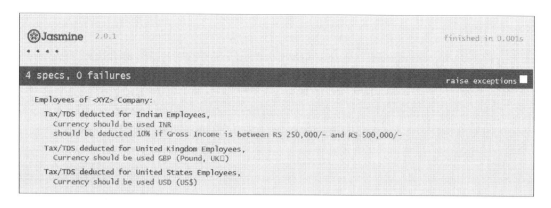

```
⊛ Jasmine   2.0.1                                        finished in 0.001s
 •  •  •  •

4 specs, 0 failures                                       raise exceptions ▪

  Employees of <XYZ> Company:
    Tax/TDS deducted for Indian Employees,
      Currency should be used INR
      should be deducted 10% if Gross Income is between RS 250,000/- and RS 500,000/-

    Tax/TDS deducted for United Kingdom Employees,
      Currency should be used GBP (Pound, UK£)

    Tax/TDS deducted for United States Employees,
      Currency should be used USD (US$)
```

How it works...

Let's take a look at what we did in the preceding recipe.

In steps 1 to 10, we defined the spec and implemented test code for scenario 1. We also looked at how the application code is developed for scenario 1 through a step-by-step approach using the BDD process.

In steps 11 to 15, following the same pattern, we implemented scenario 2 and scenario 3. In step 13, we refactored the code to pass the specs for scenarios 2 and 3. Here, we added a parameter (that is, `region`) to the `Currency()` object to identify employees of a specific region. In step 14, we also refactored the test code for scenario 1, scenario 2, and scenario 3.

In step 16, we implemented the spec for scenario 4. In steps 17 to 21, we implemented scenario 4. In step 18 and step 20, we developed application code for scenario 4 as guided through a failing spec.

We developed the code for happy paths (positive scenarios). Further, I would recommend that you create a few more scenarios and see how code can be developed with the BDD process. For example, you can develop the code to handle the case if taxable income is not within the specified range.

Creating a Jasmine test for new code using TDD and BDD

Writing Jasmine tests for new code is straightforward compared to writing Jasmine tests for existing code. In this recipe, we will learn how to design specs and write tests for new code.

To write a Jasmine test for new code using TDD and BDD, let's assume that you are working with a bank in a credit card division. There are different business rules that exist to accept credit card numbers.

"As a credit card administrator, I want to validate credit card numbers so that I can check their authenticity for further processing."

Let's consider a scenario in the following context that a credit card number should be valid to shop in online store:

Scenario-1: The credit card number should have 16 digits for the "Master Card" category

Getting ready

Let's define the Scenario in the **Given/When/Then** format as follows:

- **Given**: Credit card division of a bank
- **When**: Accepted credit card number for Master Card category
- **Then**: Should have 16 numerical digits

How to do it...

You need to perform the following steps to write Jasmine tests for new code using TDD and BDD processes:

1. Create a spec file `CreditCard_spec.js` under the `/spec` folder and code the following lines to define spec for scenario 1:

```
describe("Credit Card Division of a Bank: ",function() {
   describe("Accept Credit Card Number for Master Card
Category",function(){
      it("Should be equal to 16 digits", function() {
      });
   });
});
```

2. Run the spec file `CreditCard_spec.js` with the Jasmine runner and you will see that an empty spec (that is, without test code) passes:

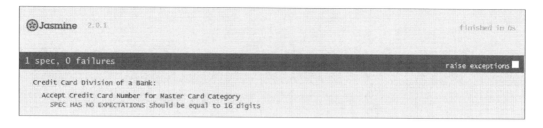

3. Now, implement the test condition as per scenario-1. Use the following code:

```
describe("Credit Card Division of a Bank: ",function() {
    describe("Accept Credit Card Number for Master Card
Category",function(){
        it("-should be having 16 numerical digits", function() {
            expect(validateCreditCardNumber("9999-9999-9999-9999")).
toBeTruthy();
        });
    });
});
```

4. Next, run the spec file `CreditCard_spec.js` with the Jasmine runner and you will see **'validateCreditCardNumber' is undefined**, as shown in the following screenshot:

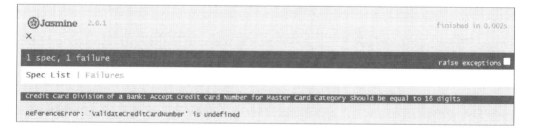

5. Next, let's create a `CreditCard.js` file under the `/src` folder and define the `validateCreditCardNumber` function, by using the following code:

```
function validateCreditCardNumber(number) {
    if (number.length==16) {
        return (true);
    }
    else {
        return (false);
    }
}
```

Here, notice that we are writing new code to implement the functionality of scenario 1 and there is no dependency on any existing code.

6. Now, add the reference of the `CreditCard.js` file to the Jasmine runner and run the spec file `CreditCard_spec.js` with the Jasmine runner. You will see that the spec fails for scenario 1:

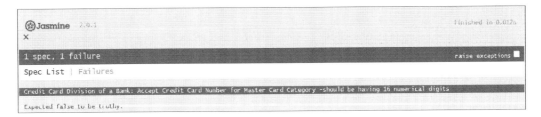

7. As indicated in the previous step, let's refactor the code as follows:

```
function validateCreditCardNumber(number) {
    return (number.replace(/-/g, "").length === 16);
};
```

8. Next, run the spec file `CreditCard_spec.js` with the Jasmine runner and you will see that the spec passes for scenario 1:

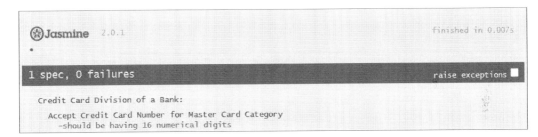

How it works...

In steps 1 to 8, we defined the spec and implemented test code for scenario 1. We also looked at how the Jasmine spec and test code are implemented while working with new code or developing new independent features.

Let's take a look at the steps of this recipe.

In step 1, we defined specs for scenario 1 as per the **Given/When/Then** format. In step 2, we executed the test with an empty spec. In the next step, we implemented the test code corresponding to the spec (that is, the credit card number should have 16 numerical digits).

In steps 4 to 7, we developed and refactored the code for scenario 1 as guided through a failing spec. In step 8, we successfully executed the test with the Jasmine runner.

Designing Jasmine tests for existing code using TDD and BDD

Writing Jasmine tests for existing code is tricky compared to writing Jasmine tests for new code. Consider that you are updating the existing code against a change request. Then, there can be the following situations where you write Jasmine tests with the existing code:

- The existing code is developed without using TDD and BDD processes and no test is written for the existing code.

- The existing code is developed without using TDD and BDD processes. However, Jasmine tests are developed for the existing code.

- The existing code is developed using TDD and BDD processes and Jasmine tests are already written for the existing code.

Whatever the scenario is valid for you from the above list, but when we implement a new feature or functionality, it's recommended to develop Jasmine tests only for the new piece of code. Also, if Jasmine tests are not written for the existing code, then we need to develop the tests only for the code that is impacted by the new implementation.

In this recipe, you will learn how to design specs and write tests with the existing code, which is developed using TDD and BDD processes.

Getting ready

You will learn this recipe with help of the first recipe in this chapter. For more information, refer to the first recipe in this chapter, *Writing a Jasmine test using TDD and BDD processes*.

To understand when and how to write Jasmine tests with existing code using TDD and BDD, let's consider two more scenarios in the **Given/When/Then** format:

Define **scenario-1** as follows:

- **Given**: Employees of <XYZ> Company
- **When**: Tax deducted for Indian employee
- **Then**: Should be deducted 20 percent if gross income is between Rs. 500,000 and Rs. 1,000,000

Define **scenario-2** as follows:

- **Given**: Employees of <XYZ> Company
- **When**: Tax deducted for Indian employee
- **Then**: Should be deducted 30 percent if Gross Income is >RS. 1,000,000/-

How to do it...

You need to perform the following steps to write Jasmine tests for existing code using TDD and BDD processes:

1. First, you need to create a spec file (`TDS_existing_spec.js`) under the `/spec` folder and get the following code from the spec file (`TDS_spec.js`) created in the first recipe of this chapter, *Writing a Jasmine test using TDD and BDD processes*:

```javascript
describe("Employees of <XYZ> Company:",function(){
  //Scenario -1
  describe("Tax deducted for Indian Employees, ", function(){
    it("Currency should be used INR", function(){
      var myCurrency = new Currency("INDIA");
      expect(myCurrency.currency).toBe("INR");
    });

    //Scenario -4
    it("Should be deducted 10% if Gross Income is " +
    "between RS 250,000/- and RS 500,000/-", function(){
      var myTaxableIncome = new TaxIndiaEmp();
      //Let's assume the taxable income is RS 300,000/-
      myTaxableIncome.setIncome(300000);
      expect(myTaxableIncome.calculateTDS()).toEqual(5000);
    });
  });

  //Scenario -2
  describe("Tax deducted for United Kingdom Employees, ",
  function(){
    it("Currency should be used GBP (Pound, UK£)", function(){
      var myCurrency = new Currency("UK");
      expect(myCurrency.currency).toBe("UK£");
    });
  });

  //Scenario -3
  describe("Tax deducted for United States Employees, ",
  function(){
    it("Currency should be used USD (US$)", function(){
      var myCurrency = new Currency("US");
      expect(myCurrency.currency).toBe("US$");
    });
  });
});
```

On analyzing the preceding code snapshot, notice that scenario 1 and scenario 2 need to be implemented under the suite (or group) `Tax deducted for Indian Employees`. Also, the `calculateTDS()` methods needs to be modified in order to implement scenario 5 and scenario 6.

 Before we start writing Jasmine tests for the existing code, it is recommended to analyze and see the impact of new code (or its implementation) over the existing code. Also, identify the affected method(s) by the new implementation.

2. Next, define the specs corresponding to scenario 1 and scenario 2 using the following code:

```
describe("Employees of <XYZ> Company:",function(){
  //Scenario -1
  describe("Tax deducted for Indian Employees, ", function(){
    it("Currency should be used INR", function(){
      var myCurrency = new Currency("INDIA");
      expect(myCurrency.currency).toBe("INR");
    });

    //Scenario -4
    it("Should be deducted 10% if Gross Income is " +
        "between RS 250,000/- and RS 500,000/-", function(){
      var myTaxableIncome = new TaxIndiaEmp();
      //Let's assume the taxable income is RS 300,000/-
      myTaxableIncome.setIncome(300000);
      expect(myTaxableIncome.calculateTDS())
      .toEqual(5000);
    });

    //Scenario -5 (Scenario -1 for this recipe)
    it("Should be deducted 20% if Gross Income is " +
        "between RS 500,000/- and RS 1,000,000/-", function(){
    });

    //Scenario -6 (Scenario -2 for this recipe)
    it("Should be deducted 30% if Gross Income " +
        "is >RS 1,000,000/-", function(){
    });
  });
```

```
//Scenario -2
  describe("Tax deducted for United Kingdom Employees, ",
function(){
    it("Currency should be used GBP (Pound, UK£)", function(){
      var myCurrency = new Currency("UK");
      expect(myCurrency.currency).toBe("UK£");
    });
  });


  //Scenario -3
  describe("Tax deducted for United States Employees, ",
function(){
    it("Currency should be used USD (US$)", function(){
      var myCurrency = new Currency("US");
      expect(myCurrency.currency).toBe("US$");
    });
  });
});
```

3. Let's implement the test code for scenario 1 and scenario 2, Using the following code:

```
//Scenario -5 (Scenario -1 for this recipe)
  it("Should be deducted 20% if Gross Income is " +
      "between RS 500,000/- and RS 1,000,000/-", function(){
    var myTaxableIncome = new TaxIndiaEmp();
    //Let's assume the taxable income is RS 700,000/-
    myTaxableIncome.setIncome(700000);
  expect(myTaxableIncome.calculateTDS())
  .toEqual(40000);
    });


  //Scenario -6 (Scenario -2 for this recipe)
  it("Should be deducted 30% if Gross Income " +
      "is >RS 1,000,000/-", function(){
    var myTaxableIncome = new TaxIndiaEmp();
    //Let's assume the taxable income is RS 1,300,000/-
    myTaxableIncome.setIncome(1300000);
  expect(myTaxableIncome.calculateTDS())
  .toEqual(90000);
    });
```

Here, notice that we created two more Jasmine tests along with the existing tests to validate the code corresponding to scenarios 1 and 2.

4. Next, run the spec file `TDS_existing_spec.js` with the Jasmine runner (that is, `SpecRunner.html`) and you will see that both tests fail:

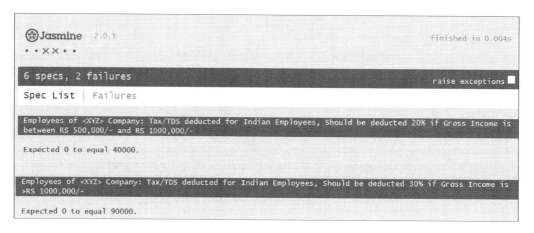

5. As indicated in the previous step, let's refactor the JavaScript code in the `TaxIndiaEmp.js` file to implement scenario 1 and scenario 2, Using the following code:

```javascript
var TaxIndiaEmp = function() {
  var grossTaxableIncome;
    //getters and setters
    this.getIncome    = function()        { return
grossTaxableIncome || 0; };
    this.setIncome    = function (grossIncome) {
grossTaxableIncome = grossIncome;};
};
TaxIndiaEmp.prototype.calculateTDS = function()
{
  var myTax = 0;
  if (this.getIncome() > 250000 && this.getIncome() <= 500000) {
    myTax = (this.getIncome()-250000) * 10/100;
    return myTax;
  }
  else if (this.getIncome() > 500000 && this.getIncome() <=
1000000) {
    myTax = (this.getIncome()-500000) * 20/100;
    return myTax;
  }
```

```
        else if (this.getIncome() > 1000000) {
           myTax = (this.getIncome()-1000000) * 30/100;
           return myTax;
        }
   };
```

6. Run the spec file `TDS_existing_spec.js` with the Jasmine runner and you will see that all the new and existing tests pass:

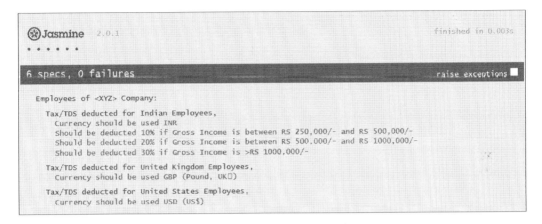

How it works...

In steps 1 to 6, we defined the spec and implemented test code for scenario 1 and scenario 2. We also looked at how the Jasmine spec and test code is implemented while working with existing code.

Let's take a look at the steps of this recipe.

In step 1, we got the entire code from the spec file `TDS_spec.js` and analyzed that scenario 1 and scenario 2 will impact the code of existing method `calculateTDS`. In step 2, we defined the specs for scenario 1 and scenario 2 as per the **Given/When/Then** format. In the next step, we implemented the test code for scenario 1 and scenario 2 according to the scenarios' test conditions.

In step 5, we refactored the code as guided through the failing spec.

In step 6, we successfully executed the Jasmine tests for both the scenarios.

Defining nested suites to write more meaningful specs

Sometimes, we need to refactor Jasmine specs by defining a suite or suites within a suite (that is, nested suites) to make it more granular and readable. This helps all stakeholders to understand the functionality from a holistic perspective. Moreover, you can easily identify and map the failing spec(s) with an exact piece of code. In this recipe, you will learn to design specs with nested suites.

 In Jasmine, we can define suites using the `describe` global function. This function accepts two parameters (`string` and `function()`). The `string` parameter is for naming the collection of specs and `function()` is a block of code that implements the suite.

Getting ready

You will learn this recipe with the help of a previous recipe in this chapter. For more information, refer to the *Designing the Jasmine test for existing code using TDD and BDD* recipe.

To understand when and how to define nested test suites to write more meaningful specs, let's consider a few more Scenarios in the **Given/When/Then** format:

Define **scenario-1** as follows:

- ▶ **Given**: Employees of <XYZ> Company
- ▶ **When**: Tax deducted for United Kingdom employee
- ▶ **Then**: Should be deducted 20 percent if gross annual income is between £10,000 and £32,000

Define **scenario-2** as follows:

- ▶ **Given**: Employees of <XYZ> Company
- ▶ **When**: Tax deducted for United States employee
- ▶ **Then**: Should be deducted 35 percent of gross taxable income if employee's status is SINGLE

Define **scenario-3** as follows:

- ▶ **Given**: Employees of <XYZ> Company
- ▶ **When**: Tax deducted for United States employee
- ▶ **Then**: Should be deducted 30 percent of gross taxable income if employee's status is MARRIED

How to do it...

To write a Jasmine test with nested suites, you need to perform the following steps:

1. First, you need to create a spec file (TDS_nested_spec.js) under the /spec folder and get the following code from the spec file (TDS_existing_spec.js) created in the previous recipe of this chapter, _Designing the Jasmine test for existing code using TDD and BDD_:

```
describe("Employees of <XYZ> Company:",function(){
  //Scenario -1
  describe("Tax deducted for Indian Employees, ", function(){
    it("Currency should be used INR", function(){
      var myCurrency - new Currency("INDIA");
      expect(myCurrency.currency).toBe("INR");
    });

    //Scenario -4
    it("Should be deducted 10% if Gross Income is " +
        "between RS 250,000/- and RS 500,000/-", function(){
      var myTaxableIncome = new TaxIndiaEmp();
      //Let's assume the taxable income is RS 300,000/-
      myTaxableIncome.setIncome(300000);
      expect(myTaxableIncome.calculateTDS())
      .toEqual(5000);
    });

    //Scenario -5
    it("Should be deducted 20% if Gross Income is " +
        "between RS 500,000/- and RS 1,000,000/-", function(){
      var myTaxableIncome = new TaxIndiaEmp();
      //Let's assume the taxable income is RS 700,000/-
      myTaxableIncome.setIncome(700000);
      expect(myTaxableIncome.calculateTDS())
      .toEqual(40000);
    });

    //Scenario -6
    it("Should be deducted 30% if Gross Income " +
        "is >RS 1,000,000/-", function(){
      var myTaxableIncome = new TaxIndiaEmp();
      //Let's assume the taxable income is RS 1,300,000/-
      myTaxableIncome.setIncome(1300000);
      expect(myTaxableIncome.calculateTDS())
      .toEqual(90000);
    });
  });
});
```

```
      //Scenario -2
      describe("Tax deducted for United Kingdom Employees, ",
  function(){
          it("Currency should be used GBP (Pound, UK£)", function(){
              var myCurrency = new Currency("UK");
              expect(myCurrency.currency).toBe("UK£");
          });
      });


      //Scenario -3
      describe("Tax deducted for United States Employees, ",
  function(){
          it("Currency should be used USD (US$)", function(){
              var myCurrency = new Currency("US");
              expect(myCurrency.currency).toBe("US$");
          });
      });
  });
```

2. Next, let's define the spec for scenario 1, Using the following code:

```
      //Scenario -2
      describe("Tax deducted for United Kingdom Employees, ",
  function(){
          it("Currency should be used GBP (Pound, UK£)", function(){
              var myCurrency = new Currency("UK");
              expect(myCurrency.currency).toBe("UK£");
          });


          //Scenario -7 (Scenario -1 for this recipe)
      xit("Should be deducted 20% " +
          "if Gross Annual Income is " +
          "between £10,000/- and  £32,000", function(){
      });
      });
```

In the preceding code snapshot, notice that we defined the spec for scenario 1 and marked it as **pending** by declaring the it block as a xit function. For more information on pending specs, refer to the recipe, *Declaring pending specs with Jasmine tests*, in *Chapter 3, Customizing Matchers and Jasmine Functions*.

Pending specs do not run, but their names will be displayed in the test results as **pending**.

3. Let's define the specs for scenarios 2 and 3 and mark them as pending using the following code:

```
describe("Tax deducted for United States Employees, ",
function(){
    //Scenario -3
    it("Currency should be used USD (US$)", function(){
        var myCurrency = new Currency("US");
        expect(myCurrency.currency).toBe("US$");
    });

    //Scenario -8 (Scenario -2 for this recipe)
    xit("Should be deducted 35% " +
        "of Gross Taxable Income " +
        "if employee status is SINGLE", function(){
    });

    //Scenario -9 (Scenario -3 for this recipe)
    xit("Should be deducted 30% " +
        "of Gross Taxable Income " +
        "if employee status is MARRIED", function(){
    });
});
```

4. Run the spec file (TDS_nested_spec.js) with the Jasmine runner and you will see the following output:

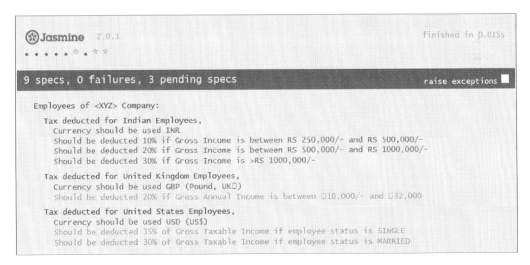

In the preceding screenshot, notice that all the three scenarios defined in steps 2 and 3 are displayed as **pending**.

5. Next, let's refactor the specs to make them more understandable. Also, identify the common code across the specs. Using the following code:

```
describe("Employees of <XYZ> Company:",function(){
  describe("Tax/TDS Currency", function(){
    //Scenario -1
    it("Currency should be used INR", function(){
      var myCurrency = new Currency("INDIA");
      expect(myCurrency.currency).toBe("INR");
    });

    //Scenario -2
    it("Currency should be used GBP (Pound, UK£)", function(){
      var myCurrency = new Currency("UK");
      expect(myCurrency.currency).toBe("UK£");
    });

    //Scenario -3
    it("Currency should be used USD (US$)", function(){
      var myCurrency = new Currency("US");
      expect(myCurrency.currency).toBe("US$");
    });
  });
  describe("Tax/TDS", function(){
    describe("For Indian Employees, ", function(){

      //Scenario -4
      it("Should be deducted 10% if Gross Income is " +
         "between RS 250,000/- and RS 500,000/-", function(){
        var myTaxableIncome = new TaxIndiaEmp();
        //Let's assume the taxable income is RS 300,000/-
        myTaxableIncome.setIncome(300000);
        expect(myTaxableIncome.calculateTDS())
        .toEqual(5000);
      });

      //Scenario -5
      it("Should be deducted 20% if Gross Income is " +
         "between RS 500,000/- and RS 1,000,000/-", function(){
        var myTaxableIncome = new TaxIndiaEmp();
        //Let's assume the taxable income is RS 700,000/-
        myTaxableIncome.setIncome(700000);
```

```
        expect(myTaxableIncome.calculateTDS())
        .toEqual(40000);
      });

      //Scenario -6
      it("Should be deducted 30% if Gross Income " +
          "is >RS 1,000,000/-", function(){
    var myTaxableIncome = new TaxIndiaEmp();
          //Let's assume the taxable income is RS 1,300,000/-
    myTaxableIncome.setIncome(1300000);
          expect(myTaxableIncome.calculateTDS())
          .toEqual(90000);
      });
    });
    describe("For United Kingdom Employees, ", function(){

      //Scenario -7 (Scenario -1 for this recipe)
      xit("Should be deducted 20% " +
          "if Gross Annual Income is " +
          "between £10,000/- and  £32,000", function(){
      });
    });
    describe("For United States Employees, ", function(){

      //Scenario -8 (Scenario -2 for this recipe)
      xit("Should be deducted 35% " +
          "of Gross Taxable Income " +
          "if employee status is SINGLE", function(){
      });

      //Scenario -9 (Scenario -3 for this recipe)
      xit("Should be deducted 30% " +
          "of Gross Taxable Income " +
          "if employee status is MARRIED", function(){
      });
    });
  });
});
```

In the preceding code snapshot, notice that we reorganized all the specs and highlighted the common test code across the specs.

6. Now, run the spec file (`TDS_nested_spec.js`) with the Jasmine runner and you will see that all the tests are reorganized according to related functionality:

```
*Jasmine  2.0.1                                    finished in 0.006s
• • • • • • ☆ ☆ ☆

9 specs, 0 failures, 3 pending specs
                                                   raise exceptions ■

Employees of <XYZ> Company:

  Tax/TDS Currency
    Currency should be used INR
    Currency should be used GBP (Pound, UK□)
    Currency should be used USD (US$)

  Tax/TDS

    For Indian Employees,
      Should be deducted 10% if Gross Income is between RS 250,000/- and RS 500,000/-
      Should be deducted 20% if Gross Income is between RS 500,000/- and RS 1000,000/-
      Should be deducted 30% if Gross Income is >RS 1000,000/-

    For United Kingdom Employees,
      Should be deducted 20% if Gross Annual Income is between □10,000/- and □32,000

    For United States Employees,
      Should be deducted 35% of Gross Taxable Income if employee status is SINGLE
      Should be deducted 30% of Gross Taxable Income if employee status is MARRIED
```

7. To optimize the test code, let's refactor the common code under the suite `Tax/TDS Currency` using the following code:

```javascript
    describe("Tax/TDS Currency", function(){
var index = 0;
var myRegion, myCurrency;
beforeEach(function() {
  myRegion = ["INDIA", "UK", "US"];
  myCurrency = new Currency(myRegion[index]);
  });
afterEach(function() {
  index=index+1;
});
    //Scenario -1
    it("Currency should be used INR", function(){
      expect(myCurrency.currency).toBe("INR");
    });

    //Scenario -2
    it("Currency should be used GBP (Pound, UK£)", function(){
      expect(myCurrency.currency).toBe("UK£");
    });
```

```
                //Scenario -
  3
        it("Currency should be used USD (US$)", function(){
          expect(myCurrency.currency).toBe("US$");
        });
      });
```

8. Next, let's refactor the common code under the suite `For Indian Employees` (a spec within the `Tax/TDS` group). Using the following code:

```
        describe("For Indian Employees, ", function(){
          var index=0;
          var grossTaxableIncome, myTaxableIncome;
          beforeEach(function() {
            grossTaxableIncome = [300000, 700000, 1300000];
            myTaxableIncome = new TaxIndiaEmp();
            myTaxableIncome.setIncome(grossTaxableIncome[index]);
            });
          afterEach(function() {
            index=index+1;
          });

          //Scenario -4
          it("Should be deducted 10% if Gross Income is " +
              "between RS 250,000/- and RS 500,000/-", function(){
            //Let's assume the taxable income is RS 300,000/-
            expect(myTaxableIncome.calculateTDS())
            .toEqual(5000);
          });

          //Scenario -5
          it("Should be deducted 20% if Gross Income is " +
              "between RS 500,000/- and RS 1,000,000/-", function(){
            //Let's assume the taxable income is RS 700,000/-
            expect(myTaxableIncome.calculateTDS())
            .toEqual(40000);
          });

          //Scenario -6
          it("Should be deducted 30% if Gross Income " +
              "is >RS 1,000,000/-", function(){
            //Let's assume the taxable income is RS 1,300,000/-
            expect(myTaxableIncome.calculateTDS())
            .toEqual(90000);
          });
        });
```

9. Now, run the spec file (`TDS_nested_spec.js`) with the Jasmine runner and you will see that all the tests pass after optimizing the test code:

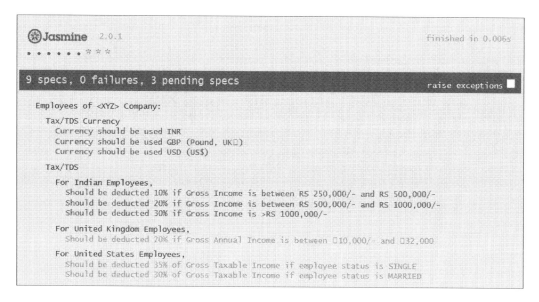

How it works...

Let's take a look at the steps of this recipe.

In steps 1 to 7, we saw that how nested suites help in defining and categorizing the related functionality. In steps 2 to 3, we defined the specs for scenarios 1 to 3 and marked them as **pending** using `xit`.

In step 5, to define the specs meaningfully, we refactored the specs according to related functionality. In steps 7 to 8, to optimize the test code, we refactored the common code using the `beforeEach` and `afterEach` functions.

Great work! Step outside and grab a cup of coffee for having learned the BDD approach; and while you're at it, go ahead and share what you just learned with your peers as well.

3
Customizing Matchers and Jasmine Functions

In this chapter, we will cover:

- ▶ Writing a Jasmine test using a custom equality tester function
- ▶ Writing Jasmine tests with Custom Matchers
- ▶ Writing Jasmine tests for exceptions
- ▶ Declaring Pending specs with Jasmine tests

Introduction

A matcher is used to evaluate an assertion of an object. If the expected and actual values match, the assertion passes, or else, the assertion fails. Jasmine provides a rich set of built-in matchers to test JavaScript applications. To know more about Jasmine's built-in matchers, refer to the *Applying different matchers to the Jasmine test* recipe in *Chapter 1, Getting Started with Jasmine Framework*. In addition to the built-in matchers, Jasmine also provides various functions and enables you to create custom matchers to test JavaScript code. Custom matchers help to document the intent of the spec and can also help to remove code duplication across specs. In this chapter, we will investigate the need of such custom matchers and find out how to develop these in order to validate a specific test condition or scenario. In addition, you will learn how to test the scenarios that expect JavaScript exceptions to be thrown.

Writing a Jasmine test using a custom equality tester function

You can customize how Jasmine determines whether two objects are equal by defining your own custom equality tester. A custom equality tester is a function, which takes two arguments. This function returns either `true` or `false` based on the arguments. Also, if it is unable to compare the argument values, then the custom equality tester function will return `undefined`.

In this recipe, you will learn how to compare the equality of two objects using such custom equality tester functions.

Let's consider a scenario where the equality of two strings should be decided using a custom equality tester function.

"As a JavaScript developer, I want to develop a mechanism to check the equality of two strings so that I can compare and categorize objects."

> ▶ **Scenario-1**: Two strings should be equal if the first word of both strings is `Packt`

How to do it...

You need to perform the following steps:

1. First, you need to create a spec file (`custom_equality_spec.js`) under the `/spec` folder and code the following lines to define and implement the spec for scenario 1:

```
describe("Custom Equality Function: ", function() {
   describe("Strings: ", function(){
      it("should be custom equal if first word of both the strings
is Packt", function() {
         expect("Packt Jasmine Book").toEqual("Packt Java
Cookbook");
      });
   });
});
```

2. Run the spec file `custom_equality_spec.js`. You will see that the Jasmine test fails, as shown in the following screenshot:

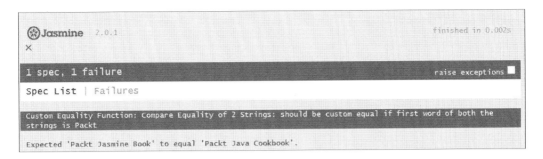

3. Now, let's define the `MyCustomEquality` custom equality tester function within the spec file `custom_equality_spec.js` to determine the equality of two strings using the following code:

```
var MyCustomEquality = function(strFirstString, strSecondString) {
    if (typeof strFirstString == "string" && typeof strSecondString
== "string") {
        return strFirstString.substr(0,5) == strSecondString.
substr(0,5);
    };
};
```

The `MyCustomEquality` function receives the first argument (that is, **Actual Value**) as the value passed to `expect()` and the value passed to the `toEqual` matcher itself as the second argument or **Expected Value**.

4. Next, use the following code to implement scenario 1 using a custom equality tester function:

```
describe("Custom Equality Function: ", function() {
    beforeEach(function() {
        jasmine.addCustomEqualityTester(MyCustomEquality);
    });
    describe("Strings: ", function(){
        it("should be custom equal if first word of both the strings
is Packt", function() {
            expect("Packt Jasmine Book").toEqual("Packt Java
Cookbook");
        });
    });
});
```

Here, note how we registered the `MyCustomEquality` custom equality tester function inside the `beforeEach` function.

 Once a custom equality tester function is registered in the `beforeEach` function, it will first be checked before the default equality logic.

5. Finally, run the spec file `custom_equality_spec.js` with the Jasmine runner (that is, `SpecRunner.html`). You will see that the Jasmine test passes:

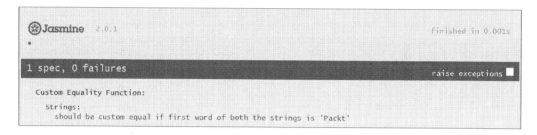

How it works...

In steps 1 and 2, we implemented scenario 1 using the `toEqual` matcher.

In step 3, we defined the `MyCustomEquality` custom equality tester function to determine the equality of two strings.

In steps 4 and 5, we implemented scenario 1 using the custom equality tester function.

Writing Jasmine tests with custom matchers

Jasmine's built-in matchers are very useful and work well in most scenarios. However, sometimes we need to develop custom matchers to implement specific scenarios. For example, we need to create the custom matchers to override the failure message or to define a new message (or custom error message). Also, a custom matcher can be created when you find a piece of code that tests the same set of properties over and over again across the different specs, and you want to bundle the fragment into a single assertion. By writing your own matcher, you eliminate code duplication and make tests more readable. In other words, by defining your own matchers, you develop a **Domain-Specific Language** (**DSL**) to describe the intent of tests in a more readable and expressive way.

To write a Jasmine test using custom matchers, let's assume that the task is to develop an online ordering module for <XYZ> company's website. There are some business rules to fill the online order.

"As an administrator, I want to validate all the business rules on submission of an online order so that I can process orders"

Let's consider some scenarios, that is, all business rules should be validated before accepting the online order:

- **Scenario-1**: Person's age should be greater than or equal to 21
- **Scenario-2**: Person's first and last names are mandatory to process the online order

Now, to understand the concept of custom matchers, consider that whenever a Jasmine test fails, a user-defined error message should be displayed for both scenarios, as follows:

- **Error message for Scenario-1**: Minimum person's age should be 21 years to place the order online
- **Error message for Scenario-2**: Person's first name and last name are mandatory to process the online order

How to do it...

You need to perform the following steps to write Jasmine tests using custom matchers:

1. Create a spec file `Custom_Matcher_spec.js` under the `/spec` folder and code the following lines to define a spec for scenario 1:

```
describe("<XYZ> Company: Online Order Module", function() {
    describe("When to place the online order: ", function(){
        it("Age should be greater than " +
            "or equal to 21 years", function() {
        });
    });
});
```

2. Now, run the spec file `Custom_Matcher_spec.js` with the Jasmine runner (that is, `SpecRunner.html`). You will see that an empty spec (that is, a spec without any expectation) passes:

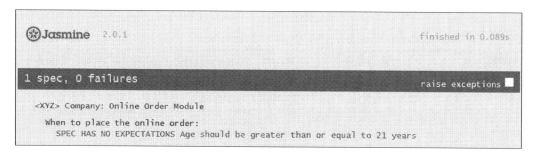

3. Next, let's add the reference of the custom matcher to display the error message for scenario 1 using the following code:

```
describe("<XYZ> Company: Online Order Module", function() {
    describe("When to place the online order: ", function(){
        beforeEach(function() {
            jasmine.addMatchers(personAgeValidationMatcher);
        });
        it("Age should be greater than " +
            "or equal to 21 years", function() {
        });
    });
});
```

Note, how we added the reference of a custom matcher (`personAgeValidationMatcher`) to the `beforeEach` function.

Before applying a custom matcher to any expectation, its reference needs to be added in the `beforeEach` function.

4. Run the spec file `Custom_Matcher_spec.js`. You will see that the spec fails in the absence of the **personAgeValidationMatcher** custom matcher function:

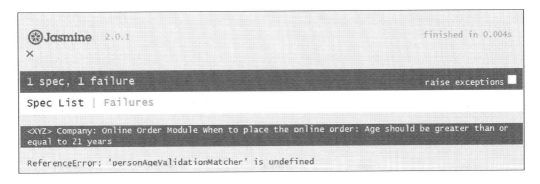

5. As indicated in the previous step, let's define the custom matcher `personAgeValidationMatcher` within the spec file `Custom_Matcher_spec.js` using the following code:

```
var personAgeValidationMatcher  = {
    toBeOlderThan: function() {
      return {
        compare: function(actualAge, expectedAge) {
          if (expectedAge === undefined) {
            throw "Expected value is required";
          }
          if (actualAge>=expectedAge) {
            return {
              pass:true
            };
          }else {
            return {
              pass:false
            };
          };
        }
      };
    }
};
```

Here, note that we created the `toBeOlderThan` method to validate a person's age within the `personAgeValidationMatcher` custom matcher. Also, a `compare` function is created with two parameters.

The `compare` function receives the first argument as **Actual Value,** which is passed to `expect()` and it receives the second argument as **Expected Value**, which is passed to the matcher itself.

The `compare` function returns a result object with a property called `pass` that is the `Boolean` result of matcher. The `pass` property tells the expectation whether the matcher is successful (`true`) or unsuccessful (`false`).

6. Now, let's create the `Person.js` file under the `/src` folder and define the `Person()` object to get one's age and name. Use the following code to define the `Person()` object:

```
var Person = function (age, firstName, lastName) {
this.age=age;
this.firstName = firstName;
this.lastName = lastName;
};
```

7. Next, use the following code to implement scenario 1:

```
describe("<XYZ> Company: Online Order Module", function() {
  describe("When to place the online order: ", function(){
    beforeEach(function() {
        jasmine.addMatchers(personAgeValidationMatcher);
    });
    it("Age should be greater than " +
        "or equal to 21 years", function() {
        var myPerson = new Person(25, "James", "Smith");
      expect(myPerson.age).toBeOlderThan(20);
    });
  });
});
```

Here, you can observe that we are using the `toBeOlderThan()` function to validate a person's age, which is defined within the custom matcher (`personAgeValidationMatcher`).

8. Now, add the reference of the `Person.js` file to the Jasmine runner and run the spec file `Custom_Matcher_spec.js`. You will see that the spec passes:

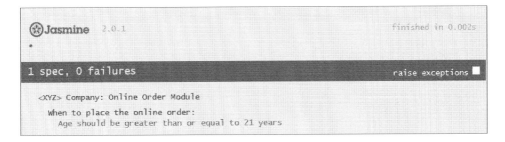

9. Before implementing the custom failure message for scenario 1, let's use the following code to fail it:

```
describe("<XYZ> Company: Online Order Module", function() {
    describe("When to place the online order: ", function(){
        beforeEach(function() {
            jasmine.addMatchers(personAgeValidationMatcher);
        });
        it("Age should be greater than " +
            "or equal to 21 years", function() {
            var myPerson = new Person(18, "James", "Smith");
            expect(myPerson.age).toBeOlderThan(20);
        });
    });
});
```

10. Run the spec file `Custom_Matcher_spec.js` with the Jasmine runner. You should see the following failure message:

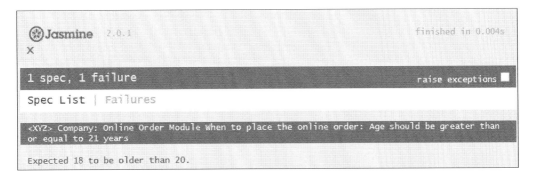

In the preceding screenshot, you can see that the expectation generated an error message for the matcher: **Expected 18 to be older than 20**.

In the absence of a user-defined error message, the expectation will generate a default error message for the matcher.

11. Now, let's implement a user-defined error message for scenario 1 using the following code:

```
var personAgeValidationMatcher  = {
    toBeOlderThan: function() {
      return {
        compare: function(actualAge, expectedAge) {
          if (expectedAge === undefined) {
            throw "Expected value is required";
          }
          if (actualAge>=expectedAge) {
            return {
              pass:true,
              message:"Person is eligible to place online order"
            };
          }else {
            return {
              pass:false,
              message:"Minimum person's age should be 21 years to
place the order online"
            };
          };
        }
      };
    }
  };
```

In the preceding code snapshot, notice how we defined a custom message using the `message` property.

12. Run the spec file `Custom_Matcher_spec.js`. You will see a user-defined failure message, as shown in the following screenshot:

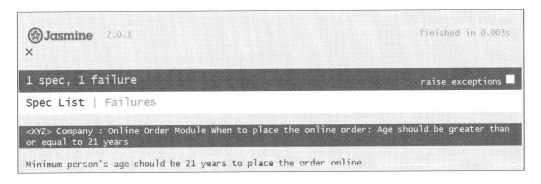

In the preceding screenshot, you can see that a user-defined message is displayed: **Minimum person's age should be 21 years to place order online**.

13. Next, to implement scenario 2, let's create a custom matcher (`personNameValidationMatcher`) within the spec file `Custom_Matcher_spec.js` using the following code:

```
var personNameValidationMatcher = {
  toContainFirstAndLastName: function() {
     return {
       compare: function(actual) {
          if (actual.firstName != undefined && actual.lastName !=
undefined){
             return {
               pass:true,
               message:"Person is eligible to place the online order"
             };
          } else {
             return {
               pass:false,
               message:"First name and last name are mandatory to
process the online order"
             };
          };
       }
     };
  }
};
```

Here, you can observe that we created the `toContainFirstAndLastName` method to validate the person's full name. Also, we defined a custom message using the `message` property. This will be displayed if the Jasmine test fails.

14. Now, following the same pattern, let's define and implement the spec for scenario 2 using the following code:

```
describe("<XYZ> Company : Online Order Module ", function() {
    describe("When to place the online order: ", function(){
        beforeEach(function() {
            jasmine.addMatchers(personAgeValidationMatcher );
            jasmine.addMatchers(personNameValidationMatcher);
        });
        //Scenario 1
        it("Age should be greater than " +
            "or equal to 21 years", function() {
            var myPerson = new Person(25, "James", "Smith");
          expect(myPerson.age).toBeOlderThan(20);
        });
        //Scenario 2
        it("First Name and Last Name are required " +
            "to place the online order", function() {
            var myPerson = new Person(23, "James", "Smith");
          expect(myPerson).toContainFirstAndLastName();
        });
    });
});
```

In the preceding code snapshot, you will observe that we added the reference to the custom matcher (that is, `personNameValidationMatcher`) inside the `beforeEach` function.

15. Finally, run the spec file `Custom_Matcher_spec.js`. You will see that the specs pass for both the scenarios:

How it works...

In steps 1 to 15, we looked at how Jasmine tests are developed using custom matchers. We also saw how the custom messages are generated when the test fails.

Let's take a look at what we did throughout this recipe.

In steps 1 to 8, we implemented scenario 1 using custom matchers. In step 3, we added the reference to the custom matcher (`personAgeValidationMatcher`) using the `beforeEach` function. In step 5, we created the `personAgeValidationMatcher` custom matcher in the spec file `Custom_Matcher_spec.js`. In step 6, to implement the functionality of scenario 1, we defined the `Person` object. In step 7, we implemented specs for scenario 1.

In steps 9 to 12, we implemented a user-defined failure message for scenario 1 using a custom matcher.

In steps 13 to 15, following the same methodology, we defined and implemented the specs for scenario 2.

Writing Jasmine tests for exceptions

In this recipe, you will learn to write Jasmine tests for JavaScript exceptions using the `toThrow()` and `toThrowError()` matchers. Also, you will learn how to write Jasmine tests to validate user-defined messages.

To write the Jasmine test for Exceptions, let's assume that you are developing an application for <ABC> company. Currently, you are developing an error handling module, which handles user-defined or system errors.

"As a JavaScript developer, I want to handle all the errors and validate error messages so that the end user should not get stuck during any process."

Let's consider some scenarios in the current context, that is, all the system and user-defined errors should be handled throughout the application:

 ▶ **Scenario-1**: Error should be thrown on any unexpected behavior or malfunction.

 ▶ **Scenario-2**: Error messages should be consistent throughout the application.

How to do it...

You need to perform the following steps to write Jasmine tests for exceptions:

1. Create a spec file `Exception_spec.js` under the `/spec` folder and code the following lines to define the spec for scenario 1:

    ```
    describe("JavaScript Exceptions: ", function(){
      describe("Validate Errors:", function(){
        it("Error should be thrown on any " +
            "unexpected behavior or malfunctioning", function(){
        });
      });
    });
    ```

2. Run the spec file `Exception_spec.js`. You will see that an empty spec passes, as shown in the following screenshot:

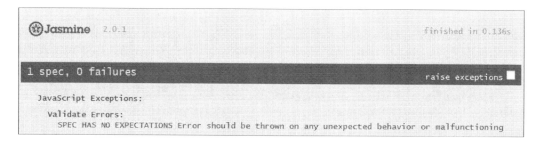

3. Create the `Exception.js` file and put it under the `/src` folder. Using the following code:

    ```
    function addTwonumbers(num1, num2){
      return num1 + num2;
    };
    function generateMaxValue(maxValue){
      var intVar=maxValue;
      if (intVar===undefined){
          throw new ParameterException("No value is assigned to variable
    intVar!");
      }
      intVar=intVar+1;
      if (maxValue<1 || maxValue>1000){
    ```

```
    throw new ArgumentOutOfRangeException("Maximum value should be
between 0 and 1000");
  }
  return intVar;
};


function ParameterException(message) {
    this.name = "ParameterException";
    this.message = message || "Default Message";
}
ParameterException.prototype = Object.create(Error.prototype);
ParameterException.prototype.constructor = ParameterException;

function ArgumentOutOfRangeException(message) {
  this.name = "ArgumentOutOfRangeException";
  this.message = message || "Default Message";
}
ArgumentOutOfRangeException.prototype = Object.create(Error.
prototype);
ArgumentOutOfRangeException.prototype.constructor =
ArgumentOutOfRangeException;
```

You can see in the preceding code snapshot that an error will be thrown along with
a user-defined error message if the `intVar` variable is undefined or the value of the
`maxValue` argument is not between 0 and 1000.

4. Now, use the following test code to implement scenario 1:

```
describe("JavaScript Exceptions: ", function(){
  describe("Validate Errors:", function(){
    it("Error should be thrown on any " +
        "unexpected behavior or malfunctioning", function(){
      expect(addTwonumbers).not.toThrow();
      expect(generateMaxValue).toThrow();
      expect(generateMaxValue).toThrowError();
    });
  });
});
```

In the preceding code snapshot, you can see that both functions `addTwonumbers`
and `generateMaxValue` are used without parenthesis. It means that we are not
passing any arguments to both functions.

5. Next, to test the functions' arguments, let's implement the code for scenario 1 along with function parameters, using the following code:

```
describe("JavaScript Exceptions: ", function(){
  describe("Validate Errors:", function(){
    //Scenario 1
    it("Error should be thrown on any " +
        "unexpected behavior or malfunctioning", function(){
      expect(addTwonumbers).not.toThrow();
      expect(generateMaxValue).toThrow();
      expect(generateMaxValue).toThrowError();
    });
    it("Error should be thrown on passing any " +
        "unexpected or wrong arguments", function(){
      /*Assertions to test parameters
       * of addTwonumbers() function*/
      expect(addTwonumbers.bind(null,1,2)).not.toThrow();
      expect(addTwonumbers.bind(null,1,2)).not.toThrowError();
      expect(function(){addTwonumbers(1,4);}).not.toThrow();
      /*Assertions to test parameters
       * of generateMaxValue() function*/
      expect(generateMaxValue.bind(null,5)).not.toThrow();
      expect(generateMaxValue.bind(this,5)).not.toThrow();
      expect(function() {generateMaxValue(2000);}).toThrow();
      expect(function() {generateMaxValue(2000);}).toThrowError();
    });
  });
});
```

Here, you can see that we passed the arguments in two ways – using the bind function and prefixed `function()` to test (`AddTwonumbers` and `GenerateMaxValue`).

To validate parameters of a function, You can pass the arguments with the bind function. This function was introduced in ECMAScript 5. The first parameter needs to be passed as `null` or `this`. Thereafter, you can pass the actual parameter(s) of the function to be tested.

Another way to pass the arguments is simply to prefix `function()` with the function to be tested.

6. Now, add the reference of the `Exception.js` file to the Jasmine runner (that is, `SpecRunner.html`) and run the spec file `Exception_spec.js`. You will see that both the specs pass for scenario 1:

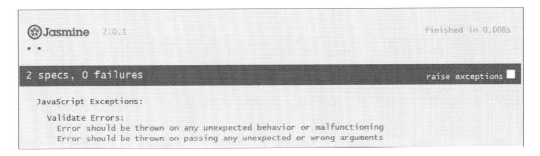

7. Let's use the following code to implement scenario 2:

```
describe("Validate Error Messages: ", function(){
    it("Error messages should be consistent " +
        "throughout the application", function(){
        expect(generateMaxValue).toThrow(new Error("No value is
assigned to variable intVar!"));
        expect(generateMaxValue).toThrowError("No value is
assigned to variable intVar!");
        expect(generateMaxValue.bind(null,5000)).toThrow(new
Error("Maximum value should be between 0 and 1000"));
        expect(generateMaxValue.bind(null,5000)).
toThrowError("Maximum value should be between 0 and 1000");
        expect(function() {generateMaxValue(5000);}).
toThrowError("Maximum value should be between 0 and 1000");
    });
});
```

In the preceding code snapshot, you will observe that we are using the `toThrow` and `toThrowError` matchers to validate user-defined error messages.

8. Now, to execute both scenarios, run the spec file `Exception_spec.js`. You will see that both scenarios are pass:

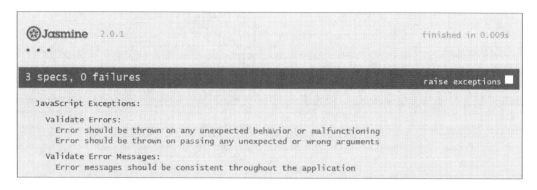

9. Next, let's fail scenario 2 by passing a message, which is different from the JavaScript code, using the following code:

```
describe("Validate Error Messages: ", function(){
    it("Error messages should be consistent " +
        "throughout the application", function(){
        expect(generateMaxValue).toThrow(new Error("No value is
assigned to variable intVar!"));
        expect(generateMaxValue).toThrowError("No value is
assigned to variable intVar!");
        expect(generateMaxValue.bind(null,5000)).toThrow(new
Error("Maximum value should be between 0 and 1000"));
        expect(generateMaxValue.bind(null,5000)).
toThrowError("Maximum value should be between 0 and 1000");
        expect(function() {generateMaxValue(5000);}).
toThrowError("Value should be between 0-1000");
    });
});
```

In the preceding test code, you can see that the error message has been changed. Now, the message is **Value should be between 0 and 1000** instead of **Maximum value should be between 0 and 1000**, which is defined with JavaScript code in the `Exception.js` file.

10. Run the spec file `Exception_spec.js` with the Jasmine runner. You will see that the spec fails for scenario 2:

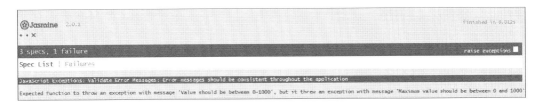

You will observe in the preceding screenshot that the test fails because of inconsistent error messages.

How it works...

In steps 1 to 10, we saw how to write Jasmine tests to validate JavaScript exceptions/errors using the `toThrow` and `toThrowError` matchers. We also looked at how to write tests to validate error messages.

Let's take a look at the steps of this recipe.

In steps 1 to 2, we defined the empty spec for scenario 1.

In step 3, to write Jasmine tests for exception, we developed JavaScript code in the `Exception.js` file. Here, we defined two functions: `AddTwonumbers()` and `GenerateMaxValue(maxValue)`. Also, to handle argument errors for the `GenerateMaxValue` function, we defined two functions (that is, `ParameterException` and `ArgumentOutOfRangeException`) along with user-defined error messages.

In steps 4 to 6, we implemented scenario 1 to test JavaScript exceptions using the `toThrow` and `toThrowError` matchers. In step 5, we implemented the code to test the function's arguments using the `bind` function. Also, we passed the parameter (that is, `maxValue`) value of more than 1000 to pass the test.

In steps 7 to 8, we implemented scenario 2 to validate the consistency of messages throughout the application.

In steps 9 to 10, we implemented test code for scenario 2 to make it fail. Here, we saw how a Jasmine test fails because of inconsistent messages defined across JavaScript code and Jasmine specs.

Furthermore, I would suggest that you change the error message defined in step 10 as per step 7 (that is, `Maximum value should be between 0 and 1000`) and run the spec file with the Jasmine runner to see the test results.

 It's good practice to create Jasmine tests corresponding to exceptions to maintain the consistency of error messages.

Declaring pending specs with Jasmine tests

Sometimes, the specific functionality of an application gets changed or becomes obsolete due to new business rules or change requests raised by stakeholders. In this situation, such legacy Jasmine tests also becomes obsolete and there is a need to remove them from the existing suites. In this recipe, you will learn the usage of pending specs and how to handle the specs that get changed or obsolete.

Getting ready

You will learn this recipe with the help of the second recipe in this chapter, *Writing a Jasmine test with Custom Matchers*.

To understand the concept of pending specs, consider that a few of the business rules have been changed for both the scenarios described in the second recipe. Now, let's consider the following scenarios as per the new business rules:

- **Scenario-1**: Age is not a criteria to place the online order
- **Scenario-2**: Only the first name is required to place the online order

How to do it...

You need to perform the following steps to declare pending specs with Jasmine tests:

1. First, you need to create a spec file (`Peding_spec.js`) under the `/spec` folder and get the following code from the spec file (`Custom_Matcher_spec.js`) created in the second recipe of this chapter, *Writing a Jasmine test with Custom Matchers*:

```
describe("<XYZ> Company : Online Order Module ", function() {
  describe("When to place the online order: ", function(){
    beforeEach(function() {
      jasmine.addMatchers(personAgeValidationMatcher );
      jasmine.addMatchers(personNameValidationMatcher);
    });
```

```
        //Scenario 1
        it("Age should be greater than " +
            "or equal to 21 years", function() {
            var myPerson = new Person(25, "James", "Smith");
          expect(myPerson.age).toBeOlderThan(20);
        });
        //Scenario 2
        it("First Name and Last Name are required " +
            "to place the online order", function() {
            var myPerson = new Person(23, "James", "Smith");
          expect(myPerson).toContainFirstAndLastName();
        });
      });
    });
```

2. As per new business rules, a person's age is not a criteria and only the first name is required to process the online order. Let's use the following code to implement scenario 1 and scenario 2:

```
describe("<XYZ> Company : Online Order Module ", function() {
  describe("When to place the online order: ", function(){
    beforeEach(function() {
        jasmine.addMatchers(personAgeValidationMatcher );
        jasmine.addMatchers(personNameValidationMatcher);
    });

    //Scenario 1
    xdescribe("Given: Age is not a " +
        "criteria to place online order", function(){
      it("Age should be greater than " +
          "or equal to 21 years", function() {
          var myPerson = new Person(25, "James", "Smith");
        expect(myPerson.age).toBeOlderThan(20);
      });
    });

    //Scenario 2
    xit("First Name and Last Name are required " +
        "to place the online order", function() {
        var myPerson = new Person(23, "James", "Smith");
      expect(myPerson).toContainFirstAndLastName();
    });
  });
});
```

You can see in the highlighted code that we created a new `xdescribe` block to implement scenario 1.

> In Jasmine, if any suite is declared with `xdescribe`, then specs created inside the suite are skipped. Also, when the suite is executed, it will not appear in the test results.

Furthermore, we assumed that JavaScript code is not developed corresponding to scenario 2 and marked the spec as pending using `xit`. Now, the spec will be ignored during the test execution.

> If any spec is declared with `xit`, then it is marked as `pending`. However, it will appear in the test results as a pending spec.
>
> It is good practice to mark all the specs as pending until the code is not refactored as per a new business rule or change request.

3. Next, run the spec file `Peding_spec.js`. You will see that only one spec is executed instead of two and it is marked as pending:

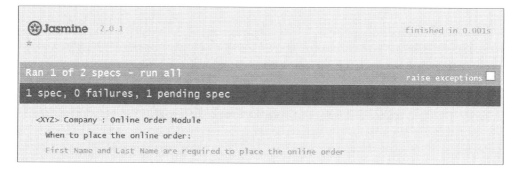

4. Let's use the following code for scenario 2 to mark the spec as pending using different options provided by Jasmine:

```
//Scenario 2
xit("First Name and Last Name are required " +
    "to place the online order", function() {
    var myPerson = new Person(23, "James", "Smith");
    expect(myPerson).toContainFirstAndLastName();
});
it("First Name and Last Name are required " +
    "to place the online order");
```

```
it("First Name and Last Name are required " +
    "to place the online order", function() {
  pending();
    var myPerson = new Person(23, "James", "Smith");
  expect(myPerson).toContainFirstAndLastName();
});
```

You will observe in the preceding code snapshot that we the declared pending specs using different options.

In Jasmine, a spec is considered as pending in the following situations:

  ▸ It the spec is declared with `xit`
  ▸ If the `pending()` function is called within the spec
  ▸ If the `it` function is declared without a function body

5. Run the spec file `Peding_spec.js`. You will see that three specs ran out of four and all three specs are marked as pending:

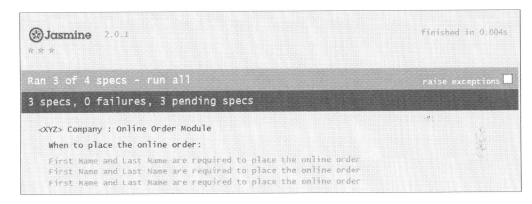

Now, you know how and why to declare the pending specs. Furthermore, I would suggest that you implement the code for scenario 2 as per the new business rule (that is, only a first name is required to place the online order).

4

Designing Specs from Requirement

In this chapter, we will cover:

- ▶ Writing useful specs by analyzing the test requirements
- ▶ Implementing the Jasmine test corresponding to the specs
- ▶ Implementing Acceptance Criteria to the Jasmine test
- ▶ Organizing Jasmine specs into groups and subgroups

Introduction

Whenever, there is a need to design and develop a new application or new component, we gather functional and nonfunctional requirements from various sources. For example, we collect the system/product requirements by reviewing and analyzing existing processes, interviewing or brainstorming with stakeholders, or by conducting the requirements workshop. Thereafter, to put together all the functional and nonfunctional requirements, we develop corresponding artifacts such as **Product Requirement Document** (**PRD**), **Software Requirement Specification** (**SRS**), Use Cases or User Stories. As per the needs of the project/stakeholders or from an implementation perspective, requirements can also be prioritized and categorized.

In this chapter, you will learn how to write Jasmine tests for test requirements and organize them into groups and subgroups. Also, you will learn how to implement acceptance criteria for a user story.

Writing useful specs by analyzing the test requirements

Generally, we develop the test requirements from PRD, SRS, Use Cases, or User Stories. Test requirements are developed in the form of test scenarios or test cases. In this recipe, we will define test requirements from the User Story in the form of test cases. Also, you will learn how to design Jasmine Specs for the test cases.

Let's assume that you are working with <ABC> Money Exchange Company. As per the new requirements, a component (or module) needs to be developed, which manages and converts currency across the continents, that is, Asia, Europe, North America, South America, and Africa. The company follows the agile methodology to design and develop their products. You are playing the role of a white box engineer (or quality engineer) in the scrum team. Your responsibility is to create all the test cases based on the requirements, and design the corresponding Jasmine specs. Thereafter, a JavaScript developer will implement the code corresponding to the specs. To know more about agile and scrum, you can visit the following websites:

- `http://en.wikipedia.org/wiki/Agile_software_development`
- `http://en.wikipedia.org/wiki/Scrum_(software_development)`

Based on the information provided here, let's consider the following user story:

"As a travel agent, I want to check the value of converted currency across the regions/countries using the Money Exchange facility of <ABC> company so that I can provide the exact details of currency conversion to tourists"

Considering that the Money Exchange company deals across the continents, the white box engineer defined the following test requirements in the form of test cases corresponding to the preceding User Story:

- **Test Case-1**: Verify that Indian Rupees (INR) are converted to US Dollars (USD)
- **Test Case-2**: Verify that Indian Rupees (INR) are converted to Japanese Yen (JPY)
- **Test Case-3**: Verify that Hong Kong Dollars (HKD) are converted to US Dollars (USD)
- **Test Case-4**: Verify that Japanese Yen (JPY) are converted to US Dollars (USD)
- **Test Case-5**: Verify that UAE Dirhams (AED) are converted to US Dollars (USD)
- **Test Case-6**: Verify that British Pound Sterlings are (GBP) converted to US Dollars (USD)
- **Test Case-7**: Verify that South African Rands (ZAR) are converted to Indian Rupees (INR)
- **Test Case-8**: Verify that US Dollars (USD) are converted to Hong Kong Dollars (HKD)
- **Test Case-9**: Verify that US Dollars (USD) are converted to Japanese Yen (JPY)

How to do it...

You need to perform the following steps to define the Jasmine specs corresponding to the test cases:

1. Create a spec file `CurrencyConverter_spec.js` under the `/spec` folder and code the following lines to define the spec for Test Case-1:

```
describe("<ABC> Money Exchange Company: Currency Converter
Module", function() {
    describe("When Convert Currency Across Region: ", function(){
        xit("Verify that Indian Rupees (INR) " +
            "converted to Us Dollars (USD)", function() {
        });
    });
});
```

Note that we defined the spec using `xit`. Now, the spec will be ignored during test execution. However, it will appear in the test results as a `pending` spec. To know more about pending specs, refer to the *Declaring pending specs with Jasmine tests* recipe in *Chapter 3, Customizing Matchers and Jasmine Functions*.

 It is good practice to mark the spec as pending until the code corresponding to the spec is not implemented.

2. Now, run the spec file `CurrencyConverter_spec.js` with the Jasmine runner (that is, `SpecRunner.html`). You will see that the spec is marked as pending for Test Case 1:

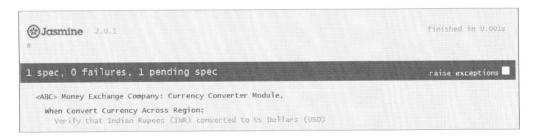

3. Next, let's define the Jasmine specs for Test Cases 2 to 9 using the following code:

```
describe("<ABC> Money Exchange Company: Currency Converter Module,
", function() {
    describe("When Convert Currency Across Region: ", function(){
        xit("Verify that Indian Rupees (INR) " +
```

```
                "converted to Us Dollars (USD)", function() {
            });
            xit("Verify that Indian Rupees (INR) " +
                "converted to Japanese Yen (JPY)", function() {
            });
            xit("Verify that Hong Kong Dollars (HKD) " +
                "converted to US Dollars (USD)", function() {
            });
            xit("Verify that Japanese Yen (JPY) " +
                "converted to US Dollars (USD)", function() {
            });
            xit("Verify that UAE Dirham (AED) " +
                "converted to US Dollars (USD)", function() {
            });
            xit("Verify that British Pound Sterling (GBP) " +
                "converted to US Dollars (USD)", function() {
            });
            xit("Verify that South African Rand (ZAR) converted to " +
                "Indian Rupees (INR)", function() {
            });
            xit("Verify that US Dollars (USD) " +
                "converted to Hong Kong Dollars (HKD)", function() {
            });
            xit("Verify that US Dollars (USD) " +
                "converted to Japanese Yen (JPY)", function() {
            });
        });
    });
```

4. Run the spec file `CurrencyConverter_spec.js` with the Jasmine runner. You will see that all the Jasmine specs corresponding to test cases are pending:

How it works...

In steps 1 to 4, we looked at how Jasmine specs are designed for the test requirements.

In step 1, we defined the Jasmine spec for Test Case 1. Also, we marked the spec as pending using `xit`.

In steps 2 to 4, following the same pattern, we designed the Jasmine specs for Test Cases 2 to 9.

Implementing the Jasmine test corresponding to the specs

In the previous recipe, *Writing useful specs by analyzing the test requirements*, we defined the Jasmine specs against test requirements. In this recipe, you will learn to write Jasmine tests and the corresponding JavaScript code for the specs designed in the previous recipe. For details, please refer to the previous recipe in this chapter.

How to do it...

You need to perform the following steps to write Jasmine tests corresponding to the specs:

1. First, you need to create a spec file (`CurrencyConverter_tests_spec.js`) under the `/spec` folder and get the following code from the spec file (`CurrencyConverter_spec.js`) created in the previous recipe:

```
describe("<ABC> Money Exchange Company: Currency Converter Module,
", function() {
  describe("When Convert Currency Across Region: ", function(){
    xit("Verify that Indian Rupees (INR) " +
        "converted to Us Dollars (USD)", function() {
    });
    xit("Verify that Indian Rupees (INR) " +
        "converted to Japanese Yen (JPY)", function() {
    });
    xit("Verify that Hong Kong Dollars (HKD) " +
        "converted to US Dollars (USD)", function() {
    });
    xit("Verify that Japanese Yen (JPY) " +
        "converted to US Dollars (USD)", function() {
    });
    xit("Verify that UAE Dirham (AED) " +
        "converted to US Dollars (USD)", function() {
    });
    xit("Verify that British Pound Sterling (GBP) " +
```

```
            "converted to US Dollars (USD)", function() {
        });
        xit("Verify that South African Rand (ZAR) converted to " +
            "Indian Rupees (INR)", function() {
        });
        xit("Verify that US Dollars (USD) " +
            "converted to Hong Kong Dollars (HKD)", function() {
        });
        xit("Verify that US Dollars (USD) " +
            "converted to Japanese Yen (JPY)", function() {
        });
    });
});
```

2. Let's define the test code to implement specs corresponding to Test Case 1 and Test Case 2 (that is, converting Indian Currency (INR) into US Dollars and Japanese Yen) using the following code:

```
describe("<ABC> Money Exchange Company: Currency Converter Module,
", function() {
    describe("When Convert Currency Across Region: ", function(){
        it("Verify that Indian Rupees (INR) " +
            "converted to Us Dollars (USD)", function() {
          var myCurrency = new CurrencyConverter(60, "INR", "USD");
          expect(myCurrency.convertedCurrency()).toEqual(1.002);
        });
        it("Verify that Indian Rupees (INR) " +
            "converted to Japanese Yen (JPY)", function() {
          var myCurrency = new CurrencyConverter(1, "INR", "JPY");
          expect(myCurrency.convertedCurrency()).toEqual(1.7756);
        });
    });
});
```

3. Run the spec file `CurrencyConverter_tests_spec.js` with the Jasmine runner. You will see that the Jasmine specs for both the test cases fail:

4. As indicated in the previous step, let's create the `CurrencyConverter.js` file and define the corresponding JavaScript code for Test Case 1 and Test Case 2 using the following code:

```javascript
var CurrencyConverter = function(number, fromCurrency, toCurrency,
currencyExchangeRate){
  this.number = number;
  this.fromCurrency=fromCurrency.toUpperCase();
  this.toCurrency=toCurrency.toUpperCase();
  this.predefinedExchangeRate=0;
  this.currencyExchangeRate=currencyExchangeRate || 0;
  this.convertedCurrency=0;
  /* Start - Configured Predefined Exchange Rates */
  var objExchangeRate =
    {
      "INR": {"USD": 0.0167, 'JPY': 1.7756}
    };
  /* End - Configured Predefined Exchange Rates */
  for(var indexfromCurrency in objExchangeRate) {
      var objPredefinedExchangeRate = objExchangeRate[indexfromCur
rency];
      if(this.fromCurrency==indexfromCurrency){
        for(var indextoCurrency in objPredefinedExchangeRate){
          if(this.toCurrency==indextoCurrency){
            this.predefinedExchangeRate= currencyExchangeRate ||
objPredefinedExchangeRate[indextoCurrency];
            this.convertedCurrency = convertCurrencyValue;
          }
        }
      }
  }
};
function convertCurrencyValue() {
  if (this.number > 10000) {
    // Exchange rate will be increased by 10%
    // if currency value is more than 10,000
    this.predefinedExchangeRate = this.predefinedExchangeRate +
(this.predefinedExchangeRate * 0.10);
    return Math.round(this.number * this.predefinedExchangeRate);
  } else {
    return this.number * this.predefinedExchangeRate;
  };
};
```

In the preceding code snapshot, you can see that we created an object (that is, `objExchangeRate`) inside the constructor function to configure the predefined exchange rate. For example, in our case, we defined an exchange rate to convert Indian Rupees, INR, into US Dollar, USD, (0.0167) and Japanese Yen, JPY, (1.7756). Further, we developed the mechanism to parse the `objExchangeRate` object and called the `convertCurrencyValue` function.

5. Run the spec file `CurrencyConverter_tests_spec.js`. You will see that both the specs pass:

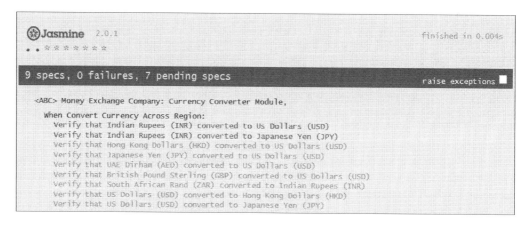

6. Next, following the same pattern, let's define the test code to implement Jasmine specs corresponding to Test Cases 3 to 9 using the following code:

```
describe("<ABC> Money Exchange Company: Currency Converter Module,
", function() {
  describe("When Convert Currency Across Region: ", function(){
    it("Verify that Indian Rupees (INR) " +
      "converted to Us Dollars (USD)", function() {
      var myCurrency = new CurrencyConverter(60, "INR", "USD");
      expect(myCurrency.convertedCurrency()).toEqual(1.002);
    });
    it("Verify that Indian Rupees (INR) " +
      "converted to Japanese Yen (JPY)", function() {
      var myCurrency = new CurrencyConverter(1, "INR", "JPY");
      expect(myCurrency.convertedCurrency()).toEqual(1.7756);
    });
    it("Verify that Hong Kong Dollars (HKD) " +
      "converted to US Dollars (USD)", function() {
```

```
    var myCurrency = new CurrencyConverter(1, "HKD", "USD");
    expect(myCurrency.convertedCurrency()).toEqual(0.1289);
  });
  it("Verify that Japanese Yen (JPY) " +
      "converted to US Dollars (USD)", function() {
    var myCurrency = new CurrencyConverter(1, "JPY", "USD");
    expect(myCurrency.convertedCurrency()).toEqual(0.54);
  });
  it("Verify that UAE Dirham (AED) " +
      "converted to US Dollars (USD)", function() {
    var myCurrency = new CurrencyConverter(1, "AED", "USD");
    expect(myCurrency.convertedCurrency()).toEqual(0.27);
  });
  it("Verify that British Pound Sterling (GBP) " +
      "converted to US Dollars (USD)", function() {
    var myCurrency = new CurrencyConverter(1, "GBP", "USD");
    expect(myCurrency.convertedCurrency()).toEqual(1.60);
  });
  it("Verify that South African Rand (ZAR) converted to " +
      "Indian Rupees (INR)", function() {
    var myCurrency = new CurrencyConverter(1, "ZAR", "INR");
    expect(myCurrency.convertedCurrency()).toEqual(5.560);
  });
  it("Verify that US Dollars (USD) " +
      "converted to Hong Kong Dollars (HKD)", function() {
    var myCurrency = new CurrencyConverter(1, "USD", "HKD");
    expect(myCurrency.convertedCurrency()).toEqual(7.750);
  });
  it("Verify that US Dollars (USD) " +
      "converted to Japanese Yen (JPY)", function() {
    var myCurrency = new CurrencyConverter(1, "USD", "JPY");
    expect(myCurrency.convertedCurrency()).toEqual(112.81);
  });
  });
});
```

Note that we are passing hardcoded expected values. However, by applying the data-driven approach, we can pass the data (input values or expected values) through a separate data file. For more information on a data-driven approach, refer to the *Implementing Jasmine Tests with Data Driven Approach* recipe in *Chapter 9, Developing JavaScript Apps Using Jasmine - A Real Time Scenario*.

7. Now, to develop the code for the specs defined in the preceding section, let's refactor the JavaScript code created in step 4 using the following code:

```javascript
var CurrencyConverter = function(number, fromCurrency, toCurrency,
currencyExchangeRate){
    this.number = number;
    this.fromCurrency=fromCurrency.toUpperCase();
    this.toCurrency=toCurrency.toUpperCase();
    this.predefinedExchangeRate=0;
    this.currencyExchangeRate=currencyExchangeRate || 0;
    this.convertedCurrency=0;
    /* Start - Configured Predefined Exchange Rates */
    var objExchangeRate =
    {
        "INR": {"USD": 0.0167, 'JPY': 1.7756},
        "HKD": {"USD": 0.1289},
        "JPY": {"USD": 0.5400},
        "AED": {"USD": 0.27},
        "GBP": {"USD": 1.60},
        "ZAR": {"INR": 5.560},
        "USD": {"HKD": 7.750, 'JPY': 112.81}
    };
    /* End - Configured Predefined Exchange Rates */
    for(var indexfromCurrency in objExchangeRate) {
        var objPredefinedExchangeRate = objExchangeRate[indexfromCur
rency];
        if(this.fromCurrency==indexfromCurrency){
            for(var indextoCurrency in objPredefinedExchangeRate){
                if(this.toCurrency==indextoCurrency){
                    this.predefinedExchangeRate= currencyExchangeRate ||
objPredefinedExchangeRate[indextoCurrency];
                    this.convertedCurrency = convertCurrencyValue;
                }
            }
        }
    }
};
function convertCurrencyValue() {
    if (this.number > 10000) {
        // Exchange rate will be increased by 10%
        // if currency value is more than 10,000
        this.predefinedExchangeRate = this.predefinedExchangeRate +
(this.predefinedExchangeRate * 0.10);
        return Math.round(this.number * this.predefinedExchangeRate);
    } else {
```

```
        return this.number * this.predefinedExchangeRate;
    };
};
```

In the preceding code snapshot, you can see that we configured the values of the predefined exchange rate for all the test cases.

8. Finally, run the spec file `CurrencyConverter_tests_spec.js` with the Jasmine runner. You will see that all the specs passes:

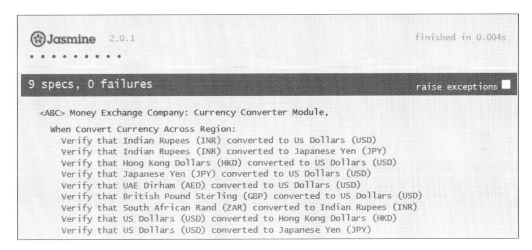

How it works...

In steps 1 to 5, we implemented Jasmine specs for Test Case 1 and Test Case 2. In step 4, we created the `CurrencyConverter.js` file and developed JavaScript code corresponding to Jasmine specs for Test Case 1 and Test Case 2. Here, we created a `CurrencyConverter` construction function with four arguments. In this function, we defined the fourth (optional) parameter as `currencyExchangeRate` to provide a user-defined exchange rate. In the absence of the `currencyExchangeRate` argument, currency will be converted with a predefined currency exchange rate. To configure the values of pre-defined exchange rates, we created an object (that is, `objExchangeRate`) and assigned corresponding values to it. Further, we developed a logic to parse the `objExchangeRate` object and assigned the value of the predefined exchange rate to the `predefinedExchangeRate` variable. Furthermore, we defined the `convertCurrencyValue` function to obtain the converted value of currency. In this function, we also modified the code when the currency value is more than 10,000. Though corresponding specs are not developed, we will discuss this in the *Increasing code coverage for existing code* recipe, in *Chapter 7, Code Coverage with Jasmine Tests*.

In steps 6 to 8, following the same pattern, we implemented the Jasmine specs for Test Cases 3 to 9.

Applying Acceptance Criteria to the Jasmine test

Normally, we define Acceptance Criteria to clarify the intended behavior of a User Story. Acceptance Criteria defines the boundary for a feature and provides clarity to all stakeholders on what needs to be achieved from a user story. It works as a completion criteria for a user story.

Let's assume that you are developing a component (or module) for the <XYZ> Money Exchange company, which manages and converts currency used in the Asia region. This company follows the agile methodology to design and develop their products. You are playing the role of a developer in the scrum team. Your responsibility is to implement the Jasmine specs for a user story. Also, the product owner is accountable to ensure whether the scrum team is delivering value to the business or not. Once the user story is completed, the product owner will accept the user story based on the Acceptance Criteria. To know more about agile, scrum, and the product owner, you can visit the following websites:

- `http://en.wikipedia.org/wiki/Agile_software_development`
- `http://en.wikipedia.org/wiki/Scrum_(software_development)`
- `http://en.wikipedia.org/wiki/Scrum_(software_development)#Role_of_Product_Owner_in_defining_and_communicating_product_requirements`

Based on the information provided here, let's consider the following user story:

"As a financial administrator of <XYZ> company, I want to check the value of the converted currency across Japan, Hong Kong, and India so that I can get the exact value of currency conversion for further usage."

Now, let's consider the following Acceptance Criteria for the preceding user story:

- **Japanese Yen** (**JPY**) should be converted to INR (Indian Rupee) with the exchange rate 0.5500
- **Hong Kong Dollar** (**HKD**) should be converted to INR (Indian Rupee) with exchange rate 9.00

How to do it...

You need to perform the following steps to write Jasmine tests for the Acceptance Criteria:

1. Create a spec file `AcceptanceCriteria_spec.js` under the `/spec` folder and code the following lines to define spec for Acceptance Criteria:

```
describe("<XYZ> Money Exchange Company: Currency Converter Module,
", function() {
  describe("When Convert the Currency Across Asian Countries: ",
function(){
    it("Japanese Yen (JPY) should be converted " +
        "to Indian Rupee (INR) " +
        "with user defined exchange rate", function() {
    });
    it("Hong Kong Dollar (HKD) should be converted " +
        "to Indian Rupee (INR) with " +
        "user defined exchange rate", function() {
    });
  });
});
```

2. Run the spec file `AcceptanceCriteria_spec.js` with the Jasmine runner (that is, `SpecRunner.html`). You will see that both the empty specs pass:

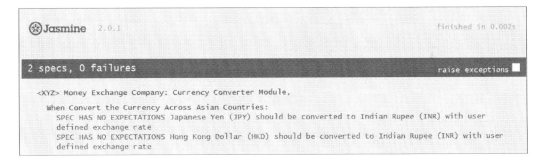

3. Now, let's implement the Acceptance Criteria using the following code:

```
describe("<XYZ> Money Exchange Company: Currency Converter Module,
", function() {
  describe("When Convert the Currency Across Asian Countries: ",
function(){
    it("Japanese Yen (JPY) should be converted " +
        "to Indian Rupee (INR) " +
```

```
        "with user defined exchange rate", function() {
        var myCurrency = new CurrencyConverter(1, "JPY",
"INR",0.5500);
            expect(myCurrency.convertedCurrency()).toEqual(0.5500);
        });
        it("Hong Kong Dollar (HKD) should be converted " +
            "to Indian Rupee (INR) with " +
            "user defined exchange rate", function() {
        var myCurrency = new CurrencyConverter(10000, "HKD",
"INR",9.0);
            expect(myCurrency.convertedCurrency()).toEqual(90000);
        });
    });
});
```

4. Run the spec file `AcceptanceCriteria_spec.js` with the Jasmine runner; this will let you know that both the specs defined for Acceptance Criteria are fail:

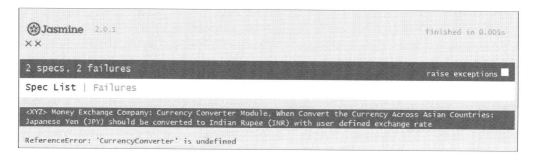

5. As indicated in the previous step, JavaScript code needs to be developed corresponding to the specs. Let's use the same code/JavaScript file `CurrencyConverter.js` created in the previous recipe, *Implementing the Jasmine test corresponding to the specs*, and define the predefined exchange rate as follows:

```
/* Start - Configured Predefined Exchange Rates */
var objExchangeRate =
{
  "INR": {"USD": 0.0167, "JPY": 1.7756},
  "HKD": {"USD": 0.1289, "INR": 8.0},
  "JPY": {"USD": 0.5400, "INR": 0.0089},
  "AED": {"USD": 0.27},
  "GBP": {"USD": 1.60},
  "ZAR": {"INR": 5.560},
  "USD": {"HKD": 7.750, "JPY": 112.81}
};
/* End - Configured Predefined Exchange Rates */
```

6. Finally, add the reference of the `CurrencyConverter.js` file to the Jasmine runner and run the spec file `CurrencyConverter_spec.js`. You will see that all the Jasmine specs corresponding to the Acceptance Criteria pass:

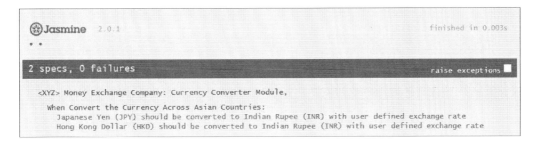

How it works...

Let's take a look at the steps of this recipe.

In step 1, we defined the empty Jasmine specs corresponding to the Acceptance Criteria.

In step 3, we implemented the test code corresponding to the specs. Here, we called the construction function with user-defined exchange rates as defined by the Acceptance Criteria.

In step 5, we configured the predefined exchange rate to convert Japanese Yen and Hong Kong Dollars to Indian Rupees.

Organizing Jasmine specs into groups and subgroups

Whenever code expands and becomes complex, we can segregate and categorize the Jasmine specs corresponding to a specific feature or component. In this recipe, you will learn how to organize Jasmine specs into groups and subgroups. Jasmine provides the `describe` global function to define group-related specs. The `string` parameter of the `describe` function is used to name the collection of specs, which represents a specific feature or component. This helps in finding specs and corresponding JavaScript code in a large suite. The name of the collection of specs is further concatenated with the name(s) of subgroup(s) to make a spec's full name. Moreover, if we name them well, we can read specs as a full sentence.

You will learn this recipe with the help of the second recipe in this chapter, *Implementing the Jasmine test corresponding to the specs*.

How to do it...

You need to perform the following steps to write the organized Jasmine specs into groups and subgroups:

1. First, you need to create a spec file (CurrencyConverter_tests_group_
   spec.js) under the /spec folder and get the following code from the spec file
   (CurrencyConverter_tests_spec.js) created in the second recipe of this
   chapter:

```javascript
describe("<ABC> Money Exchange Company: Currency Converter Module.
", function() {
  describe("When Convert Currency Across Region: ", function(){
    it("Verify that Indian Rupees (INR) " +
      "converted to Us Dollars (USD)", function() {
      var myCurrency = new CurrencyConverter(60, "INR", "USD");
      expect(myCurrency.convertedCurrency()).toEqual(1.002);
    });
    it("Verify that Indian Rupees (INR) " +
      "converted to Japanese Yen (JPY)", function() {
      var myCurrency = new CurrencyConverter(1, "INR", "JPY");
      expect(myCurrency.convertedCurrency()).toEqual(1.7756);
    });
    it("Verify that Hong Kong Dollars (HKD) " +
      "converted to US Dollars (USD)", function() {
      var myCurrency = new CurrencyConverter(1, "HKD", "USD");
      expect(myCurrency.convertedCurrency()).toEqual(0.1289);
    });
    it("Verify that Japanese Yen (JPY) " +
      "converted to US Dollars (USD)", function() {
      var myCurrency = new CurrencyConverter(1, "JPY", "USD");
      expect(myCurrency.convertedCurrency()).toEqual(0.54);
    });
    it("Verify that UAE Dirham (AED) " +
      "converted to US Dollars (USD)", function() {
      var myCurrency = new CurrencyConverter(1, "AED", "USD");
      expect(myCurrency.convertedCurrency()).toEqual(0.27);
    });
    it("Verify that British Pound Sterling (GBP) " +
      "converted to US Dollars (USD)", function() {
      var myCurrency = new CurrencyConverter(1, "GBP", "USD");
      expect(myCurrency.convertedCurrency()).toEqual(1.60);
    });
```

```
      it("Verify that South African Rand (ZAR) converted to " +
          "Indian Rupees (INR)", function() {
        var myCurrency = new CurrencyConverter(1, "ZAR", "INR");
        expect(myCurrency.convertedCurrency()).toEqual(5.560);
      });
      it("Verify that US Dollars (USD) " +
          "converted to Hong Kong Dollars (HKD)", function() {
        var myCurrency = new CurrencyConverter(1, "USD", "HKD");
        expect(myCurrency.convertedCurrency()).toEqual(7.750);
      });
      it("Verify that US Dollars (USD) " +
          "converted to Japanese Yen (JPY)", function() {
        var myCurrency = new CurrencyConverter(1, "USD", "JPY");
        expect(myCurrency.convertedCurrency()).toEqual(112.81);
      });
    });
  });
});
```

2. Next, let's categorize and place the Jasmine specs under different groups and subgroups to make it granular and more understandable using the following code:

```
describe("<ABC> Money Exchange Company: Currency Converter
Module. ", function() {
  describe("When Convert The Currency ", function(){
    describe("Across The Continents, ", function(){
      describe("For Asian Countries. Then: ", function(){
        it("Verify that Indian Rupees (INR) " +
            "converted to Us Dollars (USD)", function() {
          var myCurrency = new CurrencyConverter(60, "INR",
"USD");
          expect(myCurrency.convertedCurrency()).toEqual(1.002);
        });
        it("Verify that Indian Rupees (INR) " +
            "converted to Japanese Yen (JPY)", function() {
          var myCurrency = new CurrencyConverter(1, "INR", "JPY");
          expect(myCurrency.convertedCurrency()).toEqual(1.7756);
        });
        it("Verify that Hong Kong Dollars (HKD) " +
            "converted to US Dollars (USD)", function() {
          var myCurrency = new CurrencyConverter(1, "HKD", "USD");
          expect(myCurrency.convertedCurrency()).toEqual(0.1289);
        });
        it("Verify that Japanese Yen (JPY) " +
```

```
            "converted to US Dollars (USD)", function() {
            var myCurrency = new CurrencyConverter(1, "JPY", "USD");
            expect(myCurrency.convertedCurrency()).toEqual(0.54);
        });
        it("Verify that UAE Dirham (AED) " +
            "converted to US Dollars (USD)", function() {
            var myCurrency = new CurrencyConverter(1, "AED", "USD");
            expect(myCurrency.convertedCurrency()).toEqual(0.27);
        });
    });
    describe("For European Countries. Then: ", function(){
        it("Verify that British Pound Sterling (GBP) " +
            "converted to US Dollars (USD)", function() {
            var myCurrency = new CurrencyConverter(1, "GBP", "USD");
            expect(myCurrency.convertedCurrency()).toEqual(1.60);
        });
    });
    describe("For African Countries. Then: ", function(){
        it("Verify that South African Rand (ZAR) converted to " +
            "Indian Rupees (INR)", function() {
            var myCurrency = new CurrencyConverter(1, "ZAR", "INR");
            expect(myCurrency.convertedCurrency()).toEqual(5.560);
        });
    });
    describe("For North America Countries. Then: ", function(){
        it("Verify that US Dollars (USD) " +
            "converted to Hong Kong Dollars (HKD)", function() {
            var myCurrency = new CurrencyConverter(1, "USD", "HKD");
            expect(myCurrency.convertedCurrency()).toEqual(7.750);
        });
        it("Verify that US Dollars (USD) " +
            "converted to Japanese Yen (JPY)", function() {
            var myCurrency = new CurrencyConverter(1, "USD", "JPY");
            expect(myCurrency.convertedCurrency()).toEqual(112.81);
        });
    });
  });
 });
});
```

In the preceding code snapshot, you can see how we defined different groups and subgroups using the `describe` global function.

3. Now, run the spec file `CurrencyConverter_tests_group_spec.js` with the Jasmine runner (that is, `SpecRunner.html`). You will see that all the Jasmine specs fail:

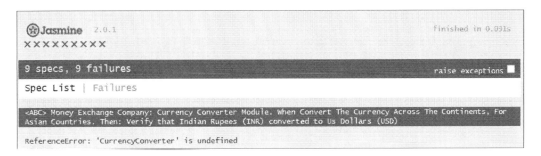

4. As indicated in the previous step, let's add the reference of the `CurrencyConverter.js` file to the Jasmine runner, which we created in the second recipe of this chapter and run the spec file `CurrencyConverter_tests_group_spec.js`. You will that all the Jasmine specs pass:

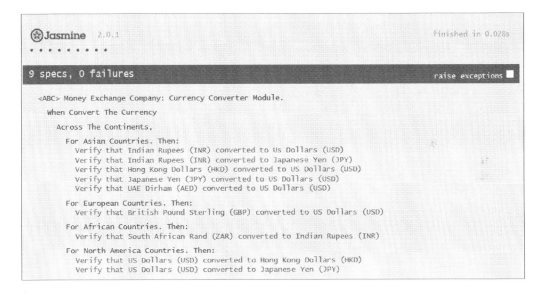

In the preceding screenshot, you can see how we created different groups and subgroups and organized Jasmine's specs for currency conversion according to continents and countries.

5
Jasmine Spies

In this chapter, we will cover:

▶ Writing Jasmine tests using the `spyOn()` method and special matchers for spies

▶ Writing Jasmine tests using tracking properties

▶ Writing Jasmine tests with your own custom spy method

▶ Using `jasmine.any` and `jasmine.objectContaining`

▶ Writing Jasmine tests to mock the JavaScript timeout functions

Introduction

The primary objective of unit testing is to test a method, object, or component in isolation and see how it behaves in different circumstances. However, there are situations where a method/object has dependencies on other methods or objects. In this scenario, we need to design tests/specs across the units/methods or components to validate behavior or simulate a real-time scenario. However, due to non-availability of dependent methods/objects or a staging/production environment, it is quite challenging to write Jasmine tests for methods that have dependencies on other methods/objects. This is where **mocks** come into the picture. A mock is a fake object that replaces the original object/method and imitates the behavior of the real object, without going into the nitty-gritty of creating the real object/method.

Mocks work by implementing the proxy model. Whenever we create a mock object, it creates a proxy object, which replaces the real object/method. In our test method, we can define the methods that are called and their returned values. Mocks can then be utilized to retrieve runtime statistics on the mocked function, such as:

▸ The number of times that the mocked function/object method was called

▸ The value that the function returned to the caller

▸ The number of arguments that the function was called with

In this chapter, you will learn how to write Jasmine tests using mock objects. Also, you will learn to develop custom/user-defined mock functions.

Writing Jasmine tests using the spyOn() method and special matchers for spies

In Jasmine, mocks are referred to as **spies**. Spies are used to mock a function/object method. A spy can stub any function and tracks calls and all its arguments. Jasmine provides a rich set of functions and properties to enable mocking. There are special matchers to interact with spies that are, `toHaveBeenCalled` and `toHaveBeenCalledWith`. In this recipe, you will learn how to mock a function using Jasmine's `spyOn()` function and special matchers.

To write the Jasmine tests using spies, let's assume that you are developing an application for <ABC> company, which provides solutions for the health care industry. Currently, there is a need to design a component that can get a person's details (such as name, age, blood group, details of diseases, and so on) and process it for further usage. Now, assume that you are developing a component that verifies a person's blood or organ donation details. There are also a few factors/biological rules that exist to donate or receive blood.

"As a doctor/physician, I want to validate all the factors/biological rules so that I can accept someone's blood for further usage"

Let's consider some scenarios in the current context, that is, all factors/biological rules should be validated before receiving/donating one's blood:

▸ **Scenario-1**: The person's age should be greater than or equal to 18

▸ **Scenario-2**: The person should not be HIV+

▸ **Scenario-3**: In Europe, the person's age should be greater than or equal to 16

Getting ready

Now, to understand the concept of Jasmine spies with the help of scenarios described in the preceding section, we need JavaScript code. Let's create the `check_person_eligibility.js` file and consider the following JavaScript code:

```javascript
var Person = function(name, DOB, bloodgroup, donor_receiver) {
    this.myName = name || "Larry Page";
  this.myDOB = DOB || "10/25/1990";
  this.myBloodGroup = bloodgroup || "B-";
  this.donor_receiver = donor_receiver;
  this.ValidateAge    = function(myDOB) {
      this.myDOD - myDOD || DOB;
      return this.getAge(this.myDOB);
    };
    this.ValidateHIV    = function(personName,personDOB,personBloodGr
oup) {
      this.myName = personName || this.myName;
      this.myDOB = personDOB || this.myDOB;
      this.myBloodGroup = personBloodGroup || this.myBloodGroup;
      return this.checkHIV(this.myName, this.myDOB, this.
myBloodGroup);
    };
};
Person.prototype.getAge = function(birth){
  console.log("getAge() function is called");
  var calculatedAge=0;
  // Logic to calculate person's age will be implemented later

  if (calculatedAge<18) {
    throw new ValidationError("Person must be 18 years or older");
  };
  return calculatedAge;
};
Person.prototype.checkHIV = function(pName, pDOB, pBloodGroup){
  console.log("checkHIV() function is called");
  bolHIVResult=true;
  // Logic to verify HIV+ will be implemented later

  if (bolHIVResult == true) {
    throw new ValidationError("A person is infected with HIV+");
  };
```

```
    return bolHIVResult;
};
// Define custom error for validation
function ValidationError(message) {
    this.message = message;
}
ValidationError.prototype = Object.create(Error.prototype);
```

In the preceding code snapshot, we created an object as `Person`, which accepts four parameters, that is, name of the person, date of birth, person's blood group, and whether the person is a donor or receiver. Further, we defined the following functions within the person's object to validate biological factors for the scenarios described in the preceding section:

▶ `ValidateAge()`: This function accepts an argument as the date of birth and returns the person's age by calling the `getAge` function.

▶ `ValidateHIV()`: This function accepts three arguments as name, date of birth, and the person's blood group. This function verifies whether the person is infected with HIV, or not, by calling the `checkHIV` function.

How to do it...

You need to perform the following steps to write Jasmine tests with spies:

1. Create a spec file `check_person_eligibility_spec.js` under the `/spec` folder and code the following lines to define the spec for scenario 1:

```
describe("<ABC> Company: Health Care Solution, ", function() {
    describe("When to donate or receive blood, ", function(){
        it("Person's age should be greater than " +
            "or equal to 18 years", function() {
        });
    });
});
```

2. Run the spec file `check_person_eligibility_spec.js` with the Jasmine runner (that is, `SpecRunner.html`). You will see that an empty spec passes for scenario 1:

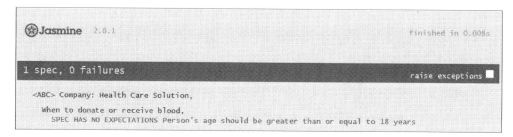

3. Now, let's implement a Jasmine test for scenario 1 with spies or mock functions using the following test code:

```
describe("<ABC> Company: Health Care Solution, ", function() {
    describe("When to donate or receive blood, ", function(){
        it("Person's age should be greater than " +
            "or equal to 18 years", function() {
        var testPersonCriteria = new Person();
        spyOn(testPersonCriteria, "getAge");
        testPersonCriteria.ValidateAge("10/25/1990");
        expect(testPersonCriteria.getAge).toHaveBeenCalled();
        expect(testPersonCriteria.getAge).
toHaveBeenCalledWith("10/25/1990");
        });
    });
});
```

In the preceding code snapshot, you can see that we mocked the function getAge using spyOn(). Further, you will observe that we used the toHaveBeenCalled matcher to verify whether the function getAge is called or not. Also, to validate the argument of the getAge function, we used the toHaveBeenCalledWith matcher.

> Jasmine provides the spyOn() function to mock any JavaScript function. A spy can stub any function and tracks calls and all arguments. A spy only exists in the describe or it block it is defined in, and will be removed after each spec.
>
> Jasmine provides special matchers toHaveBeenCalled and toHaveBeenCalledWith to interact with spies. The toHaveBeenCalled matcher returns true if the spy was called. The toHaveBeenCalledWith matcher will return true if the argument list matches any of the recorded calls to the spy.

4. Now, add the reference of the check_person_eligibility.js file to the Jasmine runner and run the spec file check_person_eligibility_spec.js. You will see that the spec passes for scenario 1:

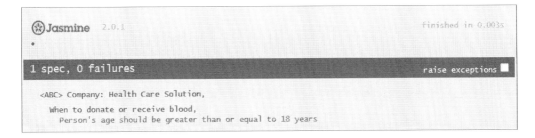

While executing the Jasmine test, you can see that the log message, which we defined within the `getAge()` function, is not printed in the browser console window.

Whenever we spy a method/function using Jasmine's `spyOn()` function, it replaces the original method of the object with a proxy method.

5. Next, following the same pattern, let's implement scenario 2 with Jasmine spies using the following code:

```
describe("<ABC> Company: Health Care Solution, ", function() {
    describe("When to donate or receive blood, ", function(){
        //Scenario 1
        it("Person's age should be greater than " +
            "or equal to 18 years", function() {
            var testPersonCriteria = new Person();
            spyOn(testPersonCriteria, "getAge");
            testPersonCriteria.ValidateAge("10/25/1990");
            expect(testPersonCriteria.getAge).toHaveBeenCalled();
            expect(testPersonCriteria.getAge).
toHaveBeenCalledWith("10/25/1990");
        });
        //Scenario 2
        it("A person should not be " +
            "infected with HIV+", function() {
            var testPersonCriteria = new Person();
            spyOn(testPersonCriteria, "checkHIV");
            testPersonCriteria.ValidateHIV();
            expect(testPersonCriteria.checkHIV).toHaveBeenCalled();
        });
    });
});
```

Note that we again spied on the `checkHIV` function using the `spyOn()` function.

6. Run the spec file `check_person_eligibility_spec.js` with the Jasmine runner. You will see that both the specs pass:

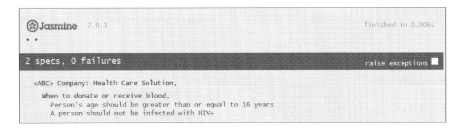

7. Let's chain the `spyOn()` function with `.and.callThrough` for scenario 1 using the following code:

```
//Scenario 1
it("Person's age should be greater than " +
    "or equal to 18 years", function() {
  var testPersonCriteria = new Person();
  spyOn(testPersonCriteria, "getAge").and.callThrough();
  testPersonCriteria.ValidateAge("10/25/1990");
  expect(testPersonCriteria.getAge).toHaveBeenCalled();
  expect(testPersonCriteria.getAge).
toHaveBeenCalledWith("10/25/1990");
    });
```

Whenever the `spyOn()` function is chained with `.and.callThrough`, the spy will still track all calls to it. However, in addition, it will delegate the control back to the actual implementation/function.

8. Run the spec file `check_person_eligibility_spec.js` with the Jasmine runner. You will see that the spec fails:

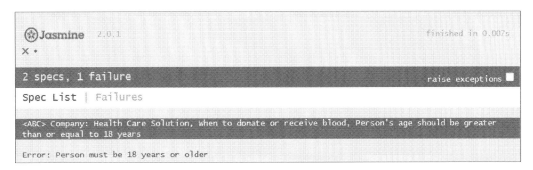

While executing the spec file, you can see that a log message is printed to the console (that is, the `getAge()` function is called).

9. Next, let's implement scenario 1 by chaining the `spyOn()` function with `.and.callFake`. Use the following code:

```
//Scenario 1
it("Person's age should be greater than " +
    "or equal to 18 years", function() {
  var testPersonCriteria = new Person();
  spyOn(testPersonCriteria, "getAge").and.callFake(function()
{
    return 18;
  });
  testPersonCriteria.ValidateAge("10/25/1990");
  expect(testPersonCriteria.getAge).toHaveBeenCalled();
  expect(testPersonCriteria.getAge).
toHaveBeenCalledWith("10/25/1990");
  expect(testPersonCriteria.getAge()).toEqual(18);
});
```

In the preceding code snapshot, you can notice that we chained the `spyOn()` function with `.and.callFake` and set the return value to 18.

> Whenever the `spyOn()` function is chained with `.and.callFake`, all calls to the spy will delegate to the supplied function.

10. Run the spec file `check_person_eligibility_spec.js` with the Jasmine runner. You will see that both the specs pass:

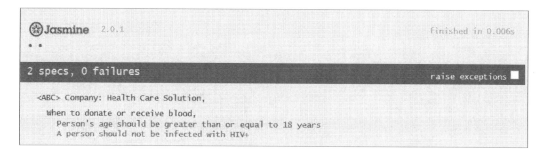

11. Let's implement scenario 3 by chaining the `spyOn()` function with `.and.returnValue` using the following code:

```
//Scenario 3
it("In Europe, Person's age should " +
    "be greater than or equal to 16 years", function() {
  var testPersonCriteria = new Person();
  spyOn(testPersonCriteria, "getAge").and.returnValue(16);
  testPersonCriteria.ValidateAge("10/25/1990");
  expect(testPersonCriteria.getAge).toHaveBeenCalled();
  expect(testPersonCriteria.getAge()).toEqual(16);
});
```

In the preceding code snapshot, you can see that we chained the `spyOn()` function with `.and.returnValue` and set the desired return value for the `getAge` function.

> Whenever the `spyOn()` function is chained with `.and.returnValue`, you can get a specific value from the spied function/method as per your requirements.

12. Run the spec file `check_person_eligibility_spec.js` with the Jasmine runner. You will see that all the specs pass:

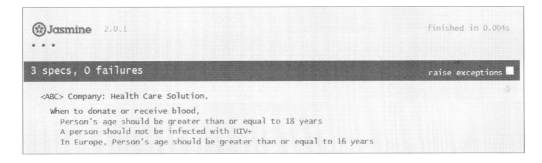

How it works...

Let's take a look at what we did throughout this recipe.

In steps 1 to 4, we looked at how tests are designed with Jasmine spies using the `spyOn()` function. We also saw the usage of special matchers (`toHaveBeenCalled` and `toHaveBeenCalledWith`), which interacted with the Jasmine spies.

In step 5, following the same pattern, we implemented scenario 2.

In steps 7 to 12, we looked at how the spyOn() function can be chained to get a specific/desired value. In step 7, we looked at how the control goes back to the actual (or original) method by chaining the spyOn() function with .and.callThrough.

In step 9, we chained the spyOn() function with .and.callFake. Here, we set the return value of the spied function (that is, getAge) as 18.

In step 11, we implemented scenario 3 by chaining the spyOn() function with .and. returnValue.

Writing Jasmine tests using tracking properties

Jasmine provides a rich set of tracking properties, meaning every call to a spy (or spied function/object method) can be tracked and exposed using the calls property of Jasmine spies. We can also track the details of arguments that are passed to the spied function. In this recipe, you will learn how to a track a call(s) to spied function/object method using tracking properties.

To understand this recipe, let's assume that you are developing a JavaScript application and you have to implement test code for various scenarios by applying different tracking properties of Jasmine spies.

"As a JavaScript developer, I want to apply different tracking properties so that I can implement a test condition successfully."

Let's consider some scenarios in the current context, that is, tracking properties of Jasmine spies should be applied for different test conditions:

- **Scenario-1**: The .calls.any() property should return false if the spy is not called at all
- **Scenario-2**: The .calls.any() property should return true if the spy is called once
- **Scenario-3**: The .calls.count() property should track the number of times the spy is called
- **Scenario-4**: The .calls.argsFor(index) property should return the argument(s) corresponding to each call
- **Scenario-5**: The .calls.allArgs() property should return the arguments to all calls
- **Scenario-6**: The .calls.mostRecent() property should return the context (the this keyword) and arguments for the most recent call
- **Scenario-7**: The .calls.first() property should return the context (the this keyword) and arguments for the first call
- **Scenario-8**: The .calls.reset() property should clear all tracking for a spy

How to do it...

To apply tracking properties to Jasmine tests, you need to perform the following steps:

1. Create the `spies_tracking_properties_spec.js` file under the `/spec` folder and code the following lines:

```
describe("Jasmine Spies: ", function() {
  describe("Tracking Properties, ", function(){
    describe(".calls.any() property ", function(){
      it("should return 'false' if spy is not called at
all",function(){
      });
      it("should return 'true' if spy is called once",function(){
      });
    });
  });
});
```

2. Run the spec file `spies_tracking_properties_spec.js` with the Jasmine runner (that is, `SpecRunner.html`). You will see that the empty specs pass for scenario 1 and scenario 2:

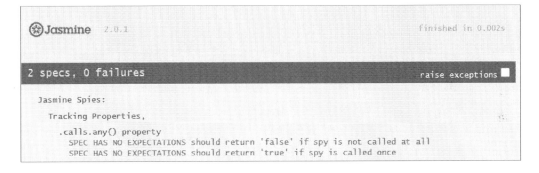

3. Let's add the reference of the `check_person_eligibility.js` file to the Jasmine runner, which we created in the previous recipe of this chapter. Also, use the following code to implement scenarios 1 and 2:

```
describe("Jasmine Spies: ", function() {
  describe("Tracking Properties, ", function(){
    beforeEach(function() {
      this.testPersonCriteria = new Person();
      spyOn(this.testPersonCriteria, "getAge");
      });
    //Scenario 1 and 2
```

```
describe(".calls.any() property ", function(){
  it("should return 'false' " +
      "if spy is not called at all",function(){
    expect(this.testPersonCriteria.getAge.calls.any())
    .toEqual(false);
  });
  it("should return 'true' " +
      "if spy is called once",function(){
    this.testPersonCriteria.ValidateAge("10/25/1990");
    expect(this.testPersonCriteria.getAge.calls.any())
    .toEqual(true);
  });
});
});
});
```

4. Run the spec file `spies_tracking_properties_spec.js` with the Jasmine runner. You will see that both the specs pass

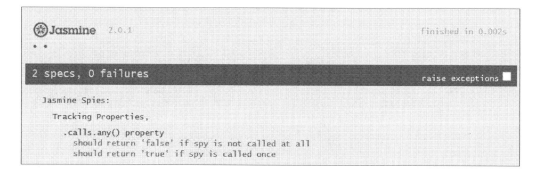

5. Next, let's implement scenario 3 using the following code:

```
describe("Jasmine Spies: ", function() {
  describe("Tracking Properties, ", function(){
    beforeEach(function() {
      this.testPersonCriteria = new Person();
      spyOn(this.testPersonCriteria, "getAge");
      spyOn(this.testPersonCriteria, "checkHIV");
    });
    //Scenario 3
    describe(".calls.count() property ", function(){
      it("should track the number of times " +
          "the spy is called",function(){
```

```
                    expect(this.testPersonCriteria.getAge.calls.count())
                    .toEqual(0);
                    this.testPersonCriteria.ValidateAge("10/25/1990");
                    this.testPersonCriteria.ValidateAge("10/25/1990");
                    expect(this.testPersonCriteria.getAge.calls.count())
                    .toEqual(2);
                });
            });
        });
    });
```

6. Now, run the spec file `spies_tracking_properties_spec.js` (for scenario 3). You will see that the test passes:

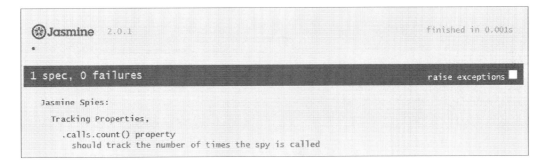

7. Use the following code to implement scenario 4:

```
describe("Jasmine Spies: ", function() {
    describe("Tracking Properties, ", function(){
        beforeEach(function() {
            this.testPersonCriteria = new Person();
            spyOn(this.testPersonCriteria, "checkHIV");
        });
        //Scenario 4
        describe(".calls.argsFor(index) property ", function(){
            it("should return the argument(s) " +
                "corresponding to each call",function(){
            this.testPersonCriteria.ValidateHIV("Name1", "10/25/1990",
"B+"); // Call 1
            this.testPersonCriteria.ValidateHIV("Name2", "10/25/1990",
"B+"); // Call 2
            this.testPersonCriteria.ValidateHIV("Name3", "10/25/1990",
"B+"); // Call 3
                expect(this.testPersonCriteria.checkHIV.calls.argsFor(0))
                .toEqual(["Name1", "10/25/1990", "B+"]);
```

```
            expect(this.testPersonCriteria.checkHIV.calls.argsFor(1))
            .toEqual(["Name2", "10/25/1990", "B+"]);
            expect(this.testPersonCriteria.checkHIV.calls.argsFor(2))
            .toEqual(["Name3", "10/25/1990", "B+"]);
          });
        });
      });
    });
```

8. To execute scenario 4, run the spec file `spies_tracking_properties_spec.js` with Jasmine. You will see that all the test conditions defined for scenario 4 pass:

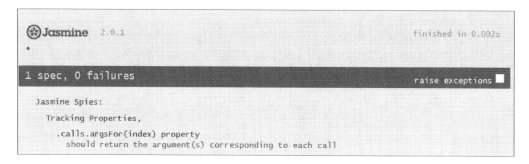

9. Next, use the following code to implement scenario 5:

```
describe("Jasmine Spies: ", function() {
  describe("Tracking Properties, ", function(){
    beforeEach(function() {
      this.testPersonCriteria = new Person();
      spyOn(this.testPersonCriteria, "checkHIV");
    });
    //Scenario 5
    describe(".calls.allArgs() property ", function(){
      it("should return the arguments " +
        "for all calls",function(){
        this.testPersonCriteria.ValidateHIV("Name1", "10/25/1990",
"B+"); // Call 1
        this.testPersonCriteria.ValidateHIV("Name2", "10/25/1990",
"B+"); // Call 2
        this.testPersonCriteria.ValidateHIV("Name3", "10/25/1990",
"B+"); // Call 3
        expect(this.testPersonCriteria.checkHIV.calls.allArgs())
        .toEqual([["Name1", "10/25/1990", "B+"],
            ["Name2", "10/25/1990", "B+"],
            ["Name3", "10/25/1990", "B+"]]);
      });
```

```
      });
    });
  });
```

10. Run the spec file `spies_tracking_properties_spec.js` with the Jasmine runner to execute scenario 5. You will see that the spec passes:

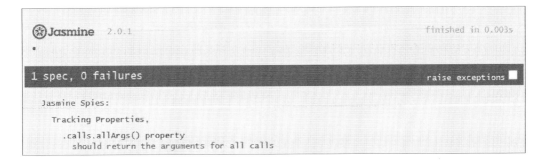

11. Now, use the following code to implement scenarios 6 and 7:

```
describe("Jasmine Spies: ", function() {
  describe("Tracking Properties, ", function(){
    beforeEach(function() {
      this.testPersonCriteria = new Person();
      spyOn(this.testPersonCriteria, "getAge");
      spyOn(this.testPersonCriteria, "checkHIV");
    });
    //Scenario 6
    describe(".calls.mostRecent() property ", function(){
      it("should return the context (the this) and " +
          "arguments for the most recent call",function(){
        this.testPersonCriteria.ValidateHIV("Name1", "10/25/1990",
"B+"); // Call 1
        this.testPersonCriteria.ValidateHIV("Name2", "10/25/1990",
"B+"); // Call 2
        expect(this.testPersonCriteria.checkHIV.calls.
mostRecent())
          .toEqual({object: this.testPersonCriteria, args: ["Name2",
"10/25/1990", "B+"]});
        expect(this.testPersonCriteria.checkHIV.calls.
mostRecent().object)
          .toBe(this.testPersonCriteria);
      });
    });
    //Scenario 7
```

```
        describe(".calls.first() property ", function(){
          it("should return the context (the this) " +
            "and arguments for the first call",function(){
            this.testPersonCriteria.ValidateAge("10/25/1990"); //Call
  1
            this.testPersonCriteria.ValidateAge("11/20/1988"); //Call
  2
            expect(this.testPersonCriteria.getAge.calls.first())
            .toEqual({object: this.testPersonCriteria, args:
  ["10/25/1990"]});
            expect(this.testPersonCriteria.getAge.calls.first().
  object)
            .toBe(this.testPersonCriteria);
          });
        });
      });
    });
```

12. Now, to execute scenario 6 and scenario 7, run the spec file `spies_tracking_properties_spec.js` with the Jasmine runner. You will see that both the specs pass:

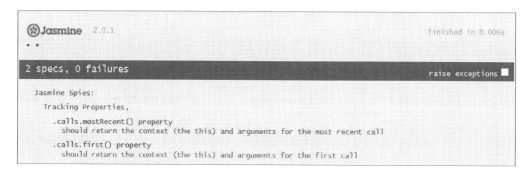

13. Next, use the following code to implement scenario 8:

```
describe("Jasmine Spies: ", function() {
  describe("Tracking Properties, ", function(){
    beforeEach(function() {
      this.testPersonCriteria = new Person();
      spyOn(this.testPersonCriteria, "getAge");
    });
    //Scenario 8
    describe(".calls.reset() property ", function(){
      it("should clear all " +
        "tracking for a spy",function(){
        this.testPersonCriteria.ValidateAge("10/25/1990");
        expect(this.testPersonCriteria.getAge.calls.any())
        .toEqual(true);
```

```
            this.testPersonCriteria.getAge.calls.reset();
              expect(this.testPersonCriteria.getAge.calls.any())
              .toBe(false);
         });
       });
     });
   });
```

14. Run the spec file (for scenario 8) with the Jasmine runner and you will see that the spec passing:

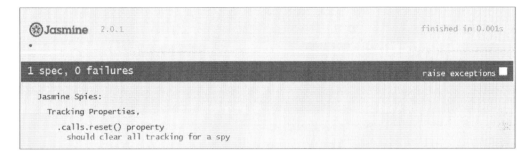

15. Finally, to run all the eight scenarios in one go, make a single spec file with the entire test code and run the spec file `spies_tracking_properties_spec.js` with the Jasmine runner. You will see that all the eight specs pass:

How it works...

Let's take a look at what we did throughout the preceding recipe.

In steps 1 to 4, we looked at how calls can be tracked to the spied function using the `.calls.any()` tracking property of Jasmine spies. In step 3, we implemented test code for scenario 1 and scenario 2 to track the calls corresponding to the spied function (that is, `getAge`).

In steps 5 to 6, we implemented scenario 3 using the `.calls.count()` property. Here, the `ValidateAge()` function is called twice. Intrinsically, this function calls the `getAge` function. Therefore, the `.calls.count()` property returns the value 2.

In steps 7 to 8, we implemented scenario 4. Here, the `.calls.argsFor(index)` property returns the argument(s) of the function/method corresponding to each call.

In steps 9 to 10, we implemented scenario 5 using the `.calls.allArgs()` property.

In steps 11 to 12, we implemented scenario 6 and scenario 7 using the `.calls.mostRecent()` and `.calls.first()` property.

In step 13, we implemented scenario 8 using the `.calls.reset()` property. Once the `.calls.reset()` property is applied, it clears all tracking for a spy.

Writing Jasmine tests with your own custom spy method

In the previous two recipes, we looked at how we can spy on a function and track all the function's calls/arguments using the tracking properties of spies. Now, let's assume that there is no function that exists to spy on. There are several cases when one may need to replace the original method. For example, the original function/method takes a long time to execute, or it depends on another object(s) (or third party system) that is/are not available in the test environment. In this situation, it is beneficial to replace the original method with a fake/custom spy method for testing purposes. Jasmine provides a method called `jasmine.createSpy` to create your own custom spy method. In this recipe, you will learn to develop a custom spy method. Also, you will learn how to track all the calls/arguments of the custom spy method.

Getting ready

You will learn this recipe with the help of the first recipe in this chapter. For more information, refer to the *Writing Jasmine tests using the spyOn() method and special matchers for Spies* recipe.

To understand how to write Jasmine tests with your own custom method, let's consider a few more scenarios as follows:

- **Scenario-1**: Person with O+ blood group can receive blood from a person with O+ blood group

- **Scenario 2**: Person with O+ blood group can give blood to a person with A+ blood group

- **Scenario 3**: Person with B- blood group can receive blood from a person with B- blood group

- **Scenario 4**: Person with B- blood group can receive blood from a person with O- blood group

Now, let's update the JavaScript file `check_person_eligibility.js` created in the first recipe of this chapter and add a new method `ValidateBloodGroup` to the `Person` object using the following code:

```
this.ValidateBloodGroup     = function(callback){
  var _this = this;
  var matchBloodGroup;
  this.MatchBloodGroupToGiveReceive(function (personBloodGroup) {
    _this.personBloodGroup = personBloodGroup;
    matchBloodGroup = personBloodGroup;
    callback.call(_this, _this.personBloodGroup);
  });
  return matchBloodGroup;
  };
};
Person.prototype.MatchBloodGroupToGiveReceive = function(callback){
  var matchBloodGroup;
  if (this.donor_receiver == null || this.donor_receiver == undefined)
{
    throw new ValidationError("Argument (donor_receiver) is missing
");
  };
  if (this.myBloodGroup == "O+" && this.donor_receiver.toUpperCase()
== "RECEIVER"){
    matchBloodGroup = ["O+"];
  }else if (this.myBloodGroup == "O+" && this.donor_receiver.
toUpperCase() == "DONOR"){
    matchBloodGroup = ["A+"];
  }else if (this.myBloodGroup == "B-" && this.donor_receiver.
toUpperCase() == "RECEIVER"){
  matchBloodGroup = ["B-", "O-"];
  };
  callback.call(this, matchBloodGroup);
};
```

In the preceding code snippet, you can see that the `ValidateBloodGroup()` function accepts an argument as the `callback` function. The `ValidateBloodGroup()` function returns matching/eligible blood group(s) for the receiver/donor by calling the `MatchBloodGroupToGiveReceive` function.

How to do it...

Let's create the Jasmine tests with the custom spy method using the following steps:

1. First, you need to create a spec file `custom_spy_spec.js` under the `/spec` folder and code the following lines to define specs for scenarios 1 and 2:

```
describe("<ABC> Company: Health Care Solution, ", function() {
    describe("When to donate or receive blood, ", function(){
        describe("Person With O+ Blood Group: ", function(){
            it("can receive the blood of the " +
                "person with O+ blood group", function() {
            });
            it("can give the blood to the " +
                "person with A+ blood group", function() {
            });
        });
    });
});
```

2. Run the spec file with the Jasmine runner. You will see that both the empty specs pass:

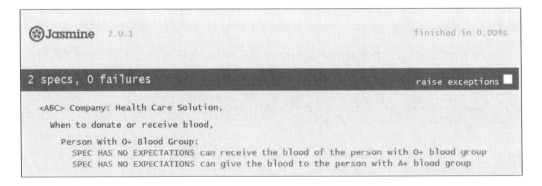

3. Let's implement scenario 1 and scenario 2 using the following test code:

```
describe("<ABC> Company: Health Care Solution, ", function() {
    describe("When to donate or receive blood, ", function(){
        describe("Person With O+ Blood Group: ", function(){
```

```
        it("can receive the blood of the " +
            "person with O+ blood group", function() {
        var testPersonCriteria = new Person("John Player",
"10/30/1980", "O+", "Receiver");
        spyOn(testPersonCriteria, "MatchBloodGroupToGiveReceive").
and.callThrough();
        var callback = jasmine.createSpy();
        testPersonCriteria.ValidateBloodGroup(callback);
        //Verify, callback method is called or not
        expect(callback).toHaveBeenCalled();
        expect(callback.calls.any()).toEqual(true);
        expect(callback.calls.count()).toEqual(1);
        //Verify, MatchBloodGroupToGiveReceive is
        // call and check whether control goes back
        // to the function
        expect(testPersonCriteria.MatchBloodGroupToGiveReceive).
toHaveBeenCalled();
        expect(testPersonCriteria.MatchBloodGroupToGiveReceive.
calls.any()).toEqual(true);
        expect(testPersonCriteria.MatchBloodGroupToGiveReceive.
calls.count()).toEqual(1);
        expect(testPersonCriteria.ValidateBloodGroup(callback)).
toContain("O+");
    });
    it("can give the blood to the " +
        "person with A+ blood group", function() {
        var testPersonCriteria = new Person("John Player",
"10/30/1980", "O+", "Donor");
        spyOn(testPersonCriteria, "MatchBloodGroupToGiveReceive").
and.callThrough();
        var callback = jasmine.createSpy();
        testPersonCriteria.ValidateBloodGroup(callback);
        expect(callback).toHaveBeenCalled();
        expect(testPersonCriteria.MatchBloodGroupToGiveReceive).
toHaveBeenCalled();
        expect(testPersonCriteria.ValidateBloodGroup(callback)).
toContain("A+");
    });
    });
  });
});
```

In the preceding code snapshot, you can see that first we mocked the function `MatchBloodGroupToGiveReceive` using `spyOn()` and chained it with and `.callThrough()` to hand over the control back to the function. Thereafter, we created `callback` as the custom spy method using `jasmine.createSpy`. Furthermore, we tracked calls/arguments to the `callback` and `MatchBloodGroupToGiveReceive` functions using tracking properties (that is, `.calls.any()` and `.calls.count()`). For more information on tracking properties, refer to the previous recipe, *Writing Jasmine tests using tracking properties*.

> Whenever we create a custom spy method using `jasmine.createSpy`, it creates a bare spy. It is a good mechanism to test the callbacks. You can also track calls and arguments corresponding to the custom spy method. However, there is no implementation behind it.

4. Run the spec file `custom_spy_spec.js` with the Jasmine runner. You will see that both the specs pass, as shown in the following screenshot:

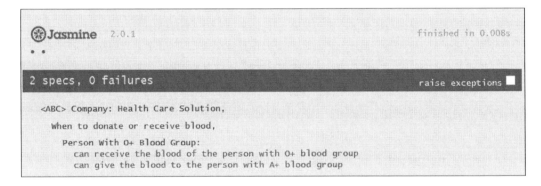

5. Next, following the same pattern, let's implement the test code for scenarios 3 and 4 under the subgroup **When to donate or receive blood**. Use the following code:

```
describe("Person With B- Blood Group: ", function(){
    it("can receive the blood of the " +
        "person with B- blood group", function() {
        var testPersonCriteria = new Person("John Player",
"10/30/1980", "B-", "Receiver");
        spyOn(testPersonCriteria, "MatchBloodGroupToGiveReceive").
and.callThrough();
        var callback = jasmine.createSpy();
```

```
        testPersonCriteria.ValidateBloodGroup(callback);
        expect(callback).toHaveBeenCalled();
        expect(testPersonCriteria.MatchBloodGroupToGiveReceive).
toHaveBeenCalled();
        expect(testPersonCriteria.ValidateBloodGroup(callback)).
toContain("B-");
    });
    it("can receive the blood of the " +
        "person with O- blood group", function() {
        var testPersonCriteria = new Person("John Player",
"10/30/1980", "B-", "Receiver");
        spyOn(testPersonCriteria, "MatchBloodGroupToGiveReceive").
and.callThrough();
        var callback = jasmine.createSpy();
        testPersonCriteria.ValidateBloodGroup(callback);
        expect(callback).toHaveBeenCalled();
        expect(testPersonCriteria.MatchBloodGroupToGiveReceive).
toHaveBeenCalled();
        expect(testPersonCriteria.ValidateBloodGroup(callback)).
toContain("O-");
    });
  });
```

6. Finally, to execute all four scenarios, run the spec file custom_spy_spec.js with the Jasmine runner. You will see that all four specs pass:

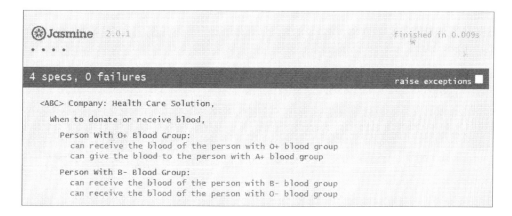

How it works...

In steps 1 to 6, we looked at how to design Jasmine specs using the custom spy method. In step 3, we implemented test code for scenario 1 and scenario 2. Here, you can see that the `ValidateBloodGroup` function accepts an argument as a `callback` function and it has dependency on the `MatchBloodGroupToGiveReceive` method, which also calls the `callback` function. To test the scenario, we created `callback` as a custom spy method using `jasmine.createSpy` and mocked the `MatchBloodGroupToGiveReceive` function using the `spyOn()` function. Further, we tracked the calls/arguments using tracking properties of spies. In step 5, we implemented the test code for scenarios 3 and 4.

Using jasmine.any and jasmine.objectContaining

In this recipe, we will design Jasmine tests using `jasmine.any` and `jasmine.objectContaining`.

The `jasmine.any` function takes a constructor/class as an expected value. It returns `true` if the constructor matches the constructor of the actual value. The `jasmine.objectContaining` compares objects with actual key/value pairs.

To understand this recipe, let's assume that you are developing a JavaScript application and you have to implement test code for various scenarios by applying `jasmine.any` and `jasmine.objectContaining`.

"As a JavaScript developer I want to develop Jasmine tests using `jasmine.any` and `jasmine.objectContaining` so that I can implement a test condition successfully."

Let's consider some scenarios in the current context, that is, `jasmine.any` and `jasmine.objectContaining` should be applied for different test conditions:

> ▶ **Scenario-1**: The `jasmine.any` function should be applied successfully for comparing types of arguments.

> ▶ **Scenario-2**: The `jasmine.objectContaining` should match/compare objects corresponding to actual key/value pairs.

> ▶ **Scenario-3**: The `jasmine.objectContaining` should be applied successfully to compare arguments with Jasmine Spies.

Getting ready

Now, to implement all the scenarios described in the preceding section, we need JavaScript code. Let's create the `phone_class.js` file and consider the following code:

```javascript
function MobilePhone(brand, color, primaryCamera, mdate, platform) {
    this.brand           = brand;
    this.color           = color;
    this.primaryCamera   = primaryCamera;
    this.manufactureDate = mdate;
    this.platform        = platform;
}
MobilePhone.prototype.reviewRating = function () {
    return this.mobileRating(this.brand, this.platform);
};
MobilePhone.prototype.mobileRating = function (brand, platform) {
    var reviewRating = '****';
    // Logic will be implemented later by collecting data/review from
a third
    // party system
    return reviewRating;
};
MobilePhone.prototype.finalPrice = function (callback) {
    var _this = this;
    this.mobilePrice(function (finalPrice) {
        _this.finalPrice = finalPrice;
        callback.call(_this, _this.finalPrice);
    });
};
MobilePhone.prototype.mobilePrice = function (callback) {
    // Let's use hard coded values for demonstration purpose
    // In JavaScript there is
    // rounding errors. Always calculate in cents not dollars.
    var price = (50.0 * 100);
    var tax   = price * 6;
    price     = (price + tax) / 100;
    callback.call(this, price);
};
```

In the preceding code snapshot, we created a `MobilePhone` object, which accepts five parameters (that are, mobile brand, color, camera, manufacturing date, and mobile platform). Here, we defined two methods `reviewRating` and `finalPrice`. Further, the `reviewRating` method called the `mobileRating` method to get the user's review rating. The `finalPrice` method called the `mobilePrice` method to evaluate the actual price of the mobile.

How to do it...

To write Jasmine tests using `jasmine.any` and `jasmine.objectContaining`, you need to perform the following steps:

1. Create the `jasmine_any_objectContaining_spec.js` file under the `/spec` folder and code the following lines to define scenario 1:

```
describe("jasmine.any", function() {
  it("should be applied successfully " +
      "for comparing arguments", function() {
  });
});
```

2. Now, let's implement the test code for scenario 1:

```
describe("jasmine.any", function() {
  it("should be applied successfully for comparing arguments",
  function() {
      var mydate = new Date("11/20/2014"); // mm//dd/yyyy
      var myMobile = new MobilePhone("Samsung","White",
        "8 Megapixels",mydate.toDateString(),
        ["Android", "Lollipop","1.2 GHz Quad Core "]);
      expect(myMobile).toEqual(jasmine.any(Object));
      expect(myMobile.mobileRating()).toEqual(jasmine.any(String),
  jasmine.any(Array));
      expect(12).toEqual(jasmine.any(Number));
  });
});
```

You can see how we compare the type of arguments using `jasmine.any` in the preceding code snapshot.

3. Now, add the `phone_class.js` file to the Jasmine runner and run the spec file `jasmine_any_objectContaining_spec.js`. You will see that the spec passes for scenario 1, as shown in the following screenshot:

4. Next, use the following code to implement scenario 2 and scenario 3:

```
describe("jasmine.objectContaining", function() {
  it("should match/compare objects " +
      "corresponding to keys/values " +
      "pairs in the actual", function() {
    var mydate = new Date("11/20/2014"); // mm//dd/yyyy
    var myMobile = new MobilePhone("Samsung",
        "White", "8 Megapixels",
        mydate.toDateString(),
        ["Android", "Lollipop","1.2 GHz Quad Core"]);
    expect(myMobile).toEqual(jasmine.objectContaining({
      brand: "Samsung",
      color: "White",
      primaryCamera: "8 Megapixels"
    }));
  });
  describe("when used with a spy", function(){
    it("should be applied successfully " +
        "for comparing arguments", function() {
      myMobile = jasmine.createSpy('myMobile');
      myMobile({
          brand: "Samsung",
          foo: "foo"
        });
    expect(myMobile).toHaveBeenCalledWith(jasmine.
objectContaining({
        brand: "Samsung",
        foo: "foo"
      }));
    });
  });
});
```

Here, you can see that we use `jasmine.objectContaining` to compare objects corresponding to actual key/value pairs.

5. Finally, run the spec file `jasmine_any_objectContaining_spec.js` with the Jasmine runner. You will see that all four specs pass:

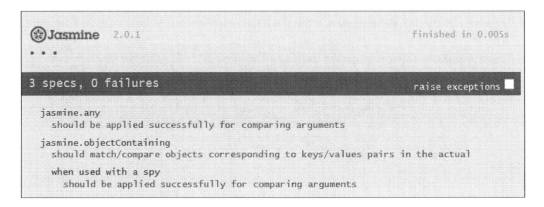

How it works...

Let's take a look at what we did throughout the preceding recipe.

In steps 1 to 3, we implemented test code for scenario 1. In step 2, we defined an object for a mobile phone (that is, `myMobile`) by creating an instance of `MobilePhone`. Here, we called the `mobileRating` function of the `myMobile` object and compared argument types using `jasmine.any`.

In steps 4 and 5, we implemented test code for scenarios 3 and 4 using `jasmine.objectContaining`.

Writing Jasmine tests to mock the JavaScript timeout functions

With JavaScript, we can create a time-dependent program/code and execute it at a specified time or time intervals using the `setTimeout()` and `setInterval()` methods. In Jasmine, we can also handle time-dependent code (or time events) using Jasmine Clock. This can be installed with a call to `jasmine.clock().install()` in a spec or suite that needs to manipulate time. In this recipe, you will learn how to mock the JavaScript timeout functions using Jasmine Clock.

To understand this recipe, let's assume that you are developing a JavaScript application and you have to implement test code to handle JavaScript timeout functions (that are, `setTimeout()` and `setInterval()`).

"As a JavaScript developer, I want to develop Jasmine tests for JavaScript timeout functions using Jasmine Clock so that I can implement a test condition successfully."

Let's consider a scenario in the current context, that is, Jasmine tests should be created for JavaScript timeout functions:

> ▶ **Scenario-1**: JavaScript Timeout function/method should be called synchronously using Jasmine Clock

How to do it...

To write Jasmine tests to mock the JavaScript Timeout functions, you need to perform the following steps:

1. Create the `jasmine_mock_TimeOut_spec.js` file under the `/spec` folder and code the following lines to define scenario 1:

```
describe("JavaScript Timeout Functions", function() {
  describe("With setTimeout() Method:", function(){
    it("should be called synchronously using Jasmin Clock",
function() {
    });
  });
  describe("With setInterval() Method:", function(){
    it("should be called synchronously using Jasmin Clock",
function() {
    });
  });
});
```

2. Run the spec file `jasmine_mock_TimeOut_spec.js` with the Jasmine runner (that is, `SpecRunner.html`). You will see that empty specs pass for scenario 1, as shown in the following screenshot:

```
⊛Jasmine  2.0.1                                              finished in 0.001s

2 specs, 0 failures                                          raise exceptions ■

  JavaScript Timeout Functions
    With setTimeout() Method:
      SPEC HAS NO EXPECTATIONS should be called synchronously using Jasmin Clock
    With setInterval() Method:
      SPEC HAS NO EXPECTATIONS should be called synchronously using Jasmin Clock
```

3. Now, use the following code to implement scenario 1:

```
describe("JavaScript Timeout Functions", function() {
  var mytimerCallback;
  beforeEach(function() {
    mytimerCallback = jasmine.createSpy("mytimerCallback");
    jasmine.clock().install();
  });
  afterEach(function() {
    jasmine.clock().uninstall();
  });
  describe("With setTimeout() Method:", function(){
    it("should be called synchronously using Jasmin Clock",
function() {
        setTimeout(function() {
          mytimerCallback();
        }, 100);
        expect(mytimerCallback).not.toHaveBeenCalled();
        jasmine.clock().tick(100);
        expect(mytimerCallback).toHaveBeenCalled();
    });
  });
  describe("With setInterval() Method:", function(){
    it("should be called synchronously using Jasmin Clock",
function() {
        setInterval(function() {
          mytimerCallback();
        }, 100);
        expect(mytimerCallback).not.toHaveBeenCalled();
        jasmine.clock().tick(101);
        expect(mytimerCallback.calls.count()).toEqual(1);
        jasmine.clock().tick(50);
        expect(mytimerCallback.calls.count()).toEqual(1);
        jasmine.clock().tick(50);
        expect(mytimerCallback.calls.count()).toEqual(2);
        jasmine.clock().tick(100);
        expect(mytimerCallback.calls.count()).toEqual(3);
    });
  });
});
```

Here, to call functions synchronously, you can see that we are ticking/moving the time forward using the `jasmine.clock().tick` function, which takes a number of milliseconds.

4. Run the spec file `jasmine_mock_TimeOut_spec.js` with the Jasmine runner. You will see that all the specs for scenario 1 pass:

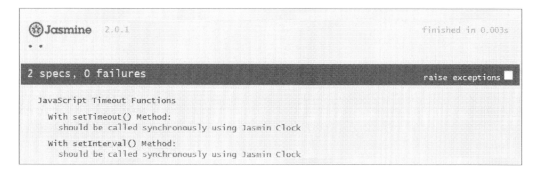

How it works...

In steps 1 to 4, we implemented scenario 1 to mock the JavaScript Timeout functions. In step 3, we created a custom spy (that is, `mytimerCallback`) using `jasmine.createSpy`. Here, we also installed Jasmine Clock using `jasmine.clock().install` within the `beforeEach` function and uninstalled the clock using `jasmine.clock().uninstall()` within the `afterEach` function to restore the original functions.

6
Jasmine with AJAX, jQuery, and Fixtures

In this chapter, we will cover:

- ▶ Writing Jasmine specs for AJAX

- ▶ Designing Jasmine specs with HTML and JSON fixtures

- ▶ Writing Jasmine specs for jQuery

- ▶ Writing Jasmine specs using custom jQuery matchers

- ▶ Writing Jasmine specs for asynchronous operations using the done() function

Introduction

Designing Jasmine specs for AJAX, jQuery, and asynchronous calls is a bit tricky. In this chapter, you will learn how to stub out AJAX calls using Jasmine and how to write tests for jQuery using spies. Also, you will learn to write tests for fixtures and asynchronous operations.

Writing Jasmine specs for AJAX

Using AJAX, we can load data in the background and display it on the web page without reloading the whole page. Whenever an AJAX request is initiated, it creates an `XMLHttpRequest` object and sends an `HttpRequest` request to the server. The server processes the request and sends the response back to the browser. In other words, AJAX allows web applications to send/retrieve data to/from a server asynchronously without interfering with the display and behavior of the existing page. It is hard to test asynchronous processes. However, the Jasmine library provides a couple of tools for handling AJAX calls. In this recipe, you will learn how to write Jasmine specs for AJAX calls.

Getting ready

Now, to write Jasmine specs for AJAX, let's consider the following HTML code:

```
<!DOCTYPE html>
<html>
<head>
<script src="myJavaScript_File.js"></script>
</head>
<body>
<div id="myID"></div>
</body>
</html>
```

In the preceding code snapshot, we simply defined a `div` tag and set a reference for a JavaScript file using the `script` tag. Now, to understand the concept, let's also consider the following JavaScript code for the `myJavaScript_File.js` file:

```
function ajaxRequest(myCallback){
    var xmlhttp  = new XMLHttpRequest();
    xmlhttp.onload = function(args) {
      myCallback(this.responseText);
    };
    xmlhttp.open("GET", "/some/url/?q=Cookbook",true);
    xmlhttp.send();
}
function myCallback(myText) {
      var myTextToDisplay = myText;
      $("#myID").html(myTextToDisplay);
}
```

In the preceding code snapshot, we created an object (that is, `xmlhttp`) of `XMLHttpRequest` and sent asynchronous requests to server using the `Get` method and the `/some/url/?q=Cookbook` url. Then, we checked the response of the server using the `onload` event. On successful execution, the server returns the response (that is, `xmlhttp.responseText`) as plain text (that is, `Jasmine Cookbook`) and the `myCallback` method gets invoked.

Now, let's consider some scenarios in the current context, that is, AJAX handling should be validated before displaying the details on the web page:

- ▶ **Scenario-1**: The `Get` method should be passed through the `XMLHttpRequest` request

- ▶ **Scenario-2**: The `url` should be passed as `/some/url/?q=Cookbook` through the `XMLHttpRequest` request

- ▶ **Scenario-3**: The `myCallback` method should be invoked on a successful response

To write tests for AJAX calls, Jasmine provides a plugin called `jasmine-ajax`. It allows AJAX calls to be mocked in tests. To use it, you need to download the `mock-ajax.js` file and add it to your Jasmine helpers.

To download and get more details about it, you can visit the following website:

```
https://github.com/jasmine/jasmine-ajax
```

How to do it...

Let's perform the following steps to write Jasmine specs for AJAX calls:

1. Create a spec file `JasmineTest_Ajax_spec.js` under the `/spec` folder and code the following lines to define a specs for scenario 1 and scenario 2:

```
describe("Ajax Calls: ", function(){
  describe("Validate using 'jasmine-ajax' Plugin", function(){
    var request, myText, myCallback;
    beforeEach(function() {
      jasmine.Ajax.install();
    });
    afterEach(function() {
      jasmine.Ajax.uninstall();
    });
    //Scenario -1
    it("Method 'GET' should be passed through XMLHttpRequest
request",function(){
    });
    //Scenario -2
    it("url should be passed as '/some/url/?q=Cookbook' through
XMLHttpRequest request",function(){
    });
  });
});
```

In the preceding code snapshot, notice that we use `jasmine.Ajax.install()` in the `beforeEach` function. This will mock out all the AJAX calls for the entire suite. Further, we use `jasmine.Ajax.uninstall()` in the `afterEach` function.

> The `jasmine-ajax` plugin stubs out the global `XMLHttpRequest` object for the page. So, to restore the original status for the specs that expect to make a real AJAX request, we need to call `jasmine.Ajax.uninstall()` in the `afterEach` function.

2. Run the spec file `JasmineTest_Ajax_spec.js` with the Jasmine runner (that is, `SpecRunner.html`). You will see that both the empty specs pass for scenarios 1 and 2, as shown in the following screenshot:

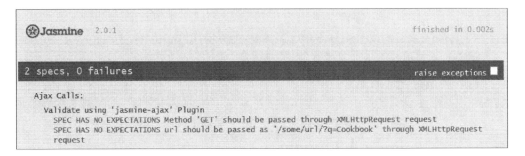

3. Now, add the reference of the `myJavaScript_File.js` file to the Jasmine runner and implement test code for both the scenarios:

```
describe("Ajax Calls: ", function(){
  describe("Validate Using 'jasmine-ajax' Plugin", function(){
    var request, myText, myCallback;
    beforeEach(function() {
      jasmine.Ajax.install();
      myCallback = jasmine.createSpy("success");
      ajaxRequest(myCallback);
      request = jasmine.Ajax.requests.mostRecent();
    });
    afterEach(function() {
      jasmine.Ajax.uninstall();
    });
    //Scenario -1
    it("Method 'GET' should be passed " +
        "through XMLHttpRequest request",function(){
      expect(request.method).toBe('GET');
      expect(myCallback).not.toHaveBeenCalled();
    });
    //Scenario -2
    it("url should be passed as " +
        "'/some/url/?q=Cookbook' through " +
        "XMLHttpRequest request",function(){
```

```
    expect(request.url).toBe('/some/url/?q=Cookbook');
    expect(myCallback).not.toHaveBeenCalled();
  });
 });
});
```

In the preceding code snapshot, observe that we created a spy for `myCallback`. Also, we sent the asynchronous requests using the `Get` method and the `/some/url/#q=Cookbook` url. Here, you can also see that the `myCallback` function is not yet called.

To learn more about spies, go through the recipes of *Chapter 5, Jasmine Spies*.

4. Next, add the reference of the `mock-ajax.js` file to the Jasmine runner and run the spec file `JasmineTest_Ajax_spec.js`. You will see that both the specs pass:

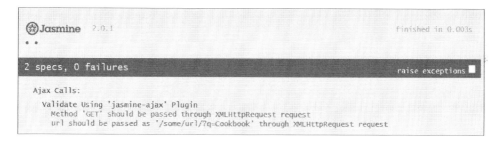

5. Let's implement scenario 3 using the following code:

```
//Scenario -3
it("myCallback should be called on " +
    "successful response",function(){
  myText = "Jasmine Cookbook";
  request.respondWith({
    "success": myCallback(myText)
  });
  expect(myCallback).toHaveBeenCalledWith("Jasmine Cookbook");
});
```

In the preceding code snapshot, observe that we are validating whether the `myCallbak` function is called or not on successful response. Further, you can test the `myCallback` function by loading HTML fixtures in DOM. For more information on HTML fixture, refer to the next two recipes, *Designing Jasmine specs with HTML and JSON fixtures* and *Writing Jasmine specs for jQuery*.

6. Run the spec file `JasmineTest_Ajax_spec.js` with the Jasmine runner. You will see that all three specs pass:

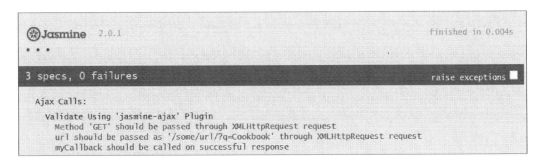

How it works...

Let's take a look at what we did throughout the preceding recipe.

In steps 1 to 4, we looked at how tests are designed for AJAX calls using the `jasmine-ajax` plugin. In step 3, we implemented scenario 1 and scenario 2. Here, we created a spy for the `myCallback` function and called the the `ajaxRequest(myCallback)` function.

In step 5, we implemented scenario 3.

Designing Jasmine specs with HTML and JSON fixtures

In this recipe, you will learn how to write Jasmine specs for JSON and HTML fixtures with the help of the `jasmine-jquery` plugin. It provides two extensions for the Jasmine JavaScript Testing Framework:

▸ An API for handling HTML and JSON fixtures in your specs

▸ A set of custom matchers for jQuery framework

The scope of this recipe is to design specs using HTML and JSON fixtures. For information on custom jQuery matchers, refer to the *Writing Jasmine specs using custom jQuery matchers* recipe.

To understand this recipe, let's assume that you are developing a JavaScript application and you have to develop test code for various scenarios using HTML and JSON fixtures.

"As a JavaScript developer, I want to apply/use HTML/JSON fixtures so that I can implement a test condition successfully."

Let's consider the following scenario in current context:

▸ **Scenario-1**: Jasmine specs should be designed using HTML and JSON fixtures

Getting ready

In order to write Jasmine specs with HTML/JSON fixtures using the `jasmine-jquery` plugin, you need to download the `jasmine-jquery.js` file and add it to your Jasmine helpers. It provides three methods (that is, `loadFixtures`, `readFixtures`, and `setFixtures`) for HTML and one method (that is, `loadJSONFixtures`) for JSON fixtures to manipulate DOM.

To download and get more details about the `jasmine-jquery` plugin, you can visit the following website:

`https://github.com/velesin/jasmine-jquery`

In this recipe, you will learn how to design specs with fixtures using `loadFixtures`, `readFixtures`, `setFixtures`, and `loadJSONFixtures` methods.

How to do it...

You need to perform the following steps to design specs with HTML and JSON fixtures:

1. Create an HTML file (that is, `HTML_Fixture.html`) under the `/spec/fixtures` folder and code the following lines:

```html
<!DOCTYPE html>
<html>
<body>
<div id="my-fixture">
<ul class = "myULClass">
<li>First Name: Munish</li>
<li>Last Name: Sethi</li>
</ul>
</div>
</body>
</html>
```

2. Next, create a JSON file (that is, `myJSONData.json`) under the `/spec/fixtures` folder and code the following lines:

```json
[
{
    "author": "Munish Sethi",
    "book": "Jasmine Cookbook"
}
]
```

3. Now, to design Jasmine Specs with HTML and JSON fixtures, let's create a spec file `jasmine_fixture_spec.js` under the `/spec` folder and code the following lines:

```
describe ("JavaScript Application:", function(){
  describe ("When Jasmine Specs designed with ", function(){
    describe("HTML Fixture: ", function(){
      beforeEach(function()  {
            jasmine.getFixtures().fixturesPath = 'spec/fixtures';
      });
      describe("'loadFixtures' Method, ", function(){
        it("Load fixture from a file", function(){
        });
      });
    });
  });
});
```

In the preceding code snapshot, observe that we changed the fixture path for HTML file to `spec/fixtures`.

 By default, fixtures are loaded from `spec/javascripts/fixtures`. You can configure this path using `jasmine.getFixtures(). fixturesPath`.

4. Let's implement scenario 1 with HTML fixtures using the `loadFixtures` method and the following code:

```
describe ("JavaScript Application:", function(){
  describe ("When Jasmine Specs designed with ", function(){
    describe("HTML Fixture: ", function(){
      beforeEach(function()  {
            jasmine.getFixtures().fixturesPath = 'spec/fixtures';
      });
      describe("'loadFixtures' Method, ", function(){
        beforeEach(function()  {
            loadFixtures('HTML_Fixture.html');
        });
        it("Load fixture from a file", function(){
            expect($('.myULClass')).toExist();
            expect($('#my-fixture')).toExist();
        });
      });
    });
  });
});
```

Here, notice that we are loading HTML code/file using the `loadFixtures` method.

 The `loadFixtures` method loads the fixture(s) from one or more HTML files and makes it available or appends it to DOM.

5. Run the spec file `jasmine_fixture_spec.js` with the Jasmine runner (that is, `SpecRunner.html`). You will see that the spec passes:

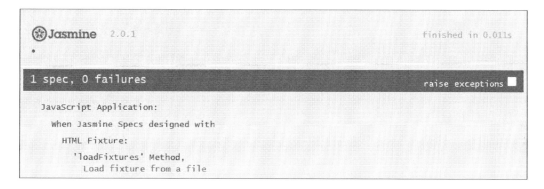

6. Let's implement test code for scenario 1 under the subgroup "**HTML Fixture:**" using the `readFixtures` method. Use the following lines of code:

```
describe("'readFixtures' Method, ", function(){
  var myFixture;
  beforeEach(function() {
        myFixture = readFixtures('HTML_Fixture.html');
  });
  it("Read fixture from a file", function(){
        expect(myFixture).toContainText(/Munish/);
        expect($(myFixture).find("li")).toHaveText(/Sethi/);
  });
});
```

In the preceding code snapshot, observe that we get the HTML fixture into a variable using the `readFixtures` method.

 The `readFixtures` method loads the fixture(s) from one or more files and returns them as a string instead of appending to the DOM. It is useful if you want to process the fixture's content in your test.

Further, we validate the HTML fixtures using custom jQuery matchers (that is, `toContainText` and `toHaveText`). For more information on jQuery custom matchers, refer to the *Writing Jasmine specs using custom jQuery matchers* recipe in this chapter.

7. Run the spec file `jasmine_fixture_spec.js` with the Jasmine runner. You will see that the specs pass:

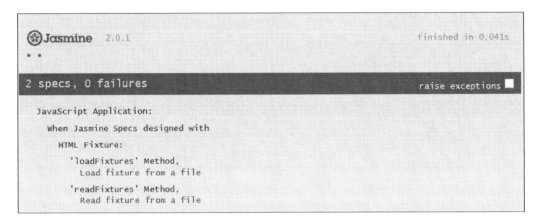

8. Now, let's implement test code for scenario 1 under the subgroup "**HTML Fixture:**" using the `setFixtures` method. Use the following code:

```
describe("'setFixtures' Method, ", function(){
   beforeEach(function() {
        setFixtures('<div class="FixtureClass">Jasmine Cookbook</
div>');
   });
   it("Receive fixture as a parameter", function(){
        expect($('.FixtureClass')).toExist();
   });
});
```

 The `setFixtures` method does not load fixtures from a string of HTML, but instead gets it directly as an HTML parameter and automatically appends the fixture to the DOM (in the fixtures container). You can also pass a jQuery object instead of an HTML string.

9. Run the spec file `jasmine_fixture_spec.js` with the Jasmine runner (that is, `SpecRunner.html`). You will see that the specs pass:

10. Finally, implement the test code for scenario 1 with the JSON fixture under the subgroup **When Jasmine Specs designed with** using the following code:

```
describe("JSON Fixture, ", function(){
  var fixtureFile, fixtures, myResult;
  beforeEach(function() {
      loadFixtures('HTML_Fixture.html');
      jasmine.getJSONFixtures().fixturesPath = 'spec/fixtures';
      fixtureFile = "myJSONData.json";
      fixtures = loadJSONFixtures(fixtureFile);
      myResult = fixtures[fixtureFile];
  });
  it("Load JSON data from a file",function(){
    $('#my-fixture').html("Jasmine Cookbook");
      expect($('#my-fixture')).toContainText("Jasmine
Cookbook");
  });
});
```

Here, observe that we changed the fixture path for the JSON file to `spec/fixtures`. Also, notice that we loaded the JSON fixture using the `loadJSONFixtures` method.

By default, JSON fixtures are loaded from `spec/javascripts/fixtures/json`. You can configure this path using `jasmine.getJSONFixtures().fixturesPath`

The `loadJSONFixtures` method loads JSON data from one or more files and parses it (that is, data from JSON file) into a JavaScript object available in your tests.

Your fixture data is loaded into an object stashed by the `JSONFixtures` structure and data can be fetched using the file name as the key. This allows you to load test data in a spec.

11. Run the spec file `jasmine_fixture_spec.js`. You will see that the specs pass, as shown in the following screenshot:

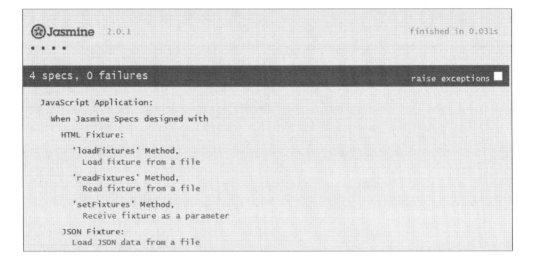

How it works...

In steps 1 to 11, we looked at how to design Jasmine specs with HTML/JSON fixtures using the `jasmine-jquery` plugin.

Let's take a look at the steps of this recipe.

In steps 1 and 2, we created an HTML and JSON file.

In step 3, we created the `jasmine_fixture_spec.js` file and configured the path for the HTML fixture.

In steps 4 to 9, we implemented scenario 1 using the `loadFixtures`, `readFixtures`, and `setFixtures` methods.

In steps 10 and 11, we configured the path for JSON file and looked at how JSON data can be loaded using the `loadJSONFixtures` method.

Writing Jasmine specs for jQuery

In the first recipe, we looked at how to write Jasmine specs for AJAX calls using the `jasmine-ajax` plugin. In this recipe, you will learn how to write tests for jQuery and DOM manipulation in Jasmine specs.

Getting ready

To understand how to write Jasmine specs with jQuery, let's create the `myfixture.html` file and consider the following code:

```html
<!DOCTYPE html>
<html>
<body>
<div id="my-fixture">something</div>
</body>
</html>
```

Here, we simply created HTML file with a `div` tag and defined `id` as `my-fixture`.

Next, let's create the `jQuery_example.js` file and consider the following code:

```javascript
function
sendRequestWithJQuery(myCallback,showErrorMessage,configurationData) {
    $.ajax({
        url: configurationData.url,
        dataType: "json",
        success: function(responseResult) {
          myCallback(responseResult);
        },
        error:showErrorMessage,
        timeout: configurationData.remainingTime
    });
}
function myCallback(ajaxResponse) {
  var out = "";
  for(i = 0; i < ajaxResponse.length; i++) {
```

```
        out += ajaxResponse[i].book + ajaxResponse[i].author;
    }
    $("#my-fixture").html(out);
}
```

In the preceding code snapshot, we created the `sendRequestWithJQuery` method that uses jQuery to retrieve JSON data from the server. It accepts three arguments `myCallback`, `showErrorMessage`, and `configurationData`. The first argument, `myCallback`, is a function which will be called on a successful response. Further, it will update the DOM/HTML based on the server response. The second argument, `showErrorMessage`, is also a function that will be called on any malfunctioning. The third argument, `configurationData`, contains attributes such as the URL and timeout in milliseconds.

Let's consider the following scenarios in current context:

▸ **Scenario-1**: The correct URL should be passed to the `$.ajax` object

▸ **Scenario-2**: The `myCallback` method should be called on successful response

▸ **Scenario-3**: The `showErrorMessage` method should be called for any malfunctioning

▸ **Scenario-4**: The DOM should be updated based on the server response

How to do it...

You need to perform the following steps to write tests for jQuery and DOM manipulation in Jasmine specs:

1. Create a spec file `jasmine_jQuery_spec.js` under the `/spec` folder and code the following lines to define scenario 1:

```
describe("jQuery",function(){
  describe("Ajax Calls:", function(){
    describe("with $.ajax", function(){
      it("Correct URL should be passed to $.ajax object",
function(){

      });
    });
  });
});
```

2. Run the spec file `jasmine_jQuery_spec.js` with the Jasmine runner (that is, `SpecRunner.html`). You will see that the empty spec passes for scenario 1:

3. Let's implement test code for scenario 1 using the following code:

```
describe("jQuery",function(){
  describe("Ajax Calls:", function(){
    describe("with $.ajax", function(){
      var configurationData = {
          url: "myData.json",
          remainingTime: 5000
      };
      it("Correct URL should be passed to $.ajax object",
function(){
          spyOn($, "ajax");
          sendRequestWithJQuery(undefined, undefined,
configurationData);
          expect($.ajax).toHaveBeenCalledWith(jasmine.
objectContaining({url: configurationData.url}));
      });
    });
  });
});
```

In the preceding code snapshot, notice that we mocked the `ajax` method using `spyOn()`. Furthermore, we validated the URL using `jasmine.objectContaining`. To know more about `spyOn()` and `jasmine.objectContaining`, go through the *Writing Jasmine tests using the spyOn() method and special matchers for Spies* and *Using jasmine.any and jasmine.objectContaining* recipes in *Chapter 5, Jasmine Spies*.

To run Jasmine specs for jQuery, you need to include the `jQuery.js`
file to Jasmine helpers either by referencing a local copy or via a CDN
(content delivery network).

4. Now, add the reference of the `jQuery.js` and `jQuery_example.js` file to the
    Jasmine helpers and run the spec file `jasmine_jQuery_spec.js`. You will see
    that the spec passes:

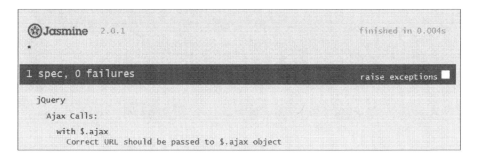

5. Next, let's implement scenario 2 using the following code:

```
//Scenario -2
it("Method 'myCallback' should be called on successful
response", function(){
        spyOn($, "ajax").and.callFake(function(e) {
            e.success({});
        });
    var myCallback;
    myCallback = jasmine.createSpy();
    showErrorMessage = jasmine.createSpy();
        sendRequestWithJQuery(myCallback,showErrorMessage,
configurationData);
        expect(myCallback).toHaveBeenCalled();
        expect(showErrorMessage).not.toHaveBeenCalled();
    });
```

Notice in the preceding code snapshot that we chained `spyOn()` with the
`.and.callFake` method. Also, to obtain a successful response, we are
passing in an anonymous function that calls the AJAX `success()` event handler.

6. Run the spec file `jasmine_jQuery_spec.js` with the Jasmine runner (that is, `SpecRunner.html`) for both the scenarios. You will see that both the specs pass:

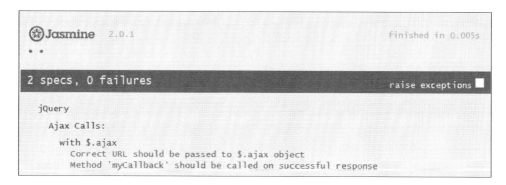

7. Next, following the same pattern, let's implement scenario 3 using the following code:

```
//Scenario -3
it("Error method showErrorMessage should be called for any
malfunctioning", function(){
    spyOn($, "ajax").and.callFake(function(e) {
        e.error({});
    });
    showErrorMessage = jasmine.createSpy();
    sendRequestWithJQuery(myCallback, showErrorMessage,
configurationData);
    expect(showErrorMessage).toHaveBeenCalled();
});
```

Here, to validate whether the `showErrorMessage` method is called or not, we chained the `spyOn()` constructor with the `.and.callFake` method and called the `error()` method explicitly.

8. Run the spec file `jasmine_jQuery_spec.js` with the Jasmine runner for all the three scenarios. You will see that all three specs pass:

```
Jasmine   2.0.1                                    finished in 0.011s
· · ·

3 specs, 0 failures                                raise exceptions ■

  jQuery
    Ajax Calls:
      with $.ajax
        Correct URL should be passed to $.ajax object
        Method 'myCallback' should be called on successful response
        Method 'showErrorMessage' should be called for any malfunctioning
```

9. Let's implement scenario 4 and code the following lines:

```
//Scenario -4
describe("DOM Manipulation", function(){
   it("Test HTML Fixture", function(){
        jasmine.getFixtures().fixturesPath = 'spec/fixtures';
        loadFixtures('myfixture.html');
        jasmine.getJSONFixtures().fixturesPath = 'spec/
fixtures';
        var FixtureUrl = "myData.json";
        var fixtures = loadJSONFixtures(FixtureUrl);
        var myResult = fixtures[FixtureUrl];
      spyOn($, "ajax").and.callFake(function(e)  {
           e.success(myResult);
        });
      showErrorMessage = jasmine.createSpy();
        sendRequestWithJQuery(myCallback,showErrorMessage,
configurationData);
        expect($('#my-fixture')).toContainText(/Jasmine Cookbook
by Munish Sethi/i);
     });
   });
```

In the preceding code snapshot, observe that we loaded both the fixture files
(that is, `myfixture.html` and `myData.json`) using the `loadFixtures`
and `loadJSONFixtures` methods respectively. Also, we validated the HTML using
the `toContainText` custom jQuery matcher. For more information on custom
jQuery matchers, refer to the next recipe, *Writing Jasmine specs using custom
jQuery matchers*.

 In order to run Jasmine specs with fixtures, you need to download the
`jasmine-jquery.js` file and add it to your Jasmine helpers. For
more information on fixtures, refer to the second recipe in this chapter,
Designing Jasmine specs with HTML and JSON fixtures.

10. Now, add the reference of `jasmine-jquery.js` to the Jasmine helpers and run the spec file `jasmine_jQuery_spec.js` for all the four scenarios. You will see that all the specs pass:

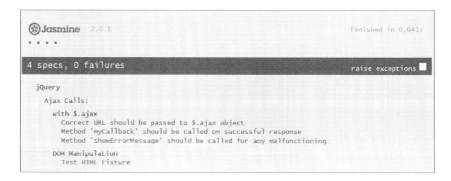

How it works...

In steps 1 to 10, we looked at how to write Jasmine specs for jQuery and validate HTML using custom matchers provided by the `jasmine-jquery` plugin.

Let's take a look at the steps of this recipe.

In steps 1 to 4, we implemented scenario 1. In step 3, we created the `configurationData` object and corresponding attributes, that is, `url` and `remainingTime`. Here, we assigned values to attributes: we set the value for `url` as `myData.json` and the value for `remainingTime` as `5000` (timeout in milliseconds). Thereafter, we mocked the `ajax` method using `spyOn()` and called the `sendRequestWithJQuery` method without defining the `myCallback` and `showErrorMessage` methods. Here, we just validated whether the correct `url` is passed or not.

In steps 5 and 6, we implemented scenario 2. Here, we created a spy for the `myCallback` and `showErrorMessage` methods and checked whether both the methods are called or not. You can notice that only `myCallback` is called.

In steps 7 and 8, following the same pattern, we implemented scenario 3. Here, we threw the error by chaining `spyOn()` with `.and.callFake` and called the `error()` method explicitly.

In steps 9 and 10, we implemented scenario 4 to manipulate DOM using JSON data.

Writing Jasmine specs using custom jQuery matchers

The `jasmine-jquery` plugin provides a rich set of custom matchers for jQuery framework. In this recipe, you will learn how to apply various custom matchers in different situations.

To understand this recipe, let's assume that you are developing an application using jQuery/JavaScript and you have to implement test code for various scenarios by applying different custom jQuery matchers.

"As a JavaScript developer I want to apply different custom jQuery matchers so that I can implement a test condition successfully."

Here are the different scenarios:

- **Scenario-1**: The `toContainText` matcher should be applied successfully to find any text in an element
- **Scenario-2**: The `toHaveText` matcher should be applied successfully to find text in an element
- **Scenario-3**: The `toHaveClass` matcher should be applied successfully to detect the class of an element
- **Scenario-4**: The `toContainHtml` matcher should be applied successfully to find an HTML element
- **Scenario-5**: The `toHaveCss` matcher should be applied successfully to find out CSS properties
- **Scenario-6**: The `toHaveId` matcher should be applied successfully to detect the ID of an element
- **Scenario-7**: The `toHaveLength` matcher should be applied successfully to find length of the ordered/unordered HTML list
- **Scenario-8**: The `toBeMatchedBy` matcher should be applied successfully to match elements for the given selector
- **Scenario-9**: The `toEqual` matcher should be applied successfully to match elements for the given selector
- **Scenario-10**: The `toBeChecked` matcher should be applied successfully to check the state/status of check box
- **Scenario-11**: The `toBeFocused` matcher should be applied successfully to detect whether an element is in focus or not
- **Scenario-12**: The `toBeDisabled` matcher should be applied successfully to detect whether an element is disabled or not

Getting ready

Now, to understand the concept and to write Jasmine specs using custom jQuery matchers, let's create `myHTMLfixture.html` and consider the following code:

```html
<!DOCTYPE html>
<html>
  <body>
    <h1>Welcome</h1>
    <div id="myFixtureOuter">
      <div id = "my-fixture" class="intro">
        <p id="Id2" class="myClass1">
          My name is Munish<span id="Lastname">Sethi</span>
        </p>
        <p id="my-Address">I live in New Delhi</p>
        <p>I have many friends:</p>
      </div>
      <ul id="Listfriends"></ul>
      <ul class="myClass">
        <li>Vipul</li>
        <li>Rahul</li>
        <li>Larry</li>
        <li>Bill Gates</li>
      </ul>
      <p>I really like Vipul!!</p>
      <h3>We are all good friends!</h3>
      <p><b>We all are very enthusiastic :</b></p>
      <div id="myStyleID">
        <div style="display: none; margin: 10px;"></div>
      </div>
    </div>
  </body>
</html>
```

Next, let's consider the following code for the `myHTML_Form_fixture.html` file:

```html
<!DOCTYPE html>
<html>
<body>
  <form>
    <input id="myCheckBox" type="checkbox" checked="checked"/>
    <input id = "mySubmit" type="submit" disabled="disabled"/>
```

```
        <input id= "myFirstName" class = "myName" type="text"
name="FirstName" value="Munish"><br>
    </form>
</body>
</html>
```

In the preceding code snapshot, we simply created two HTML files with different tags to implement custom jQuery matchers.

How to do it...

To apply different custom jQuery matchers to Jasmine specs, you need to perform the following steps:

1. Create the `jasmine_jquery_matchers.js` file under the `/spec` folder and code the following lines:

```
describe("HTML Fixture", function(){
  describe("Jasmine jQuery Custom Matchers", function(){
    beforeEach(function() {
        jasmine.getFixtures().fixturesPath = 'spec/fixtures';
        loadFixtures('myHTMLfixture.html', 'myHTML_Form_fixture.
html');
      });
    });
});
```

In the preceding code snapshot, notice that we loaded both the HTML files (that is, `myHTMLfixture.html` and `myHTML_Form_fixture.html`) using the `loadFixtures` method under the `beforeEach` function. It fetches the HTML and makes it available in DOM.

2. Let's implement test code for scenario 1 and scenario 2 using the following code:

```
describe("HTML Fixture", function(){
  describe("Jasmine jQuery Custom Matchers", function(){
    beforeEach(function() {
      jasmine.getFixtures().fixturesPath = 'spec/fixtures';
      loadFixtures('myHTMLfixture.html', 'myHTML_Form_fixture.
html');
      });
    //Scenario -1
    describe("toContainText Matcher: ", function(){
      it("should be applied successfully" +
          " for finding text in element", function(){
```

```
        expect($("h1")).toContainText("Welcome");
    });
    it("should be applied successfully" +
        " for finding any text " +
        "(or text pattern) in element", function(){
    expect($('#my-Address'))
    .toContainText(/Delhi/);
    });
});
//Scenario -2
describe("toHaveText Matcher: ", function(){
    it("should be applied successfully" +
        " for finding text in element", function(){
    expect($('#my-Address'))
    .toHaveText('I live in New Delhi');
    });
    it("should be applied successfully" +
        " for finding any text " +
        "(or text pattern) in element", function(){
    expect($('#my-Address'))
    .toHaveText(/Delhi/);
    });
});
    });
  });
});
```

In the preceding code snapshot, notice that we validated DOM contents using custom jQuery matchers corresponding to the myHTMLfixture.html file.

3. Now, add the reference of jasmine-jquery.js to the Jasmine helpers and run the spec file jasmine_jquery_matchers.js with the Jasmine runner. You will see that all the four specs pass for scenarios 1 and 2:

4. Next, let's use the following code to implement scenario 3 and scenario 4:

```
describe("HTML Fixture", function(){
  describe("Jasmine jQuery Custom Matchers", function(){
    beforeEach(function() {
      jasmine.getFixtures().fixturesPath = 'spec/fixtures';
      loadFixtures('myHTMLfixture.html', 'myHTML_Form_fixture.
html');
    });
    //Scenario -3
    describe("toHaveClass Matcher: ", function(){
      it("should be applied successfully " +
          "to detect class " +
          "of an element", function(){
        expect($('#my-fixture')).toHaveClass('intro');
      });
    });
    //Scenario -4
    describe("toContainHtml Matcher: ", function(){
      it("should be applied successfully " +
          "for finding html element", function(){
        expect($('#myFixtureOuter'))
          .toContainHtml('<ul id="Listfriends"></ul>');
      });
    });
  });
});
```

5. Run the spec file `jasmine_jquery_matchers.js` with the Jasmine runner. You will see that both the specs pass for scenarios 3 and 4:

```
Jasmine  2.0.1                                          finished in 0.015s
• •

2 specs, 0 failures                                     raise exceptions ☐

  HTML Fixture

    Jasmine jQuery Custom Matchers

      toHaveClass Matcher:
        should be applied successfully to detect class of an element

      toContainHtml Matcher:
        should be applied successfully for finding html element
```

6. Next, let's implement scenario 5, scenario 6, and scenario 7 using the following code:

```
describe("HTML Fixture", function(){
  describe("Jasmine jQuery Custom Matchers", function(){
    beforeEach(function() {
      jasmine.getFixtures().fixturesPath = 'spec/fixtures';
      loadFixtures('myHTMLfixture.html', 'myHTML_Form_fixture.
html');
    });

    //Scenario -5
    describe("toHaveCss Matcher: ", function(){
      it("should be applied successfully " +
        "to find out CSS properties", function(){
        expect($('#myStyleID').html())
        .toHaveCss({margin: "10px"});
        expect($('#myStyleID').html())
        .toHaveCss({display: "none"});
        expect($('#myStyleID').html())
        .toHaveCss({display: "none", margin: "10px"});
      });
    });

    //Scenario -6
    describe("toHaveId Matcher: ", function(){
      it("should be applied successfully " +
        "for detecting value " +
        "of Id in element", function(){
        expect($('.intro')).toHaveId('my-fixture');
      });
    });

    //Scenario -7
    describe("toHaveLength Matcher: ", function(){
      it("should be applied successfully " +
        "for finding length of " +
        "ordered/unordered HTML list", function(){
        expect($('ul.myClass > li')).toHaveLength(4);
      });
    });
  });
});
```

7. Run the spec file `jasmine_jquery_matchers.js` with the Jasmine runner for scenario 5, scenario 6, and scenario 7. You will see that all the specs pass:

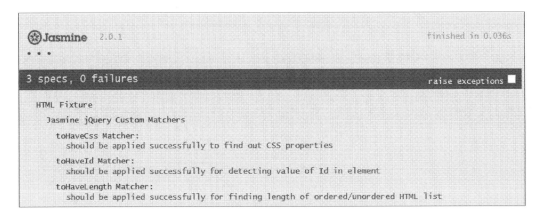

8. Let's implement scenario 8 and scenario 9 using the following code:

```
describe("HTML Fixture", function(){
  describe("Jasmine jQuery Custom Matchers", function(){
    beforeEach(function() {
      jasmine.getFixtures().fixturesPath = 'spec/fixtures';
      loadFixtures('myHTMLfixture.html', 'myHTML_Form_fixture.
html');
    });

    //Scenario -8
    describe("toBeMatchedBy Matcher: ", function(){
      it("should be applied successfully " +
          "to match elements for " +
          "the given selector", function(){
          expect($('#my-fixture')).toBeMatchedBy('.intro');
      });
    });

    //Scenario -9
    describe("toEqual Matcher: ", function(){
      it("should be applied successfully " +
          "to match elements for " +
          "the given selector", function(){
          expect($('#my-fixture')).toEqual('div');
          expect($('div.intro')).toEqual('div');
```

```
        expect($('#my-fixture')).toEqual('div#my-fixture');
        expect($('#my-fixture')).toEqual('.intro');
      });
    });
  });
});
```

9. Run the spec file `jasmine_jquery_matchers.js` for scenarios 8 and 9.
    You will see that all the test conditions pass, as shown in the following screenshot:

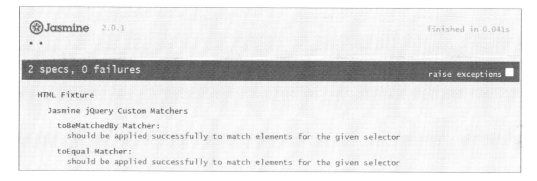

10. Now, let's implement scenario 10, scenario 11, and scenario 12 using the
    following code:

```
describe("HTML Fixture", function(){
  describe("Jasmine jQuery Custom Matchers", function(){
    beforeEach(function() {
      jasmine.getFixtures().fixturesPath = 'spec/fixtures';
      loadFixtures('myHTMLfixture.html', 'myHTML_Form_fixture.
html');
    });

    //Scenario -10
    describe("toBeChecked Matcher: ", function(){
      it("should be applied successfully " +
          "for checking the state " +
          "of check box", function(){
          expect($('#myCheckBox')).toBeChecked();
      });
    });

    //Scenario -11
    describe("toBeFocused Matcher: ", function(){
```

```
it("should be applied successfully " +
    "to detect whether element " +
    "is in focus or not", function(){
    expect($('#myFirstName').focus()).toBeFocused();
    expect($('input.myName').focus()).toBeFocused();
});
});

//Scenario -12
describe("toBeDisabled Matcher: ", function(){
    it("should be applied successfully " +
        "to detect whether element " +
        "is disabled or not", function(){
        expect($('#mySubmit')).toBeDisabled();
    });
});
});
});
```

In the preceding code snapshot, notice that we are validating DOM contents using jQuery custom matchers corresponding to myHTML_Form_fixture.html file.

11. Run the spec file jasmine_jquery_matchers.js with the Jasmine runner for scenarios 10, 11, and 12. You will see that all the specs pass, as shown in the following screenshot:

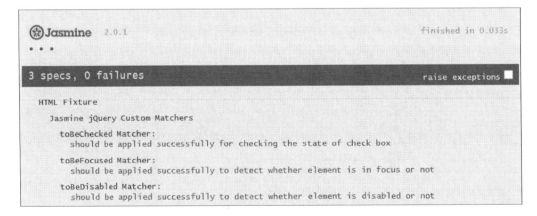

12. Finally, to run all 12 scenarios in one go, make a single spec file with the entire test code and run it (`jasmine_jquery_matchers.js`) with the Jasmine runner. You will see that all the tests pass, as shown in the following screenshot:

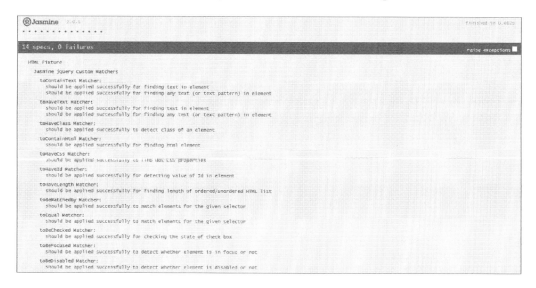

How it works...

In steps 1 to 12, we looked at how to implement custom jQuery matchers to Jasmine specs using HTML fixtures.

Let's take a look at the steps of this recipe.

In steps 1 to 9, we validated DOM contents using custom jQuery matchers corresponding to the `myHTMLfixture.html` file.

In steps 1 to 3, we implemented scenario 1 and scenario 2 using the `toContainText` and `toHaveText` custom jQuery matchers. Here, we validated the text corresponding to header `h1` and Id `my-Address`.

In steps 4 and 5, we implemented scenario 3 and scenario 4 using the `toHaveClass` and `toContainHtml` custom jQuery matchers.

In steps 6 and 7, we implemented scenario 5, scenario 6, and scenario 7. Here, we validated the properties of CSS corresponding to `myStyleID` using the `toHaveCss` custom matcher. Also, we validated the class ID and length of the unordered HTML list using the `toHaveId` and `toHaveLength` custom jQuery matchers.

In steps 8 and 9, we implemented scenario 8 and scenario 9 using the `toBeMatchedBy` and `toEqual` custom jQuery matchers. Here, we matched elements corresponding to the jQuery selector.

In steps 10 and 11, we implemented scenario 10, scenario 11, and scenario 12 using the `toBeChecked`, `toBeFocused`, and `toBeDisabled` custom jQuery matchers, respectively. Here, we validated DOM contents using jQuery custom matchers corresponding to the `myHTML_Form_fixture.html` file.

Writing Jasmine specs for asynchronous operations using the done() function

To test JavaScript's asynchronous functions/calls is a challenge. However, Jasmine 2.x provides a good way to test functions that are called asynchronously. In this recipe, you will learn to develop Jasmine specs for asynchronous operations using the `done()` function.

To understand this recipe, let's assume that you are developing an application using JavaScript and you have to design specs for asynchronous operations.

"As a JavaScript developer, I want to create Jasmine specs for asynchronous operations so that I can implement a test condition successfully."

Let's consider the following scenario in the current context:

> **Scenario-1**: Jasmine should support JavaScript asynchronous operations using the `done()` function

How to do it...

To design specs for asynchronous operations, you need to perform the following steps:

1. Create the `asynchronous_with_done_spec.js` file under the `/spec` folder and code the following lines:

```
describe("Jasmine Specs for Asynchronous Operations: ", function()
{
  //Scenario -1
  describe("With Done() function: ", function(){
    it("should support JavaScript " +
        "asynchronous operations", function() {
    });
  });
});
```

2. Run the spec file `asynchronous_with_done_spec.js` with the Jasmine runner (that is, `SpecRunner.html`). You will see that the empty spec passes for scenario 1:

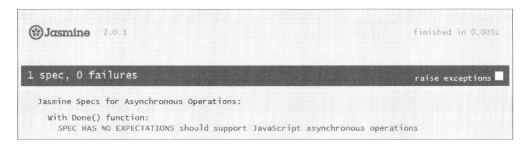

3. Let's implement the test code for scenario 1, Using the following code:

```
describe("Jasmine Specs for Asynchronous Operations: ", function()
{
  //Scenario -1
  describe("With Done() function: ", function(){
      var myCallback, showErrorMessage;
    beforeEach(function(done) {
      myCallback = jasmine.createSpy();
        $.ajax({
              url: "spec/fixtures/myData.json",
              dataType: "json",
              success: function(responseResult) {
                myCallback(responseResult);
                done();
              },
              error: showErrorMessage,
              timeout: 5000
        });
    });
    it("should support JavaScript " +
        "asynchronous operations", function() {
      expect(myCallback).toHaveBeenCalled();
    });
  });
});
```

In the preceding code snapshot, notice that `beforeEach` is taking an argument as `done`. Also, the `done()` function is called explicitly within the `beforeEach` function.

Jasmine provides the done() function to design specs for asynchronous operations.

beforeEach, it, and afterEach take an optional single argument that should be called when the asynchronous work is complete.

This spec will not start until the done() function is called in the beforeEach function.

4. Run the spec file asynchronous_with_done_spec.js with the Jasmine runner. You will see that the spec passes:

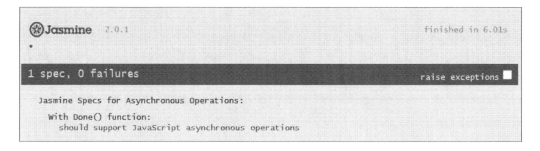

How it works...

In steps 1 to 4, we implemented scenario 1 and looked at how we can design the Jasmine specs for asynchronous operations using the done() function.

In step 3, to implement spec for asynchronous call, we passed done as an argument to the beforeEach function and called the done() function explicitly within it. Furthermore, we created jQuery to retrieve JSON data from the server. Also, we defined the myCallback function, which will be called on successful response. The showErrorMessage function will be called on any malfunctioning.

7
Code Coverage with Jasmine Tests

In this chapter, we will cover:

- ▶ Configuring code coverage tools
- ▶ Generating code coverage using karma and istanbul
- ▶ Writing Jasmine specs for uncovered branches/code
- ▶ Increasing code coverage for existing code

Introduction

Code coverage is used to determine which lines/pieces of code (or areas of a program) are not tested or exercised by a set of specs. Code coverage ensures the effectiveness of your specs/test suite, and not the quality of your product. However, if coverage is high (that is, between 90 percent and 100 percent), product quality will certainly be good. A program with high code coverage is tested thoroughly and has a lower chance of having production bugs as compared to a program with low code coverage. In other words, code coverage helps to determine whether Jasmine specs are sufficient for a specific feature/functionality or if there is a need to develop more specs in order to increase the code coverage.

To measure what percentage of code has been exercised by the specs/test suite, one or more coverage criteria/metrics are used. The major ones are statement coverage, function coverage, branch coverage, and condition coverage. To get more details about code coverage, you can visit the following website:

```
http://en.wikipedia.org/wiki/Code_coverage
```

In this chapter, you will learn to configure code coverage tools and how to get code coverage reports with Jasmine specs. We will also check the effectiveness of Jasmine specs/tests and learn how to increase code coverage for a specific functionality/feature.

Configuring code coverage tools

In this recipe, you will learn how to configure the code coverage tools istanbul and karma using npm.

istanbul is a good JavaScript code coverage tool that computes statement, line, function, and branch coverage. It supports all JavaScript coverage use cases including unit tests, server-side functional tests, and browser tests. For more details, you can visit the following website:

```
https://github.com/gotwarlost/istanbul
```

karma is a test runner that generates a code coverage report using istanbul. For more details, you can visit the following website:

```
https://github.com/karma-runner/karma-coverage
```

npm is the package manager for JavaScript. It comes with Node.js. **Node.js** is an open source server-side and networking application. There are lots of other features associated with Node.js but in the current context, we will use it to get npm. For more details on Node.js, you can visit the following websites:

- ▶ `http://nodejs.org/`
- ▶ `http://en.wikipedia.org/wiki/Node.js`

Getting ready

To configure code coverage tools using npm, first we need to install Node.js. To download Node.js, visit the following website:

```
http://nodejs.org/download/
```

As shown in the following screenshot, you can see that various installers are available on the website for different platforms:

	Windows Installer node-v0.10.34-x86.msi	Macintosh Installer node-v0.10.34.pkg	Source Code node-v0.10.34.tar.gz
Windows Installer (.msi)	32-bit		64-bit
Windows Binary (.exe)	32-bit		64-bit
Mac OS X Installer (.pkg)	Universal		
Mac OS X Binaries (.tar.gz)	32-bit		64-bit
Linux Binaries (.tar.gz)	32-bit		64-bit
SunOS Binaries (.tar.gz)	32-bit		64-bit
Source Code	node-v0.10.34.tar.gz		

For now, let's download and install Node.js with Windows 64-bit installer (that is, `node-v0.10.33-x64`). However, you can download and get the Node.js installer as per your native platform/OS. The package manager, npm, will be installed automatically with Node.js.

> npm runs through the command line and manages dependencies for an application. It also allows users to install Node.js applications that are available on the npm registry. To get more details about npm registry, you can visit the following website:
>
> `https://www.npmjs.com/`

Once Node.js is installed, you can validate whether npm is available or not by running the following statement in the command line:

```
npm --version
```

If Node.js is installed successfully, you will get the version of npm, as shown in this screenshot:

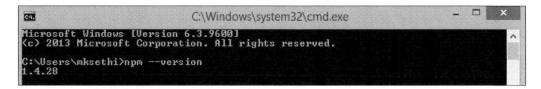

How to do it...

You need to perform the following steps to configure code coverage tools istanbul and karma:

1. First, go to the command prompt in your local project's directory and install karma with the command-line interface using the following statement:

    ```
    npm install karma-cli
    ```

    Note that if we use npm install (in package directory with no arguments), karma will be installed in your local project directory. To install the current package context as global package, you need to use the global options -g or -global with install. For example, to install karma in global mode, you can use the following statement:

    ```
    npm install -g karma-cli
    ```

    To know more about other options for npm install, you can visit the following website:

    ```
    https://docs.npmjs.com/cli/install
    ```

     It is recommended to install karma (and all the plugins your project needs) locally in the project's directory.

2. By running the statement mentioned in the preceding step, you will see the following details in the command prompt:

Notice in the preceding screenshot that karma is installed using npm.

 karma runs on Node.js and is available as an npm package.

Here, note also that a new folder `node_modules` is created in your project's directory and karma is available within this directory.

3. Now, to generate the code coverage, we need to install the plugin for coverage. Use the following statement and run it in the command-line interface:

```
npm install karma-coverage
```

4. By running the statement mentioned in the preceding step, you will see the following details in the command prompt:

5. Now go to the `node_modules` folder. You will see the following folders:

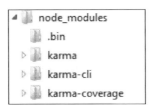

Here, notice that the `karma-coverage` package is installed and a new subfolder is created as `karma-coverage` under the `node_modules` folder.

6. Next, use the following statement and run it in the command-line interface:

npm install karma-jasmine

 To generate the code coverage with Jasmine tests using karma, we need to install karma's Jasmine plugin.

7. By running the statement mentioned in the preceding step, you will see the following details in the command prompt:

8. Now, go to the `node_modules` folder. You will see the following folders:

Here, notice that the `karma-jasmine` package is installed and a new subfolder is created as `karma-jasmine` under the `node_modules` folder.

9. Finally, use the following statement and run it in the command-line interface:

`npm install karma-chrome-launcher`

Note that we are installing the Chrome plugin for karma. karma supports various browsers to run tests (that is, Chrome, Firefox, PhantomJS, IE, and so on).

 To run the tests with karma, we need to configure one of the browsers. For more details on browsers and associated plugins, you can visit the following website:

`http://karma-runner.github.io/0.12/config/browsers.html`

10. By running the statement mentioned in the previous step, you will see the following details in the command prompt:

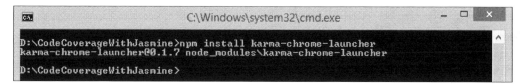

11. Now go to the `node_modules` folder. You should see the following folders:

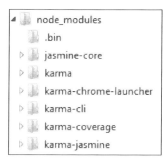

Here, notice that `karma-chrome-launcher` package is installed and a new subfolder is created as `karma-chrome-launcher` under the folder `node_modules`.

How it works...

Let's take a look what we did throughout the preceding recipe.

In steps 1 and 2, we installed karma through the command-line interface using npm package manager.

In steps 3 to 5, we installed `karma-coverage` using npm package manager. In step 5, we saw that the `karma-coverage` package is installed and a subfolder (that is, `karma-coverage`) is created under the folder `node_modules`.

In steps 6 to 8, to resolve the dependency of Jasmine tests, we installed the `karma-jasmine` plugin using npm package manager. In step 8, we looked at that how a subfolder (that is, `karma-jasmine`) is created under the folder `node_modules`.

In steps 9 to 11, to run the tests with karma using Chrome, we installed the `karma-chrome-launcher` plugin using npm package manager. In step 11, we saw that the `karma-chrome-launcher` package is installed and a subfolder (that is, `karma- chrome-launcher`) is created under the folder `node_modules`.

See also

> ▶   To know how to generate code coverage report with Jasmine tests, refer to the next two recipes, *Generating code coverage using karma and istanbul* and *Writing Jasmine specs for uncovered branches/code*.

Generating code coverage using karma and istanbul

In the previous recipe, we looked at how to configure code coverage tools and associated plugins for karma. In this recipe, you will learn how to generate code coverage reports using karma and istanbul.

Getting ready

Let's configure istanbul, karma, and associated plugins for karma. For more details, refer to the previous recipe, *Configuring Code Coverage tools*.

You will learn how to generate code coverage reports with the help of the recipe explained in *Chapter 2, Jasmine with TDD and BDD Processes*. For more information, refer to the *Designing the Jasmine test for existing code using TDD and BDD* recipe in *Chapter 2, Jasmine with TDD and BDD Processes*.

How to do it...

You need to perform the following steps to generate code coverage report using istanbul and karma:

1. First, create a `myKarma.conf.js` configuration file for karma in your local project's directory using the following code:

```
module.exports = function(config) {
  config.set({
    basePath: '',
    frameworks: ['jasmine'],
    files: [
      'src/*.js',
      'spec/TDS_existing_spec.js'
    ],
    browsers: ['Chrome'],
    singleRun: true,
    reporters: ['progress', 'coverage'],
    preprocessors: {
      'src/**/*.js': ['coverage']
    },
    coverageReporter: {
      // specify a common output directory
      dir: 'build/reports/coverage',
      reporters: [
        // reporters not supporting the 'file' property
        { type: 'html', subdir: 'report-html' },
        { type: 'lcov', subdir: 'report-lcov' },
        // reporters supporting the 'file' property, use 'subdir'
to directly
        // output them in the 'dir' directory
        { type: 'cobertura', subdir: '.', file: 'cobertura.txt' },
        { type: 'lcovonly', subdir: '.', file: 'report-lcovonly.
txt' },
        { type: 'teamcity', subdir: '.', file: 'teamcity.txt' },
        { type: 'text', subdir: '.', file: 'text.txt' },
        { type: 'text-summary', subdir: '.', file: 'text-summary.
txt' },
      ]
    }
  });
};
```

In the preceding code snapshot, notice that we specifically mentioned `frameworks` as `Jasmine` and `browsers` as `Chrome`. Also, under the `files` section, we set a reference for the spec file and corresponding JavaScript files for which we want to get code coverage details. In the current context, the spec file is `TDS_existing_spec.js` and JavaScript files are `Currency.js` and `TaxIndiaEmp.js`.

Furthermore, we defined the name of the output directory (that is, `build/reports/coverage`) under the `coverageReporter` section where the code coverage report will be generated. In order to generate a report in HTML, ICOV, and text formats, we also specified the types of coverage report under the `reporters` section. For more details on karma's configuration file, you can visit the following websites:

- https://github.com/karma-runner/karma-coverage
- http://karma-runner.github.io/0.12/config/configuration-file.html

2. Now, to get the code coverage details, we need to run tests with karma using the configuration file created in the previous step. Use the following statement and run it in the command-line interface:

```
karma start myKarma.conf.js
```

3. By running the statement mentioned in the previous step, you will see the following details in the command prompt:

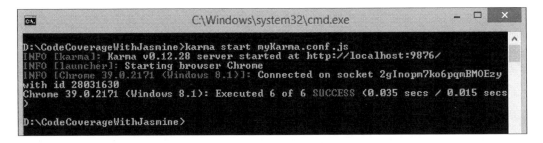

Here, notice that the karma server is started successfully and thereafter all the six Jasmine specs defined in the `TDS_existing_spec.js` file are executed successfully with Chrome launcher.

4. Now, go to your local project's directory. Here, you will see the following folders:

From the preceding screenshot, notice that a new output folder (that is, `build/reports/coverage`) is created as we mentioned in the configuration file (that is, `myKarma.conf.js`). Also, code coverage reports are generated with HTML, ICOV, and text formats.

5. Let's go to the `report-html` folder and open the code coverage report by running the `index.html` file with Chrome/Firefox/IE browser. You will see the following screenshot that has the details of code coverage:

Code coverage report for **All files**

Statements: **100%** (26 / 26) Branches: **86.67%** (13 / 15) Functions: **100%** (5 / 5) Lines: **100%** (24 / 24) Ignored: none

File		Statements		Branches		Functions		Lines	
/src\		100.00%	(26 / 26)	86.67%	(13 / 15)	100.00%	(5 / 5)	100.00%	(24 / 24)

Generated by istanbul at Thu Dec 25 2014 08:38:03 GMT+0530 (India Standard Time)

From the preceding screenshot, observe that karma uses istanbul to generate the code coverage report. istanbul parses the source files (in the current context these are `Currency.js` and `TaxIndiaEmp.js`) using **Esprima** and then adds some extra instrumentation that will be used to gather the execution statistics. To know more about Esprima, you can visit the following website:

```
http://esprima.org/
```

6. Furthermore, you can drill down the coverage report and get the details of the uncovered statements, branches, or functions. First, let's de-collapse/click on the `src` package/folder. You will see the details for both the JavaScript files separately, as shown in the following screenshot:

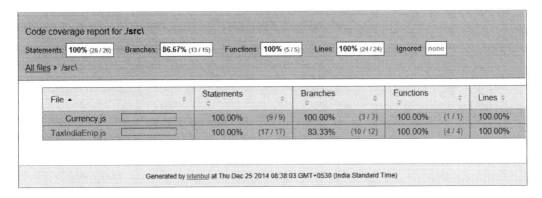

7. Now, to see the details of the uncovered branches for the `TaxIndiaEmp.js` file, let's click on it. You will see the the details of uncovered branches given in yellow, as shown in the following screenshot:

Code coverage report for **./src/TaxIndiaEmp.js**

Statements: **100%** (17 / 17) Branches: **83.33%** (10 / 12) Functions: **100%** (4 / 4) Lines: **100%** (15 / 15) Ignored: none

All files » ./src\ » TaxIndiaEmp.js

```
1   var TaxIndiaEmp = function() {
2     var grossTaxableIncome;
3     //getters and setters
4     this.getIncome     = function()        { return grossTaxableIncome || 0; };
5     this.setIncome     = function (grossIncome) { grossTaxableIncome = grossIncome;};
6   };
7   TaxIndiaEmp.prototype.calculateTDS = function()
8   {
9     var myTax = 0;
10    if (this.getIncome() > 250000 && this.getIncome() <= 500000) {
11      myTax = (this.getIncome()-250000) * 10/100;
12      return myTax;
13    }
14    else if (this.getIncome() > 500000 && this.getIncome() <= 1000000) {
15      myTax = (this.getIncome()-500000) * 20/100;
16      return myTax;
17    }
18    else E if (this.getIncome() > 1000000) {
19      myTax = (this.getIncome()-1000000) * 30/100;
20      return myTax;
21    }
22  };
```

Generated by istanbul at Thu Mar 12 2015 18:04:00 GMT+0530 (India Standard Time)

How it works...

Let's take a look at what we did throughout the preceding recipe.

In step 1, we created a configuration file for karma.

In steps 2 to 4, we executed Jasmine tests with karma and generated a code coverage report in the output folder (that is, `build/reports/coverage`) with HTML, ICOV, and text formats.

In steps 5 to 7, we looked at how to analyze a code coverage report and get the details of code for uncovered statements/branches/functions.

See also

▸ To understand how to increase the code coverage for uncovered branches/code, refer to the next recipe, *Writing Jasmine specs for uncovered branches/code*.

Writing Jasmine specs for uncovered branches/code

In the previous recipe, we looked at how to generate code coverage reports using karma. In this recipe, you will learn how to cover the code coverage for the uncovered branches or the code that is not being tested with the current test suite(s) in order to ensure the quality of code.

You will learn how to cover code coverage for uncovered branches/code with the help of the previous recipe, *Generating code coverage using karma and istanbul* and the *Designing the Jasmine test for existing code using TDD and BDD* recipe explained in *Chapter 2, Jasmine with TDD and BDD Processes*.

How to do it...

You need to perform the following steps to generate a code coverage report for uncovered branches/code:

1. First, you need to create a spec file (`TDS_existing_coverage_spec.js`) under the `/spec` folder and get the following code from the spec file (`TDS_existing_spec.js`) created during the implementation of the *Designing the Jasmine test for existing code using TDD and BDD* recipe in *Chapter 2, Jasmine with TDD and BDD Processes*:

```
describe("Employees of <XYZ> Company:",function(){
  //Scenario -1
  describe("Tax deducted for Indian Employees, ", function(){
    it("Currency should be used INR", function(){
```

```
    var myCurrency = new Currency("INDIA");
    expect(myCurrency.currency).toBe("INR");
});

//Scenario -4
it("Should be deducted 10% if Gross Income is " +
    "between RS 250,000/- and RS 500,000/-", function(){
    var myTaxableIncome = new TaxIndiaEmp();
    //Let's assume the taxable income is RS 300,000/-
    myTaxableIncome.setIncome(300000);
    expect(myTaxableIncome.calculateTDS())
    .toEqual(5000);
});

//Scenario -5
it("Should be deducted 20% if Gross Income is " +
    "between RS 500,000/- and RS 1,000,000/-", function(){
    var myTaxableIncome = new TaxIndiaEmp();
    //Let's assume the taxable income is RS 700,000/-
    myTaxableIncome.setIncome(700000);
    expect(myTaxableIncome.calculateTDS())
    .toEqual(40000);
});

//Scenario -6
it("Should be deducted 30% if Gross Income " +
    "is >RS 1,000,000/-", function(){
    var myTaxableIncome = new TaxIndiaEmp();
    //Let's assume the taxable income is RS 1,300,000/-
    myTaxableIncome.setIncome(1300000);
    expect(myTaxableIncome.calculateTDS())
    .toEqual(90000);
    });
});

//Scenario -2
describe("Tax deducted for United Kingdom Employees, ",
function(){
    it("Currency should be used GBP (Pound, UK£)", function(){
        var myCurrency = new Currency("UK");
        expect(myCurrency.currency).toBe("UK£");
    });
});

//Scenario -3
describe("Tax deducted for United States Employees, ",
function(){
    it("Currency should be used USD (US$)", function(){
        var myCurrency = new Currency("US");
```

```
      expect (myCurrency.currency).toBe ("US$");
    });
  });
});
```

2. As indicated by the code coverage report generated in the previous recipe, *Generating code coverage using karma and istanbul*, branch coverage for the `TaxIndiaEmp.js` file is 83.33 percent, and code is not written to handle the case where taxable gross income is 0. Let's refactor the code as follows:

```
var TaxIndiaEmp = function() {
  var grossTaxableIncome;
    //getters and setters
    this.getIncome      = function()        { return
grossTaxableIncome || 0; };
    this.setIncome      = function (grossIncome) {
grossTaxableIncome = grossIncome;};
  };
TaxIndiaEmp.prototype.calculateTDS = function()
{
  var myTax = 0;
  if (this.getIncome() > 250000 && this.getIncome() <= 500000) {
    myTax = (this.getIncome()-250000) * 10/100;
    return myTax;
  }
  else if (this.getIncome() > 500000 && this.getIncome() <=
1000000) {
    myTax = (this.getIncome()-500000) * 20/100;
    return myTax;
  }
  else if (this.getIncome() > 1000000) {
    myTax = (this.getIncome()-1000000) * 30/100;
    return myTax;
  }
  else {
    return myTax;
  }
};
```

From the preceding code snapshot, notice that we handled the case (that is, if gross taxable income is 0) by introducing the `else` block.

3. Now, let's create one more Jasmine spec in the spec file (`TDS_existing_ coverage_spec.js`) corresponding to the `else` block (that is, if gross taxable income is 0) using the following code:

```
    //Scenario to cover uncovered branch/code (that is, if Gross
Taxable Income is 0)
    it("Should be deducted 0 " +
        "if Gross Taxable Income is 0", function(){
```

```
var myTaxableIncome = new TaxIndiaEmp();
//Let's assume the taxable income is nil
myTaxableIncome.setIncome(0);
expect(myTaxableIncome.calculateTDS()).toEqual(0);
});
```

4. Next, update the `files` section of the configuration file (that is, `myKarma.conf.js`) created in the previous recipe, *Generating code coverage using karma and istanbul*, using the following code to update the `files` section of the configuration file:

```
files: [
 'src/*.js',
 'spec/TDS_existing_coverage_spec.js'
],
```

Here, notice that we replaced the spec file `TDS_existing_spec.js` with the `TDS_existing_coverage_spec.js` file.

 To get the code coverage report for all the suites, you can simply mention `src/*.js` and `spec/*.js` instead of referring to the name for a specific file.

5. Finally, run the tests with karma. Using the following statement and run it through the command-line interface:

`karma start myKarma.conf.js`

6. By running the statement mentioned in the previous step, you will see the following details in the command prompt:

```
C:\Windows\system32\cmd.exe
D:\CodeCoverageWithJasmine>karma start myKarma.conf.js
INFO [karma]: Karma v0.12.28 server started at http://localhost:9876/
INFO [launcher]: Starting browser Chrome
INFO [Chrome 39.0.2171 (Windows 8.1)]: Connected on socket v0ffGlEEPE3WsMqb9fzG
with id 84504747
Chrome 39.0.2171 (Windows 8.1): Executed 7 of 7 SUCCESS (0.019 secs / 0.009 secs
)
D:\CodeCoverageWithJasmine>
```

From the preceding screenshot, notice that all the seven tests are executed successfully.

7. Now, go to the output folder (that is, `build/reports/coverage`) and run the `index.html` file with Firefox/Chrome/IE from the folder `\build\reports\ coverage\report-html`. You will see that the coverage is 100 percent, as shown in the following screenshot:

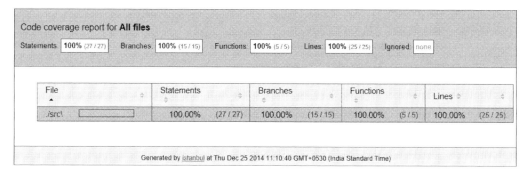

From the preceding screenshot, notice that the code coverage is 100 percent for all the branches after adding one more Jasmine test and refactoring the code.

 It's recommended to have maximum code coverage to ensure high code quality.

8. Furthermore, let's drill down the report to see the coverage details for the `TaxIndiaEmp.js` file. You will see that the coverage is 100 percent for all the branches:

Code coverage report for ./src/TaxIndiaEmp.js

Statements 100% (18/18) Branches 100% (12/12) Functions 100% (4/4) Lines 100% (16/16) Ignored none

All files » /src\ » TaxIndiaEmp.js

```
 1   var TaxIndiaEmp = function() {
 2     var grossTaxableIncome;
 3     //getters and setters
 4     this.getIncome     = function()        { return grossTaxableIncome || 0; };
 5     this.setIncome     = function (grossIncome) { grossTaxableIncome = grossIncome;};
 6   };
 7   TaxIndiaEmp.prototype.calculateTDS = function()
 8   {
 9     var myTax = 0;
10     if (this.getIncome() > 250000 && this.getIncome() <= 500000) {
11       myTax = (this.getIncome()-250000) * 10/100;
12       return myTax;
13     }
14     else if (this.getIncome() > 500000 && this.getIncome() <= 1000000) {
15       myTax = (this.getIncome()-500000) * 20/100;
16       return myTax;
17     }
18     else if (this.getIncome() > 1000000) {
19       myTax = (this.getIncome()-1000000) * 30/100;
20       return myTax;
21     }
22     else {
23       return myTax;
24     }
25   };
```

Generated by istanbul at Thu Mar 12 2015 18:09:39 GMT+0530 (India Standard Time)

How it works...

Let's take a look at the steps of this recipe.

In step 1, we created the spec file `TDS_existing_coverage_spec.js` and got the test code from the spec file `TDS_existing_spec.js`.

In step 2, we refactored the JavaScript code and handled the scenario where gross taxable income for an individual is 0.

In step 3, we created a new Jasmine test in order to handle the case where gross taxable income is 0.

In step 4, we updated the configuration file.

In steps 5 to 8, we looked at how to generate and analyze a code coverage report.

Increasing code coverage for existing code

In the previous recipe, we looked at how to generate the code coverage for the uncovered branches. In this recipe, we will extend the concept to cover the uncovered branches/code and learn how to increase the code coverage for the existing JavaScript code by adding more Jasmine tests to the current test suite.

You will learn this recipe with the help of the second recipe in this chapter, *Generating code coverage using karma and istanbul* and the *Implementing the Jasmine test corresponding to specs* recipe explained in *Chapter 4, Designing Specs from Requirement*.

How to do it...

You need to perform the following steps to generate the code coverage report for uncovered branches/code:

1. First, you need to create a spec file (`CurrencyConverter_tests_coverage_spec.js`) under the `/spec` folder and get the following code from the spec file (`CurrencyConverter_tests_spec.js`) created during the implementation of the *Implementing the Jasmine test corresponding to specs* recipe in *Chapter 4, Designing Specs from Requirement*:

```
describe("<ABC> Money Exchange Company: Currency Converter Module,
", function() {
  describe("When Convert Currency Across Region: ", function(){
    it("Verify that Indian Rupees (INR) " +
        "converted to Us Dollars (USD)", function() {
      var myCurrency = new CurrencyConverter(60, "INR", "USD");
      expect(myCurrency.convertedCurrency()).toEqual(1.002);
    });
```

```
it("Verify that Indian Rupees (INR) " +
    "converted to Japanese Yen (JPY)", function() {
  var myCurrency = new CurrencyConverter(1, "INR", "JPY");
  expect(myCurrency.convertedCurrency()).toEqual(1.7756);
});
it("Verify that Hong Kong Dollars (HKD) " +
    "converted to US Dollars (USD)", function() {
  var myCurrency = new CurrencyConverter(1, "HKD", "USD");
  expect(myCurrency.convertedCurrency()).toEqual(0.1289);
});
it("Verify that Japanese Yen (JPY) " +
    "converted to US Dollars (USD)", function() {
  var myCurrency = new CurrencyConverter(1, "JPY", "USD");
  expect(myCurrency.convertedCurrency()).toEqual(0.54);
});
it("Verify that UAE Dirham (AED) " +
    "converted to US Dollars (USD)", function() {
  var myCurrency = new CurrencyConverter(1, "AED", "USD");
  expect(myCurrency.convertedCurrency()).toEqual(0.27);
});
it("Verify that British Pound Sterling (GBP) " +
    "converted to US Dollars (USD)", function() {
  var myCurrency = new CurrencyConverter(1, "GBP", "USD");
  expect(myCurrency.convertedCurrency()).toEqual(1.60);
});
it("Verify that South African Rand (ZAR) " +
    "converted to Indian Rupees (INR)", function() {
  var myCurrency = new CurrencyConverter(1, "ZAR", "INR");
  expect(myCurrency.convertedCurrency()).toEqual(5.560);
});
it("Verify that US Dollars (USD) " +
    "converted to Hong Kong Dollars (HKD)", function() {
  var myCurrency = new CurrencyConverter(1, "USD", "HKD");
  expect(myCurrency.convertedCurrency()).toEqual(7.750);
});
it("Verify that US Dollars (USD) " +
    "converted to Japanese Yen (JPY)", function() {
  var myCurrency = new CurrencyConverter(1, "USD", "JPY");
  expect(myCurrency.convertedCurrency()).toEqual(112.81);
});
  });
});
```

2. Now, update the `files` section of the configuration file (that is, `myKarma.conf.js`) created in the second recipe of this chapter, *Generating code coverage using karma and istanbul* using the following code:

```
files: [
  'src/*.js', //Source File: CurrencyConverter.js
```

```
        'spec/CurrencyConverter_tests_coverage_spec.js' //Spec File:
CurrencyConverter_tests_coverage_spec.js
    ],
```

3. Run all the tests with karma using the configuration file (that is, `myKarma.conf.js`). Use the following statement and run it in the command-line interface:

    karma start myKarma.conf.js

4. By running the statement mentioned in the previous step, you will see the following details in the command prompt:

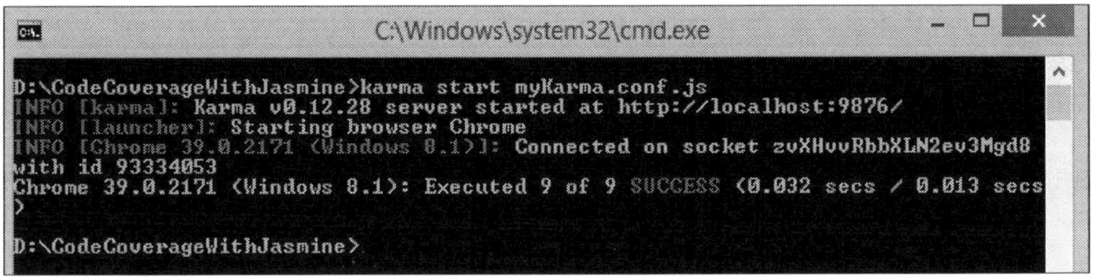

5. Let's go to the `report-html` folder and open the code coverage report by running the `index.html` file with Chrome/Firefox/IE browser. You will see the details of coverage for the `CurrencyConverter.js` file:

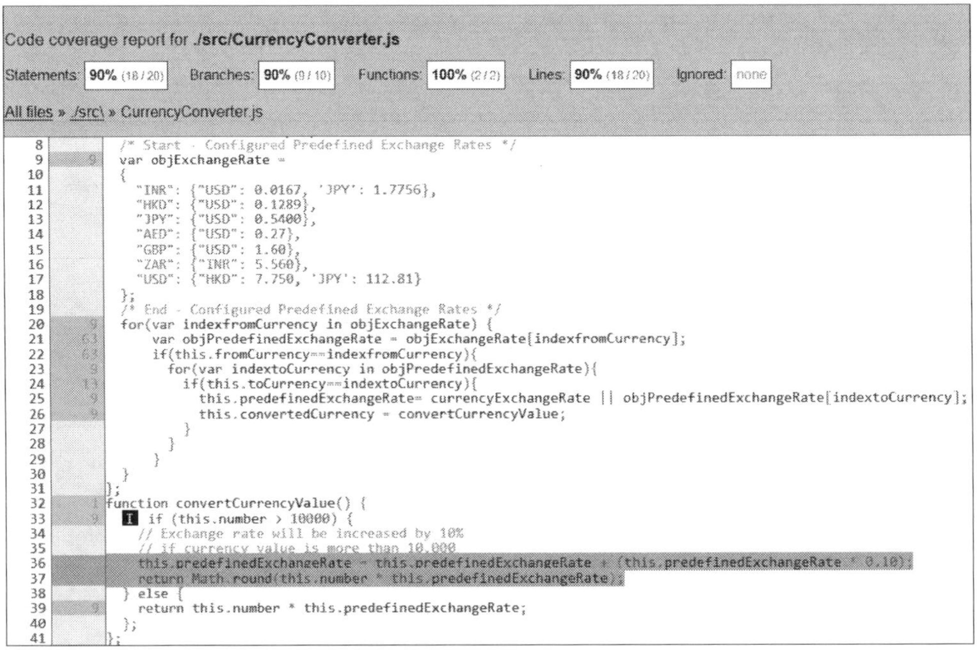

6. As indicated by the previous steps, let's create one more Jasmine test to cover the code that is not being tested with the current test suite using the following code:

```
//Created new scenario to increase code coverage
it("Verify that Indian Rupees (INR) " +
    "converted to Us Dollars (USD) " +
    "with Higher Exchange Rate", function() {
  var myCurrency = new CurrencyConverter(10500, "INR", "USD");
  expect(myCurrency.convertedCurrency()).toEqual(193);
});
```

7. Next, let's run all the tests with karma. Use the following statement and run it in the command-line interface:

```
karma start myKarma.conf.js
```

8. By running the statement mentioned in the previous step, you will see the following details in the command prompt:

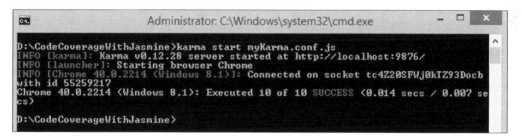

9. Let's go to the `report-html` folder and open the code coverage report by running the `index.html` file with Chrome/Firefox/IE browser. You will see that the coverage is 100 percent, as shown in the following code:

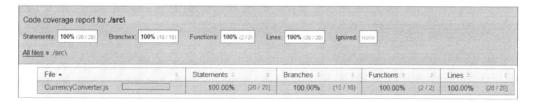

How it works...

Let's take a look at the steps of this recipe.

In steps 1 to 4, we created the spec file `CurrencyConverter_tests_coverage_spec.js` and got the entire test code from the spec file `CurrencyConverter_tests_spec.js`. Thereafter, we executed all the tests with karma.

In steps 5 and 6, we analyzed the code coverage report and created one more Jasmine tests corresponding to uncovered statements, branches, and lines.

In steps 7 to 9, we again executed all the tests with karma and generated the report with 100 percent code coverage.

8
Jasmine with Other Tools

In this chapter, we will cover:

- ▸ Writing Jasmine tests for AngularJS
- ▸ Using Jasmine with CoffeeScript
- ▸ Writing Jasmine tests for Node.js

Introduction

Until now, you have learned how to design and implement Jasmine specs for JavaScript applications. However, Jasmine also works well with other JavaScript-enabled tools/frameworks. Jasmine specs can be designed and implemented with other JavaScript-enabled platforms. In this chapter, you will learn how to develop Jasmine tests for AngularJS, CoffeeScript, and Node.js.

Writing Jasmine tests for AngularJS

AngularJS is a JavaScript framework. It extends HTML attributes with directives and binds data to HTML with expressions. The scope of this recipe is to create Jasmine tests for AngularJS code. To know more about AngularJS, you can visit the following website:

```
https://docs.angularjs.org/guide/introduction
```

In this recipe, you will learn how to create Jasmine tests for AngularJS.

To understand this recipe, let's assume that you are developing an application for a bank with AngularJS framework and you have to develop test code to implement business logic for opening a new bank account.

"As an AngularJS developer, I want to implement business logic to validate a person's age so that I can implement a test condition successfully."

Let's consider some scenarios in the current context, that is, a person's age should be greater than or equal to 18 years to open a bank account:

- **Scenario-1**: Person should be eligible to open bank account if age is greater than or equal to 18 years.

- **Scenario-2**: Person should not be eligible to open bank account if age is less than 18 years.

Getting ready

To understand how to write a Jasmine test for scenarios described in the preceding section, let's create a myDateOfBirthControllerAJS.js file with AngularJS code to handle business logic. Use the following code:

```
var myApp = angular.module("myApp", []);
myApp.controller("myDateOfBirthController", function ($scope) {
    $scope.calculateAge = function calculateAge(DateOfBirth) { //
birthday is a date
        var ageDifMs = Date.now() - DateOfBirth.getTime();
        var ageDate = new Date(ageDifMs); // milliseconds from epoch
        var myAge = Math.abs(ageDate.getUTCFullYear() - 1970);
        if (myAge >= 18){
          $scope.Eligibility = true;
        }
        else {
          $scope.Eligibility = false;
        };
    };
});
```

In the preceding code snapshot, we defined the AngularJS module with the myApp variable. Thereafter, we defined the controller (that is, myDateOfBirthController) to validate the business logic. Here, we created the calculateAge function that accepts the DateOfBirth parameter and checks whether the person is eligible to open the bank account or not.

In AngularJS, we implement the business logic using Controllers. A **Controller** is a JavaScript constructor function that is used to augment the Angular scope. To know more about Controllers, you can visit the following website:

`https://docs.angularjs.org/guide/controller`

To run AngularJS code, you need to download `angular.js` (or add a reference to the `angular.min.js` file) and add it to your Jasmine helpers. To download and get more details about `angular.js`, you can visit the following websites:

▶ `https://github.com/angular/angular.js`

▶ `https://docs.angularjs.org/misc/downloading`

In order to run Jasmine tests with AngularJS code, you need to download the `angular-mocks.js` file and add it to your Jasmine helpers. This file contains an implementation of mocks that makes testing easier for Angular applications. Your unit/integration test harness should load this file after `angular.js` is loaded.

To download and get more details about these files, you can visit the following websites:

▶ `https://github.com/angular/bower-angular-mocks`

▶ `https://docs.angularjs.org/misc/downloading`

How to do it...

You need to perform the following steps to create Jasmine tests for AngularJS:

1. First, you need to create a spec file `myDateOfBirthControllerAJS_spec.js` under the `/spec` folder and code the following lines to define a spec for scenario 1:

```
describe("Controller: To Validate Person's Age ", function() {
  describe("Check Person's Eligibility to Open Bank Account: ",
function() {
    it("should be eligible if age is greater than or equal to 18
years", function() {
    });
  });
});
```

2. Run the spec file `myDateOfBirthControllerAJS_spec.js` with the Jasmine runner (that is, `SpecRunner.html`). You will see that an empty spec is passing for scenario 1, as shown in the following screenshot:

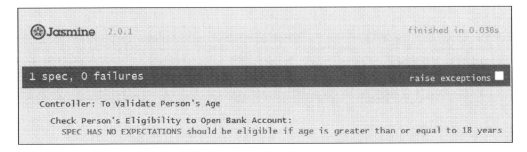

3. Now, let's implement the test code for scenario 1 using the following code:

```
describe("Controller: To Validate Person's Age ", function() {
  beforeEach(module("myApp"));
  var $controller;
  beforeEach(inject(function(_$controller_){
    $controller = _$controller_;
  }));
  describe("Check Person's Eligibility to Open Bank Account: ",
function() {
    it("should be eligible if age is greater than or equal to 18
years", function() {
      var $scope = {};
      var controller = $controller("myDateOfBirthController", {
$scope: $scope });
      var myDOB = new Date(1981,03,13);
      $scope.calculateAge(myDOB);
      expect($scope.Eligibility). toBeTruthy();
    });
  });
});
```

In the preceding code snapshot, observe that the first `beforeEach` function loads our application module `myApp` and the second `beforeEach` function injects the dependencies from AngularJS.

Controllers are not available on the global scope, so we need to use `angular.mock.inject` to inject our controller first. The `inject()` function creates a new instance of `$injector` per test, which is then used to resolve references. To know more about the inject function, you can visit the following website:

https://docs.angularjs.org/api/ngMock/function/
angular.mock.inject

Furthermore, we defined the `$controller` variable and assigned the same value with the underscore notation on both sides.

 The injector function strips out the leading and the trailing underscores when matching the parameters. The underscore rule applies only if the name starts and ends with exactly one underscore, otherwise no replacing takes place.

4. Now, add a reference of the code file `myDateOfBirthControllerAJS.js` and the spec file `myDateOfBirthControllerAJS_spec.js` to the Jasmine runner (that is, `SpecRunner.html`) and run it with the Firefox/IE/Chrome browser. You will see that the spec is passing for scenario 1, as shown in the following screenshot:

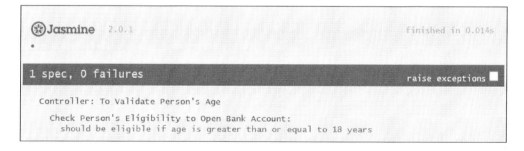

5. Next, let's implement scenario 2 using the following test code:

```
describe("Controller: To Validate Person's Age", function() {
  beforeEach(module("myApp"));
  var $controller;
  beforeEach(inject(function(_$controller_){
    $controller = _$controller_;
  }));
  describe("Check Person's Eligibility to Open Bank Account: ",
function() {
```

```
//Scenario - 1
it("should be eligible if age is greater than or equal to 18
years ", function() {
    var $scope = {};
    var controller = $controller("myDateOfBirthController", {
$scope: $scope });
    var myDOB = new Date(1981,03,13);
    $scope.calculateAge(myDOB);
    expect($scope.Eligibility).toBeTruthy();
});


//Scenario - 2
it("should not be eligible if age is less than 18 years ",
function() {
    var $scope = {};
    var controller = $controller("myDateOfBirthController", {
$scope: $scope });
    var myDOB = new Date(1999,03,13); //Format ---> yyyy/mm/dd
    $scope.calculateAge(myDOB);
    expect($scope.Eligibility). toBeFalsy();
});
});
});
```

6. Let's optimize the code as follows:

```
describe("Controller: To Validate Person's Age", function() {
  beforeEach(module("myApp"));
  var $controller;
  beforeEach(inject(function(_$controller_){
    $controller = _$controller_;
  }));
  describe("Check Person's Eligibility to Open Bank Account: ",
function() {
    var $scope, controller;
    beforeEach(function() {
      $scope = {};
      controller = $controller("myDateOfBirthController", {
$scope: $scope });
    });
    //Scenario - 1
    it("should be eligible if age is greater than or equal to 18
years", function() {
```

```
        var myDOB = new Date(1981,03,13);
        $scope.calculateAge(myDOB);
        expect($scope.Eligibility).toBeTruthy();
    });

    //Scenario - 2
    it("should not be eligible if age is less than 18 years",
function() {
        var myDOB = new Date(1999,03,13); //Format ---> yyyy/mm/dd
        $scope.calculateAge(myDOB);
        expect($scope.Eligibility).toBeFalsy();
    });
  });
});
```

7. Finally, run the spec file `myDateOfBirthControllerAJS_spec.js` for both the scenarios. You will see that the specs are passing for both the scenarios:

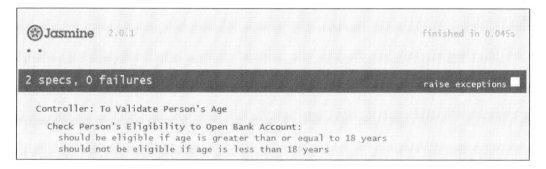

How it works...

Let's take a look at what we did throughout this recipe.

In steps 1 to 4, we implemented the test code for scenario 1. In step 3, first, we loaded the `myApp` module, and then we called the inject function within `beforeEach` to resolve the dependency.

In steps 5 to 7, we implemented scenario 2. In step 6, we optimized the test code to remove the duplicate code across both the scenarios.

Using Jasmine with CoffeeScript

CoffeeScript exposes the good parts of JavaScript in a simple and straight manner. It is a language that compiles into JavaScript. The compiled output of CoffeeScript is readable and works in every JavaScript runtime environment. To know more about CoffeeScript, you can visit the following website:

`http://coffeescript.org/`

In this recipe, you will learn how to create Jasmine tests for CoffeeScript.

To understand this recipe, let's assume that you are developing an application for a bank with CoffeeScript and you have to develop test code to implement business logic for opening a new bank account.

"As a CoffeeScript developer, I want to implement business logic to validate a person's age so that I can implement a test condition successfully."

Let's consider some scenarios in the current context, that is, the person's age should be greater than or equal to 18 years to open bank account:

- **Scenario-1**: Person should be eligible to open bank account if age is greater than or equal to 18 years.

- **Scenario-2**: Person should not be eligible to open bank account if age is less than 18 years.

Getting ready

To understand how to write a Jasmine test for the scenarios described in the preceding section, let's create the `ageCalculator.coffee` file with CoffeeScript code to handle business logic. Use the following code:

```
MS_IN_A_YEAR = 1000 * 60 * 60  * 24 * 365
class Customer
  constructor: (@dateOfBirth) ->
    @dateOfBirth = new Date(@dateOfBirth) unless @dateOfBirth
instanceof Date

  age: ->
    now = new Date().getTime()
    dob = @dateOfBirth.getTime()
    Math.round (now - dob) / MS_IN_A_YEAR
```

```
isValid: -> @age() >= 18
isValidLabel: ->
  if @isValid()
    "YES"
  else
    "NO"
```

In the preceding code snapshot, we defined a class `Customer` along with the `constructor` function, which accepts a parameter for date of birth (that is, `dateOfBirth`). Further, we defined three functions `age`, `isValid`, and `isValidLabel`. The `age` function calculates one's age with respect to the current date. The `isValid` function checks whether the age of the person is 18 years or above and accordingly returns the Boolean value. The `isValidLabel` function returns the value `YES` if the person's age is 18 years or above and `NO` if the age is below 18 years.

To run CoffeeScript code, we need to install it. Let's go to the command prompt and install CoffeeScript using the following statement:

npm install -g coffee-script

By running the previous statement, you will see the following details in the command prompt:

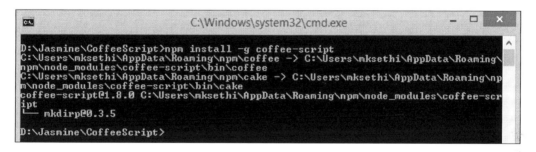

Here, notice that we installed CoffeeScript using the `npm` package manager. To know more about `npm` and how to install applications using `npm`, refer to the *Configuring code coverage tools* recipe in *Chapter 7, Code Coverage With Jasmine Tests*.

To download and get more details about CoffeeScript, you can visit the following website:

```
http://coffeescript.org/
```

How to do it...

You need to perform the following steps to create Jasmine tests for CoffeeScript code:

1. First, you need to create a spec file `ageCalculatorSpec.coffee` with CoffeeScript code under the `/spec` folder. Use the following code to define the spec for scenario 1:

```
describe "Open a New Bank Account: ", ->
  makeDateOfBirth = (age) ->
    new Date().getTime() - (age * MS_IN_A_YEAR)
  describe "#age", ->
    it "returns the age of the person in years", ->
      customer = new Customer(makeDateOfBirth 5)
      expect(customer.age()).toBe 5
  describe "Person age is 18 years or above", ->
    it "should be eligible to open a Bank Account", ->
```

In the preceding code snapshot, observe that we simply implemented a spec to get the age in years and defined the specs for scenario 1 using CoffeeScript.

2. Now, in order to run Jasmine tests with CoffeeScript code, we need to compile the CoffeeScript code. Let's compile the spec file and run it in the command-line interface using the following statement:

```
coffee -cwb ageCalculatorSpec.coffee
```

In the preceding statement, notice that we compiled the `ageCalculator.coffee` file with the `-c`, `-w`, and `-b` options.

> ▶ `-c` or `--compile` option: This compiles a `.coffee` script with a `.js` (JavaScript) file with the same name
>
> ▶ `-w` or `--watch` option: This watches for any changes in the CoffeeScript file and regenerates the .js (JavaScript) file with new updates/code
>
> ▶ `-b` or `--bare` option: This generates the JavaScript code without the top-level function safety wrapper

3. By running the statement mentioned in the preceding step, you will see the following details in the command prompt:

In the preceding screenshot, notice that the CoffeeScript spec file (that is, `ageCalculatorSpec.coffee`) is successfully compiled.

 It is recommended that you keep the command window open during the implementation of both the scenarios.

4. Now, go to the `/spec` folder. You will see the following files:

Name	Date modified	Type	Size
ageCalculatorSpec	1/8/2015 7:01 PM	COFFEE File	1 KB
ageCalculatorSpec	1/8/2015 7:32 PM	JS File	1 KB

Notice here that the `.js` (JavaScript) file is generated with the same name (that is, `ageCalculatorSpec.js`).

 Whenever we make any changes to the CoffeeScript file, the corresponding JavaScript spec file will also be regenerated with new updates/code if the CoffeeScript file is compiled with the –w option.

5. Now, following the same pattern, compile the CoffeeScript code file (that is, `ageCalculator.coffee`). Use the following statement and run it in the command-line interface:

```
coffee -cwb ageCalculator.coffee
```

6. By running the statement mentioned in the preceding step, you will see the following details in the command prompt:

In the preceding screenshot, notice that the CoffeeScript file (that is, `ageCalculator.coffee`) is successfully compiled. Now, let's keep the command window open till the implementation of both the scenarios is complete.

7. Now, go to the `/src` folder. You will see the following files:

Here, notice that the `.js` (JavaScript) file is generated with the same name (that is, `ageCalculator.js`).

8. Now, add a reference of the JavaScript code file `ageCalculator.js` and JavaScript spec file `ageCalculatorSpec.js` to Jasmine runner (that is, `SpecRunner.html`) and run it with the Firefox/IE/Chrome browser. You should see the following screenshot which indicates that empty spec is passing for scenario 1:

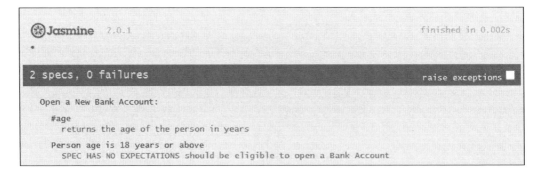

9. To implement scenario 1, let's update the test code defined in the CoffeeScript spec file (that is, `ageCalculatorSpec.coffee`) using the following code:

```
describe "Open a New Bank Account: ", ->
  makeDateOfBirth = (age) ->
    new Date().getTime() - (age * MS_IN_A_YEAR)
  describe "#age", ->
    it "returns the age of the person in years", ->
      customer = new Customer(makeDateOfBirth 5)
      expect(customer.age()).toBe 5
  describe "Person age is 18 years or above", ->
    it "should be eligible to open a Bank Account", ->
      customer = new Customer(makeDateOfBirth 18)
      expect(customer.isValid()).toBeTruthy()
      customer = new Customer(makeDateOfBirth 22)
      expect(customer.isValid()).toBeTruthy()
```

10. Next, save the CoffeeScript spec file (that is, `ageCalculatorSpec.coffee`). You will see the following details in the command prompt:

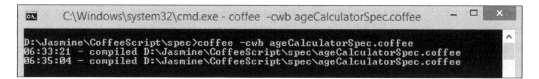

In the preceding screenshot, notice that the CoffeeScript spec file `ageCalculatorSpec.coffee` is compiled successfully.

> We compiled the CoffeeScript spec file `ageCalculatorSpec.coffee` with the `-w` option, so whenever we commit any changes to the CoffeeScript spec file (that is, `ageCalculatorSpec.coffee`), then the corresponding `.js` (JavaScript) spec file (that is, `ageCalculatorSpec.js`) will also be regenerated with new updates/code.

11. Run the JavaScript spec file `ageCalculatorSpec.js` with the Jasmine runner. You will see that the spec passes for scenario 1:

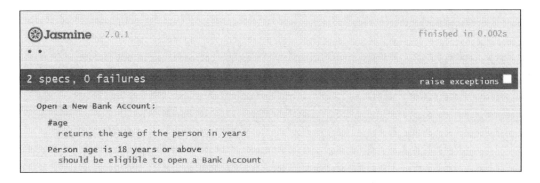

12. Now, following the same pattern, let's implement scenario 2 using the following CoffeeScript code:

```
describe "Open a New Bank Account: ", ->
  makeDateOfBirth = (age) ->
    new Date().getTime() - (age * MS_IN_A_YEAR)
  describe "#age", ->
    it "returns the age of the person in years", ->
      customer = new Customer(makeDateOfBirth 5)
      expect(customer.age()).toBe 5
  describe "Person age is 18 years or above", ->
    it "should be eligible to open a Bank Account", ->
      customer = new Customer(makeDateOfBirth 18)
      expect(customer.isValid()).toBeTruthy()
      customer = new Customer(makeDateOfBirth 22)
      expect(customer.isValid()).toBeTruthy()
  describe "Person age is below 18 years", ->
    it "should not be eligible to open a Bank Account", ->
      customer = new Customer(makeDateOfBirth 5)
      expect(customer.isValid()).toBeFalsy()
```

13. Run the spec file `ageCalculatorSpec.js` with the Jasmine runner. You should see the following screenshot letting you know that all the specs are passing:

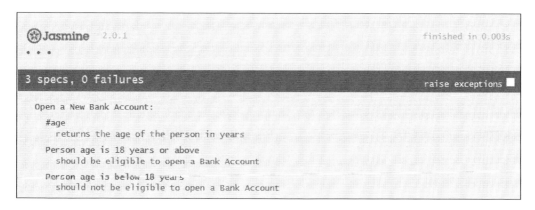

14. We can also create Jasmine specs for CoffeeScript using spies. Use the following code to implement the specs using spies:

```
describe "CoffeeScript with Jasmine Spies", ->
  describe "#isValidLabel", ->
    beforeEach ->
      @customer = new Customer(makeDateOfBirth 18)
      spyOn(@customer, "isValid")
    it "returns 'YES' when #isValid is true", ->
      @customer.isValid.and.returnValue(true)
      expect(@customer.isValidLabel()).toEqual "YES"
    it "returns 'NO' when #isValid is false", ->
      @customer.isValid.and.returnValue(false)
      expect(@customer.isValidLabel()).toEqual "NO"
```

In the preceding code snapshot, notice that we mocked the function `isValid` using `spyOn()` and set the return value as required. To know more about Jasmine spies, refer to *Chapter 5, Jasmine Spies*.

15. Finally, run the spec file `ageCalculatorSpec.js`. You will see all the specs are passing:

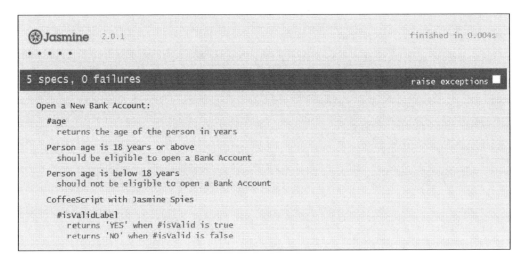

How it works...

In steps 1 to 15, we looked at that how to implement Jasmine specs using CoffeeScript.

In step 1, we defined a spec to calculate one's age in years and the empty spec for scenario 1 using the CoffeeScript code.

In steps 2 to 4, we compiled the CoffeeScript spec file `ageCalculatorSpec.coffee` with the `-c`, `-w`, and `-b` options. In step 4, we also saw that on compiling the CoffeeScript spec file `ageCalculatorSpec.coffee`, the corresponding JavaScript spec file is also generated with the same name (that is, `ageCalculatorSpec.js`).

In steps 5 to 7, following the same pattern, we compiled the CoffeeScript code file `ageCalculator.coffee` and got the corresponding JavaScript code file (that is, `ageCalculator.js`).

In steps 9 to 11, we implemented the test code using CoffeeScript for scenario 1.

In steps 12 and 13, we implemented the test code using CoffeeScript for scenario 2.

In steps 14 and 15, we looked at how Jasmine specs can be created for CoffeeScript using spies.

Writing Jasmine tests for Node.js

Node.js is a platform built on Chrome's JavaScript runtime for easily building fast and scalable network applications. It provides an event-driven architecture and a non-blocking I/O API that optimizes an application's throughput and scalability. To know more about Node.js, you can visit the following websites:

- `http://nodejs.org/`
- `http://en.wikipedia.org/wiki/Node.js`

In this recipe, you will learn how to create Jasmine tests for Node.js.

To understand this recipe, let's assume that you are developing an application for a bank with Node.js and you have to develop test code to implement business logic.

"As a Node.js developer, I want to implement business logic to validate a person's age so that I can implement a test condition successfully."

Let's consider some scenarios in the current context, that is, the person's age should be greater than or equal to 18 years to open bank account:

- **Scenario-1**: Person should be eligible to open bank account if age is greater than or equal to 18 years.
- **Scenario-2**: Person should not be eligible to open bank account if age is less than 18 years.

Getting ready

To understand how to write a Jasmine test for scenarios described in the preceding section, let's create the `checkAge.js` file with Node.js code. Use the following code:

```
(function(exports) { // customer.js
  var MS_IN_A_YEAR = 1000 * 60 * 60  * 24 * 365;
  function Customer(dob) {
    this.dateOfBirth = dob;
    if (!(this.dateOfBirth instanceof Date)) {
      this.dateOfBirth = new Date(this.dateOfBirth);
    }
  }
  Customer.prototype.age = function() {
    var now = new Date().getTime();
    var dob = this.dateOfBirth.getTime();
```

```
      return Math.round((now - dob) / MS_IN_A_YEAR);
    };
    Customer.prototype.isValid = function() {
      return (this.age() >= 18);
    };
    exports.Customer = Customer;
  })(this);
```

In the preceding code snapshot, we created a module with the function `Customer` along with the constructor function, which accepts a parameter for date of birth (that is, `dateOfBirth`). Further, we defined two functions `age` and `isValid`. The `age` function calculates one's age with respect to the current date. The `isValid` function checks whether the age of person is 18 years or above and returns the Boolean value accordingly. This function calculates one's age with respect to the current date.

To run Node.js code, we need to install it. Let's install Node.js. To learn how to install Node.js, refer to the *Configuring code coverage tools* recipe in *Chapter 7, Code Coverage with Jasmine Tests*.

Once Node.js is installed, you can validate whether it is available or not by running the following statement in the command line:

node –version

If Node.js is installed successfully, you will get the version of node as shown in the following screenshot:

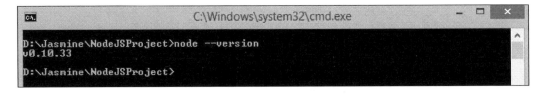

In order to run Jasmine tests with Node.js code, you need to install `jasmine-node`.

Let's install `jasmine-node` through a command-line interface using the following statement:

npm install -g jasmine-node

By running the previous statement, you should see the following details in the command prompt:

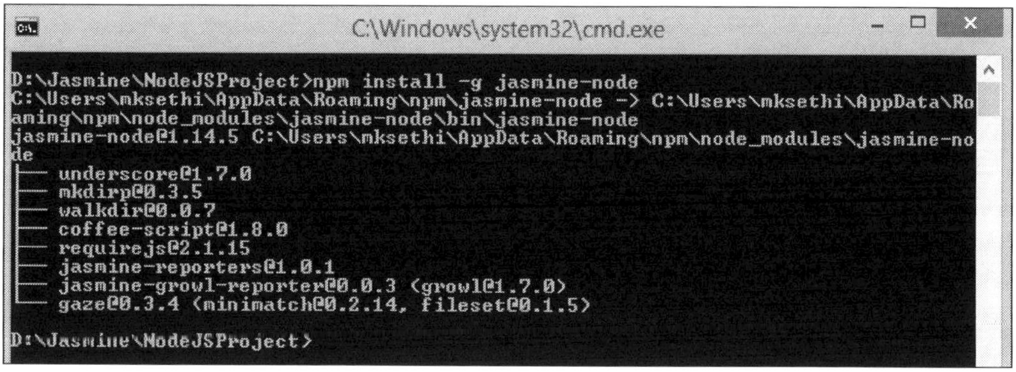

Notice here that we installed `jasmine-node` using the `npm` package manager. To know more about `npm` and how to install applications using `npm`, refer to the *Configuring code coverage tools* recipe in *Chapter 7, Code Coverage With Jasmine Tests*.

To know more about `jasmine-node`, you can visit the following website:

`https://github.com/mhevery/jasmine-node`

How to do it...

You need to perform the following steps to create Jasmine tests for Node.js:

1. First, you need to create a spec file `checkAge-spec.js` under the `/spec` folder and code the following lines to define the spec for scenario 1:

```
var checkAge = require("../src/checkAge");
var MS_IN_A_YEAR = 1000 * 60 * 60  * 24 * 365;
function makeDateOfBirth(age) {
    return new Date().getTime() - (age * MS_IN_A_YEAR);
};
describe("Open a New Bank Account: ", function() {
  describe("Person age is 18 years or above", function() {
    it('should be eligible to open a Bank Account', function() {
    });
  });
});
```

In the preceding code snapshot, notice that we included the `checkAge` module and made it accessible with the `checkAge` variable. Further, we defined a `makeDateOfBirth` function, which simply returns the person's age in years.

2. Run the spec file (that is, `checkAge-spec.js`) with jasmine-node. Use the following statement and run it through the command-line interface:

`jasmine-node spec/checkAge-spec.js`

> Note that your spec file must be named as `*spec.js`;
> Otherwise, jasmine-node will not be able find it. For example,
> `checkAge-specs.js` or `spec_checkAge.js` is wrong,
> `checkAge-spec.js` or `checkAge_spec.js` is right.

3. By running the statement mentioned in the previous step, you will see the following details in the command prompt:

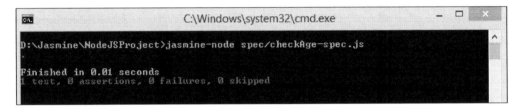

In the preceding code screenshot, notice that the empty spec is passing for scenario 1.

4. Now, let's implement the scenario 1 using the following code:

```
var checkAge = require("../src/checkAge");
var MS_IN_A_YEAR = 1000 * 60 * 60  * 24 * 365;
function makeDateOfBirth(age) {
    return new Date().getTime() - (age * MS_IN_A_YEAR);
};
describe("Open a New Bank Account: ", function() {
  describe("Person age is 18 years or above", function() {
    it('should be eligible to open a Bank Account', function() {
      var myCustomer = new checkAge.Customer(makeDateOfBirth(18));
      expect(myCustomer.isValid()).toBeTruthy();
      var myCustomer = new checkAge.Customer(makeDateOfBirth(22));
      expect(myCustomer.isValid()).toBeTruthy();
    });
  });
});
```

5. Run the spec file (that is, `checkAge-spec.js`) with jasmine-node. Use the following statement and run it in the command-line interface:

```
jasmine-node spec/checkAge-spec.js
```

6. By running the statement mentioned in the previous step, you will see the following details in the command prompt:

7. Next, let's implement scenario 2 using the following code:

```
var checkAge = require("../src/checkAge");
var MS_IN_A_YEAR = 1000 * 60 * 60  * 24 * 365;
function makeDateOfBirth(age) {
    return new Date().getTime() - (age * MS_IN_A_YEAR);
};
describe("Open a New Bank Account: ", function() {
  describe("Person age is 18 years or above", function() {
    it('should be eligible to open a Bank Account', function() {
      var myCustomer = new checkAge.Customer(makeDateOfBirth(18));
      expect(myCustomer.isValid()).toBeTruthy();
      var myCustomer = new checkAge.Customer(makeDateOfBirth(22));
      expect(myCustomer.isValid()).toBeTruthy();
    });
  });
  describe("Person age is below 18 years", function() {
    it("should not be eligible to open a new Bank Account",
function() {
      var myCustomer = new checkAge.Customer(makeDateOfBirth(5));
      expect(myCustomer.isValid()).toBeFalsy();
    });
  });
});
```

8. Run the spec file (that is, `checkAge-spec.js`) with jasmine-node. Use the following statement and run it in the command-line interface:

    jasmine-node spec/checkAge-spec.js

> You can also run `jasmine-node` with the `--autotest` option. It automatically executes the specs after each change. It is helpful when you are developing applications with TDD/BDD approach. The `jasmine-node` package provides various options to run the specs. For more information, you can visit the usage section of the following website:
>
> `https://github.com/mhevery/jasmine-node`

9. By running the statement mentioned in the previous step, you will see the following details in the command prompt:

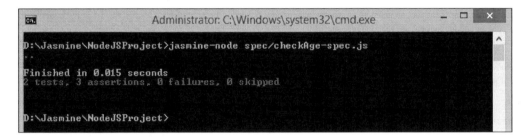

How it works...

In steps 1 to 9, we looked at how to implement Jasmine tests for Node.js using `jasmine-node`.

In steps 1 to 3, we defined the empty spec for scenario 1 and looked at how the empty spec passes by running it with `jasmine-node`.

In steps 4 to 6, we implemented scenario 1 and executed it through the command-line interface using `jasmine-node`.

In steps 7 to 9, following the same pattern, we implemented scenario 2.

9

Developing JavaScript Apps Using Jasmine – a Real-time Scenario

In this chapter, we will cover:

- ▶ Defining Jasmine specs corresponding to a user story
- ▶ Implementing Jasmine specs with Web/HTML
- ▶ Implementing Jasmine tests with the Data-Driven approach
- ▶ Creating Jasmine tests for a change request

Introduction

Sometimes, it's not feasible to test an application thoroughly for every change. Also, it is tough to update supporting documents (the requirement document, feature speciation, use cases, user stories, and so on) whenever there are any changes in the code and they become out of date quickly. An ideal approach is required to update the documents, requirements, or specifications on a continuous basis and test the application thoroughly whenever there is any change in the code. Developing the application with Behavior-Driven Development (BDD) is a good methodology. It ensures the quality of code and helps you to keep the specifications updated whenever there is any change in the code. For more information on BDD, refer to *Chapter 2, Jasmine with TDD and BDD Processes*.

In this chapter, we will learn how to develop JavaScript applications with Web/HTML using Jasmine's BDD framework. Primarily, we will elaborate and focus on the following aspects while developing an application with the BDD approach:

- How to define Jasmine specs corresponding to a user story
- How to optimize the test code and organize Jasmine specs for better understanding
- How to develop and refactor the code during development
- How to develop and test JavaScript apps with Web/HTML
- How to test an application from an E2E (end-to-end) perspective
- How to enhance and refactor the code for a change request

To explain all the preceding bullet points, we will take a real-time example to estimate tax/TDS as per individual income. Here, we will initiate the process to build a small utility/plugin (that is, a tax/TDS calculator) to estimate tax/TDS as per the United States/Federal/State Government tax rules, and demonstrate how to develop and test the JavaScript applications with Web/HTML from an E2E perspective. For more information on United States tax/TDS, you can refer to the following websites:

- `http://en.wikipedia.org/wiki/Income_tax_in_the_United_States`
- `http://www.forbes.com/sites/kellyphillipserb/2013/10/31/irs-announces-2014-tax-brackets-standard-deduction-amounts-and-more/`

Defining Jasmine specs corresponding to a user story

In this recipe, we will learn how to identify and define the Jasmine specs for a user story.

Let's assume you are working with a United States company called <ABC> Inc. As per the Federal/State government, every employee of the company has to pay tax on their income. Currently, you are developing a utility/web page with JavaScript to evaluate tax/TDS for individuals. There are different business rules (that is, tax brackets, standard deduction, child tax credit, and so on) that exist for evaluating tax/TDS for every individual.

"As a single taxpayer, I want to evaluate or estimate Tax/TDS on my income so that I can do my financial planning effectively."

So, based on the information provided in the previous paragraph, let's consider the following scenarios in the current context, that is, TDS/tax should be evaluated or estimated on the gross taxable income as per the tax brackets and rules defined by the Federal/State Government:

- ▶ **Scenario-1**: Tax/TDS should be evaluated on a gross income of $111,200 as per tax brackets and rules defined by the Federal/State Government.

- ▶ **Scenario-2**: Tax/TDS should be evaluated on a gross income of $450,000 as per tax brackets and rules defined by the Federal/State Government.

Now, to evaluate tax/TDS as per tax brackets and other tax rules, let's consider the following acceptance criteria for the single taxpayer category:

- ▶ A standard deduction of $6,200 should be applied (deducted from income) for single taxpayers

- ▶ A 10 percent tax rate should be applied if the taxable income is between $0 and $9,075

- ▶ Tax on income from $0 to $9,075 + a 15 percent tax rate should be applied if the taxable income is between $9,076 and $36,900

- ▶ Tax on income from $0 to $36,900 + a 25 percent tax rate should be applied if the taxable income is between $36,901 and $89,350

- ▶ Tax on income from $0 to $89,350 + a 28 percent tax rate should be applied if the taxable income is between $89,351 and $186,350

- ▶ Tax on income from $0 to $186,350 + a 33 percent tax rate should be applied if the taxable income is between $186,351 and $405,100

- ▶ Tax on income from $0 to $405,100 + a 35 percent tax rate should be applied if the taxable income is between $405,101 and $406,750

- ▶ Tax on income from $0 to $406,750 + a 39.6 percent tax rate should be applied if the taxable income is more than $406,750

Getting ready

Let's define both the scenarios in the **Given/When/Then** format to understand and implement the scenarios from the BDD perspective.

Define **scenario-1** as per the following points:

- ▶ **Given**: Employee of <ABC> Inc.
- ▶ **Given**: Tax filing category is single taxpayer
- ▶ **When**: Income is $111,200

> ▸ **Then**: Standard deduction should be applied

> ▸ **And** 10 percent tax rate should be applied for income between $0 and $9,075

> ▸ **And** 15 percent tax rate should be applied for income between $9,076 and $36,900

> ▸ **And** 25 percent tax rate should be applied for income between $36,901 and $89,350

> ▸ **And** 28 percent tax rate should be applied for income between $89,351 and $186,350

Define **scenario-2** as per the following points:

> ▸ **Given**: Employee of <ABC> Inc.

> ▸ **Given**: Tax filing category is single taxpayer

> ▸ **When**: Taxable income is $450,000

> ▸ **Then**: Standard deduction should be applied

> ▸ **And** 10 percent tax rate should be applied for income between $0 and $9,075

> ▸ **And** 15 percent tax rate should be applied for income between $9,076 and $36,900

> ▸ **And** 25 percent tax rate should be applied for income between $36,901 and $89,350

> ▸ **And** 28 percent tax rate should be applied for income between $89,351 and $186,350

> ▸ **And** 33 percent tax rate should be applied for income between $186,351 and $405,100

> ▸ **And** 35 percent tax rate should be applied for income between $405,101 and $406,750

> ▸ **And** 39.6 percent tax rate should be applied for income more than $406,750

How to do it...

You need to perform the following steps to define the Jasmine specs for a user story:

1. Create a spec file `US_Tax_spec.js` under the `/spec` folder and use the following code to define the spec for scenario 1:

```
describe("Employee of <ABC> Inc:",function(){
  describe("Tax Estimation:",function(){
    describe("Category: Single Taxpayer",function(){
      //Scenario-1
```

```
describe("When: Taxable income is $111,200: ",function(){
    it("standard deduction should be applied", function(){
    });
    it("10 percent Tax Rate should be applied for the income
between $0 and $9,075", function(){
    });
    it("Tax on income  $0 to $9,075 + " + "15 percent Tax Rate
should be applied for the income between $9,076 and $36,900",
function(){
    });
    it("Tax on income  $0 to $36,900 + " + "25 percent
Tax Rate should be applied for the income between $36,901 and
$89,350", function(){
    });
    it("Tax on income  $0 to $89,350 + " + "28 percent
Tax Rate should be applied for the income between $89,351 and
$186,350", function(){
    });
    });
    });
    });
});
```

Here, you can observe how we translated the Given/When/Then form at of scenario 1 into Jasmine specs.

2. Run the US_Tax_spec.js spec file with Jasmine runner (that is, SpecRunner. html). You should see the following screenshot:

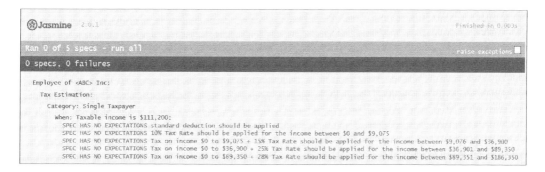

In the preceding screenshot, you can see that empty specs are passing for scenario 1.

It is a good practice to define empty Jasmine specs corresponding to user stories /use cases/features/requirements before actual implementation and get them reviewed by all stakeholders.

3. Let's define the spec for scenario 2 using the following code:

```
//Scenario-2
describe("When: Taxable income is $450,000: ",function(){
  it("standard deduction should be applied ", function(){
  });
  it("10 percent Tax Rate should be applied for the income between
$0 and $9,075", function(){
  });
  it("Tax on income  $0 to $9,075 + " + "15 percent Tax Rate
should be applied for the income between $9,076 and $36,900",
function(){
  });
  it("Tax on income  $0 to $36,900 + " + "25 percent Tax Rate
should be applied for the income between $36,901 and $89,350",
function(){
  });
  it("Tax on income  $0 to $89,350 + " + "28 percent Tax Rate
should be applied for the income between $89,351 and $186,350",
function(){
  });
  it("Tax on income  $0 to $186,350 + " + "33 percent Tax Rate
should be applied for the income between $186,351 and $405,100",
function(){
  });
  it("Tax on income  $0 to $405,100 + " + "35 percent Tax Rate
should be applied for the income between $405,101 and $406,750",
function(){
  });
  it("Tax on income  $0 to $406,750 + " + "39.6 percent Tax Rate
should be applied for the income more than $406,750", function(){
  });
});
```

4. Run the `US_Tax_spec.js` spec file for both the scenarios with Jasmine runner. You should see the following screenshot, which indicates that empty specs are passing for both the scenarios:

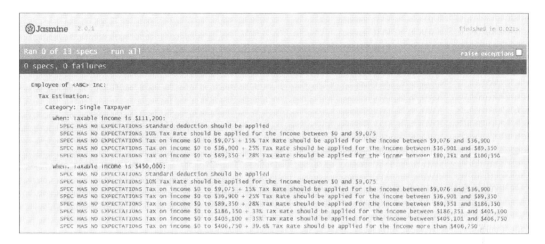

In the preceding screenshot, you can see that we defined the specs for scenario 1 and scenario 2 within different groups and subgroups. For more information on groups and subgroups, refer to the *Organizing Jasmine specs into groups and subgroups* recipe, in *Chapter 4, Designing specs from Requirement*.

See also

▶ To learn how to implement specs defined in this recipe using the BDD process, refer to the next recipe, *Implementing Jasmine specs with Web/HTML*.

Implementing Jasmine specs with Web/HTML

In *Chapter 2, Jasmine with TDD and BDD Processes*, we learned how to write incremental code with the BDD approach. In this recipe, we will learn how to develop a web application with HTML and JavaScript using the BDD approach. We will also look at how to write Jasmine specs with HTML and manipulate DOM to test the application from an E2E perspective.

The scope of this recipe is to implement Jasmine specs for both the scenarios described in the previous recipe, *Defining Jasmine specs corresponding to user story*.

Getting ready

To understand how to implement Jasmine specs with Web/HTML, let's create the
`TaxCalculator.html` file using the following HTML code:

```
<!DOCTYPE html>
<html>
<head>
  <title>Tax Calculator</title>
  <script type="text/javascript" src="src/validations.js"></script>
</head>
<body class="taxCalculator">
<div id="Wrapper" class="taxWrapper">
  <div id="main" class="taxMain">
  <div class="taxHead"><h1>Tax Estimation</h1></div>
    <div class="taxInnerWrapper">
      <div class="taxFrm">
      <form name="taxForm" class="myTaxClass">
        <h3>Income and Tax Information</h3>
        <div class="taxClass"><label for="taxStatus">Tax Filing Status
</label>
          <select name="taxFilingStatus"
id="taxFilingStatusID"><option value="S" selected="selected">Single</
option>
          <option value="H">Head of Household</option>
          <option value="MS">Married - Separately</option>
          <option value="MJ">Married - Jointly</option>
          <option value="T">Trust</option>
        </select>
      </div>
        <div class="taxClass">
        <label>Gross Annual Income</label><input type="text"
size="10" name="taxGrossIncome" value="0" id="taxGrossIncomeID" data-
validation="validation-1">
          <span id="validation-1" class="validation-output"></span>
        </div>
        <div class="taxClass">
        <label>Amount of gross income considered 'unearned'/
investment income</label><input type="text" size="10"
name="taxInvestment" value="0" id="taxInvestmentID" data-
validation="validation-2">
          <span id="validation-2" class="validation-output"></span>
        </div>
```

```
        <div class="taxClass">
            <label>Qualified Plan/IRA Contribution</label><input
type="text" size="10" name="taxIRA" value="0" id="taxIRAID" data-
validation="validation-3">
            <span id="validation-3" class="validation-output"></span>
        </div>
        <div class="taxClass">
            <label>Itemized Deductions - $0 for Standard</label><input
type="text" size="10" name="taxStandardDeduction" value="0"
id="taxStandardDeductionID" data-validation="validation-4">
            <span id="validation-4" class="validation-output"></span>
        </div>
        <div class="taxClass">
            <label>Number of Personal Exemptions</label><input
type="text" name="taxExemptions" size="10" value="0"
id="taxExemptionsID" data-validation="validation-5">
            <span id="validation-5" class="validation-output"></span>
        </div>
        <div class="taxClass">
            <label>Number of Dependent Children</label><input
type="text" name="taxDependents" size="10" value="0"
id="taxDependentsID" data-validation="validation-6">
            <span id="validation-6" class="validation-output"></span>
        </div>
        <div class="btn">
            <button type="button" class="mySubmit" id="mySubmitID" on
click="getTaxDetails()">Submit</button>   <input
type="reset" class="mySubmit" id="myCancel" onclick="" value="Reset">
        </div>
      </form>
      </div>
    </div>
    <div id="taxStatus" class="taxInnerWrapper">
      <div class="taxResult">
      <h3>Estimated Tax Calculation</h3>
      <div class="taxClass"><label>Gross Income:  </label><label id=
"myGrossIncome"></label></div>
      <div class="taxClass"><label>Qualified IRA Contributions:  </
label><label id= "myContributation"><b></b></label></div>
      <div class="taxClass"><label>Adjusted Gross Income:  </
label><label id= "myAdjustedGrossIncome"></label></div>
      <div class="taxClass"><label>Standard/Itemized Deductions:  </
label><label id= "myDeduction"></label></div>
```

```
        <div class="taxClass"><label>Personal Exemptions:  </
label><label id= "myExemption"></label></div>
        <div class="taxClass"><label>Taxable Income:  </label><label id=
"myTaxableIncome"></label></div>
        <div class="taxClass"><label>Tax Liability Before Credits:  </
label><label id= "myTaxBeforeCredit"></label></div>
        <div class="taxClass"><label>Child Tax Credits:  </label><label
id= "myChildTaxCredit"></label></div>
        <div class="taxClass"><label>Estimated Tax Liability:  </
label><label id= "myEstimatedTax"></label></div>
        </div>
      </div>
    </div>
</div>
<style type="text/css">
h3 {
    padding-left: 10px;
}
.taxHead {
    border-bottom: 1px solid;
    text-align: center;
}
.taxInnerWrapper {
    float: left;
    width: 50 percent;
}
.taxClass {
    float: left;
    margin: 5px;
    padding: 10px;
    width: 100 percent;
}
.taxFrm label {
    display: block;
    float: left;
    margin-right: 5px;
    width: 390px;
}
.taxResult label {
    display: block;
    float: left;
    width: 214px;
}
```

```
.btn {
    padding-left: 157px;
    padding-top: 20px;
}
</style>
</body>
</html>
```

In the preceding code, we simply created a web page/utility to calculate tax/TDS for individuals who pay it in the United States. Here, we collected the information which is required to estimate the tax/TDS of the end user (that is, annual income, plan/IRA contribution, itemized deductions, exemptions, and dependents). Here, we have also provided the ability to estimate tax/TDS for different categories (that is, single, head of household, married–separately, married–jointly, and trust). However, the scope of this recipe is to implement tax/TDS for the two scenarios elaborated in the previous recipe, for the single taxpayer category. You can also see that we embedded one JavaScript file (`validations.js`) with HTML. All the validations are implemented in this file to check the input values. However, the `validations.js` file is not required for creating Jasmine specs. If required, you can get it from the Packt website.

How to do it...

You need to perform the following steps to implement Jasmine specs with Web/HTML:

1. Create a `US_Tax_Estimation_spec.js` spec file under the `/spec` folder and get the following code from the `US_Tax_spec.js` spec file created in the previous recipe:

```
describe("Employee of <ABC> Inc:",function(){
  describe("Tax Estimation:",function(){
    describe("Category: Single Taxpayer",function(){
      //Scenario-1
      describe("When: Taxable income is $111,200: ",function(){
        it("standard deduction should be applied", function(){
        });
        it("10 percent Tax Rate should be applied for the income
between $0 and $9,075", function(){
        });
        it("Tax on income  $0 to $9,075 + " + "15 percent Tax Rate
should be applied for the income between $9,076 and $36,900",
function(){
        });
        it("Tax on income  $0 to $36,900 + " + "25 percent
Tax Rate should be applied for the income between $36,901 and
$89,350", function(){
        });
```

```
            it("Tax on income  $0 to $89,350 + " + "28 percent
Tax Rate should be applied for the income between $89,351 and
$186,350", function(){
            });
        });
        //Scenario-2
        describe("When: Taxable income is $450,000: ",function(){
            it("standard deduction should be applied ", function(){
            });
            it("10 percent Tax Rate should be applied for the income
between $0 and $9,075", function(){
            });
            it("Tax on income  $0 to $9,075 + " + "15 percent Tax Rate
should be applied for the income between $9,076 and $36,900",
function(){
            });
            it("Tax on income  $0 to $36,900 + " + "25 percent
Tax Rate should be applied for the income between $36,901 and
$89,350", function(){
            });
            it("Tax on income  $0 to $89,350 + " + "28 percent
Tax Rate should be applied for the income between $89,351 and
$186,350", function(){
            });
            it("Tax on income  $0 to $186,350 + " + "33 percent
Tax Rate should be applied for the income between $186,351 and
$405,100", function(){
            });
            it("Tax on income  $0 to $405,100 + " + "35 percent
Tax Rate should be applied for the income between $405,101 and
$406,750", function(){
            });
            it("Tax on income  $0 to $406,750 + " + "39.6 percent
Tax Rate should be applied for the income more than $406,750",
function(){
            });
        });
    });
  });
});
```

2. In order to develop JavaScript code along with HTML, first we need to make the fixture `TaxCalculator.html` available in the DOM. Let's implement the test code to load it using the following code and define it under the `Tax Estimation` group:

```
beforeEach(function() {
    loadFixtures('TaxCalculator.html');
});
```

In the preceding code snapshot, you can see that we defined the code within the `beforeEach` function under the `Tax Estimation` group. For more information on `beforeEach`, refer to the *Applying setup and teardown functions to the Jasmine tests* recipe, in *Chapter 1, Getting Started with the Jasmine Framework*.

We loaded the fixture `TaxCalculator.html` from the default path `spec/javascripts/fixtures/`, using the `loadFixtures` function. For more details on fixtures, refer to the *Designing Jasmine tests with HTML and JSON fixtures* recipe, in *Chapter 6, Jasmine with Ajax, jQuery, and Fixtures*.

3. Next, use the following code to trigger the `click` event:

```
//Scenario - 1
describe("When: Taxable income is $111,200: ",function(){
    beforeEach(function() {
        $("#taxFilingStatusID").val("S");
       $("#taxGrossIncomeID").val(111000);
       $('#mySubmitID').trigger("click");
    });
    //Scenario 1-- Test Code to implement scenario 1.....
    //......

    //.....End
});
```

Here, you can see that we set input values (tax filing status and gross income) and triggered the `click` event using jQuery.

4. Run the `US_Tax_Estimation_spec.js` spec file with Jasmine runner. An error will be thrown as shown in the following screenshot, which indicates that **'getTaxDetails' is undefined**:

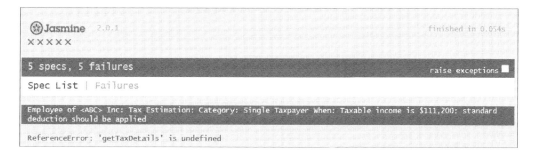

 A web server (such as Apache, Tomcat, JBoss, and so on) is required to run the test code with a fixture.

5. Let's create a `US_Tax_Estimation.js` JavaScript file and define the `getTaxDetails` function, using the following code:

```
function getTaxDetails(){
    //Define variables to collects details
    var myTaxFilingStatus, myGrossTaxableIncome, myIRAContribution,
myStandardDeduction, myExemptions, myDependent;
    var myTax =0 ; //Variable to hold the value of estimated tax
};
```

6. Now, add the reference of `US_Tax_Estimation.js` to Jasmine runner and run the `US_Tax_Estimation_spec.js` spec file. You should see the following screenshot, which indicates that all the empty specs are passing:

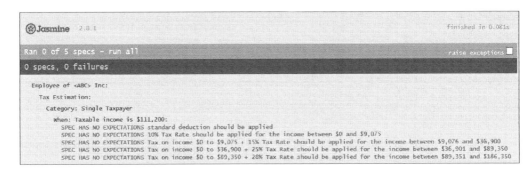

7. Let's implement the test code for spec 1, using the following code:

```
describe("Category: Single Taxpayer",function(){
    //Scenario-1
    describe("When: Taxable income is $111,200: ",function(){
        beforeEach(function() {
            $("#taxFilingStatusID").val("S");
            $("#taxGrossIncomeID").val(111000);
            $('#mySubmitID').trigger("click");
        });
        it("standard deduction should be applied", function(){
            expect(Number($("#myTaxableIncome").html())).
toEqual(105000);
        });
    });
});
```

8. Next, let's refactor the code for the `getTaxDetails` function to implement the code corresponding to the first spec (that is, the $6,200 standard deduction should be applied), using the following code:

```
function getTaxDetails(){
    //Define variables to collects details
    var myTaxFilingStatus, myGrossIncome, myIRAContribution,
myStandardDeduction, myExemptions, myDependent;
    var myTax=0; //Variable to hold the value of estimated tax
    myTaxFilingStatus = $("#taxFilingStatusID").val();
    if ($("#taxGrossIncomeID").val() > 0) {
        myGrossIncome = $("#taxGrossIncomeID").val();
    }
    else {
        myGrossIncome = 0;
    }
    if (myTaxFilingStatus != null) {
        myStandardDeduction= getStandardDeduction(myTaxFilingStatus);
        myGrossIncome = myGrossIncome - myStandardDeduction;
    }
    else {
        myStandardDeduction= 0;
    }
    $("#myTaxableIncome").html(myGrossIncome);
```

9. Run the `US_Tax_Estimation_spec.js` spec file with Jasmine.
   An error will be thrown as shown in the following screenshot, which indicates that **'getStandardDeduction' is undefined**:

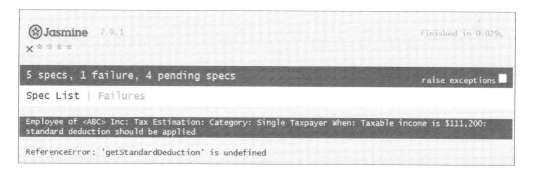

10. Let's define the `getStandardDeduction` function using the following code:

```
function getStandardDeduction(myTaxFilingStatus)
{
   var myStandardDeduction = 6200;
   return myStandardDeduction;
};
```

In the preceding code snapshot, you can see that we have written the JavaScript code and assigned $6200 as the value for standard deduction, to pass the acceptance criteria for spec 1.

11. Run the `US_Tax_Estimation_spec.js` spec file with Jasmine runner and you should see the following screenshot, which indicates that spec 1 is passing:

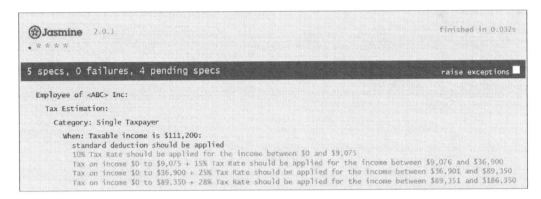

In the preceding screenshot, you can see that spec 1 is passing and the other four specs are displayed as **pending specs**. Here, we marked four specs as pending by declaring the `it` block as `xit`. In subsequent steps, we will implement all the specs one by one using the `it` block. For more information on pending specs, refer to the *Declaring Pending specs with Jasmine tests* recipe, in *Chapter 3, Customizing Matchers and Jasmine Functions*.

12. Now, let's implement the test code for spec 2, using the following code:

```
it("10 percent Tax Rate should be applied for the income between
$0 and $9,075", function(){
   expect(myTDS_TaxBracket[0]).toEqual(907.5);
});
```

13. Let's refactor the code for the `getTaxDetails` function to implement the code corresponding to the second spec (a 10 percent Tax Rate should be applied for the income between $0 and $9,075), using the following code:

```
var myTDS_TaxBracket = []; //Define variable to hold values of tax
as per US Tax Brackets
function getTaxDetails(){
  //Define variables to collects details
  var myTaxFilingStatus, myGrossIncome, myIRAContribution,
myStandardDeduction, myExemptions, myDependent;
  var myTax=0; //Variable to hold the value of estimated tax
  myTaxFilingStatus = $("#taxFilingStatusID").val();
  if ($("#taxGrossIncomeID").val() > 0) {
    myGrossIncome = $("#taxGrossIncomeID").val();
  }
  else {
    myGrossIncome = 0;
  }
  if (myTaxFilingStatus != null) {
    myStandardDeduction= getStandardDeduction(myTaxFilingStatus);
    myGrossIncome = myGrossIncome - myStandardDeduction;
  }
  else {
    myStandardDeduction= 0;
  }
  $("#myTaxableIncome").html(myGrossIncome);
  myTax= calculateTDS(myGrossIncome);
  $("#myEstimatedTax").html(myTax);
};
```

Here, you can see that we defined a `calculateTDS` function to calculate tax/TDS as per gross income.

14. Run the `US_Tax_Estimation_spec.js` spec file with Jasmine runner. An error will be thrown as shown in the following screenshot, which indicates that **'calculateTDS' is undefined**:

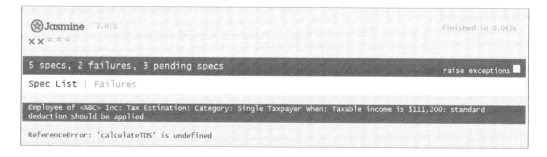

15. Let's define the `calculateTDS` function using the following code:

```
function calculateTDS(myGrossIncome)
{
  var myCalculatedTax = 0; //Declare a variable to hold the value
of estimated tax
  //Start - Calculate TDS for the Tax Bracket 0 - $9,225
  if (myGrossIncome >= 9075) { //Calculation Corresponding to tax
bracket 0 - $9,075
    myTDS_TaxBracket[0] = 9075 *(10/100);
    myCalculatedTax = myCalculatedTax + myTDS_TaxBracket[0];
  }
  else { //Calculate TDS if gross income is <$9,075
    myTDS_TaxBracket[0] = myGrossIncome*(10/100);
    myCalculatedTax = myCalculatedTax + myTDS_TaxBracket[0];
    return myCalculatedTax;
  };
  //End - Calculate TDS for the Tax Bracket 0 - $9,225
  return myCalculatedTax;
};
```

Here, you can see that we developed the code to pass the second spec (a 10 percent Tax Rate should be applied for the income between $0 and $9,075). Using BDD, we developed the code from the failing spec and refactored the code as needed. Typically with the BDD approach, we follow this process: red/green/refactor/....red/green/refactor....

16. Run the `US_Tax_Estimation_spec.js` spec file with Jasmine runner. You should see the following screenshot:

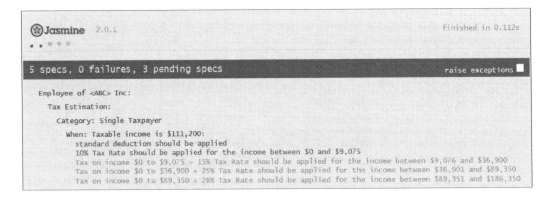

In the preceding screenshot, you can see that spec 1 and spec 2 are passing.

In BDD, first you have to define the spec, and then the corresponding code will be developed using the failing spec in a step-by-step approach.

17. Now, following the same BDD process, let's implement the JavaScript code for the remaining specs of scenario 1 and scenario 2, using the following code:

```javascript
function calculateTDS(myGrossIncome)
{
  var myCalculatedTax = 0; //Declare a variable to hold the value
of estimated tax
  //Start - Calculate TDS for the Tax Bracket 0 - $9,225
  if (myGrossIncome >= 9075) { //Calculation Corresponding to tax
bracket 0 - $9,075
    myTDS_TaxBracket[0] = 9075 *(10/100);
    myCalculatedTax = myCalculatedTax + myTDS_TaxBracket[0];
  }
  else { //Calculate TDS if gross income is <$9,075
    myTDS_TaxBracket[0] = myGrossIncome*(10/100);
    myCalculatedTax = myCalculatedTax + myTDS_TaxBracket[0];
    return myCalculatedTax;
  };//End - Calculate TDS for the Tax Bracket 0 - $9,225
  //Start - Calculation Corresponding to tax bracket $9,075 -
$36,900
  if (myGrossIncome >= 36900) {
    myTDS_TaxBracket[1] = myTDS_TaxBracket[0] + (36900-9075)
*(15/100);
    myCalculatedTax = myTDS_TaxBracket[1];
  }
  else { //Calculate TDS if gross income is >$9,225 and <37450
    myTDS_TaxBracket[1] = myTDS_TaxBracket[0]+(myGrossInco
me-9075)*(15/100);
    myCalculatedTax = myTDS_TaxBracket[1];
    return myCalculatedTax;
  };//End - Calculate TDS for the Tax Bracket $9,075 - $36,900
  //Start - Calculation Corresponding to tax bracket $36,901 -
$89,350
  if (myGrossIncome >= 89350) {
    myTDS_TaxBracket[2] = myTDS_TaxBracket[1] + (89350-36900)
*(25/100);
    myCalculatedTax = myTDS_TaxBracket[2];
  }
  else { //Calculate TDS if gross income is >$36,900 and <$89,350
    myTDS_TaxBracket[2] = myTDS_TaxBracket[1]+(myGrossInco
me-36900)*(25/100);
    myCalculatedTax = myTDS_TaxBracket[2];
    return myCalculatedTax;
  };//End - Calculate TDS for the Tax Bracket $36,901 - $89,350
```

```
//Start - Calculation Corresponding to tax bracket $89,351 -
$186,350
  if (myGrossIncome >= 186350) {
    myTDS_TaxBracket[3] = myTDS_TaxBracket[2] + (186350-89350)
*(28/100);
    myCalculatedTax = myTDS_TaxBracket[3];
  }
  else { //Calculate TDS if gross income is >$89,350 and <$186,350
    myTDS_TaxBracket[3] = myTDS_TaxBracket[2]+(myGrossInco
me-89350)*(28/100);
    myCalculatedTax = myTDS_TaxBracket[3];
    return myCalculatedTax;
  };//End - Calculate TDS for the Tax Bracket $89,351 - $186,350
  //Start - Calculation Corresponding to tax bracket $186,351 -
$405,100
  if (myGrossIncome >= 405100) {
    myTDS_TaxBracket[4] = myTDS_TaxBracket[3] + (405100-
186350)*(33/100);
    myCalculatedTax = myTDS_TaxBracket[4];
  }
  else { //Calculate TDS if gross income is >$186,350 and
<$405,100
    myTDS_TaxBracket[4] = myTDS_TaxBracket[3]+(myGrossInco
me-186350)*(33/100);
    myCalculatedTax = myTDS_TaxBracket[4];
    return myCalculatedTax;
  };//End - Calculate TDS for the Tax Bracket $186,351 - $405,100
  //Start - Calculation Corresponding to tax bracket $405,101 -
$406,750
  if (myGrossIncome >= 406750) {
    myTDS_TaxBracket[5] = myTDS_TaxBracket[4] + (406750-
405100)*(35/100);
    myCalculatedTax = myTDS_TaxBracket[5];
  }
  else { //Calculate TDS if gross income is >$405,100 and
<$406,750
    myTDS_TaxBracket[5] = myTDS_TaxBracket[4]+(myGrossInco
me-405100)*(35/100);
    myCalculatedTax = myTDS_TaxBracket[5];
    return myCalculatedTax;
  };//End - Calculate TDS for the Tax Bracket $186,351 - $405,100
  //Start - Calculation Corresponding to tax bracket if gross
income >$406,750
  if (myGrossIncome >406750) {
    myTDS_TaxBracket[6] = myTDS_TaxBracket[5] +
(myGrossIncome-406750)*(39.6/100);
    myCalculatedTax = myTDS_TaxBracket[6];
  }//End
  return myCalculatedTax;
};
```

18. Use the following test code for scenario 2:

```
//Scenario-2
describe("When: Taxable income is $450,000: ",function(){
    beforeEach(function() {
        $("#taxFilingStatusID").val("S");
        $("#taxGrossIncomeID").val(450000);
        $('#mySubmitID').trigger("click");
    });
    //Test Code to implement scenario 2.....
    it("standard deduction should be applied ", function(){
        expect(Number($("#myTaxableIncome").html())).
toEqual(443800);
    });
    it("10 percent Tax Rate should be applied for the income
between $0 and $9,075", function(){
        expect(myTDS_TaxBracket[0]).toEqual(907.5);
    });
    it("Tax on income  $0 to $9,075 + " + "15 percent Tax Rate
should be applied for the income between $9,076 and $36,900",
function(){
        expect(myTDS_TaxBracket[1]).toEqual(5081.25);
    });
    it("Tax on income  $0 to $36,900 + " + "25 percent
Tax Rate should be applied for the income between $36,901 and
$89,350", function(){
        expect(myTDS_TaxBracket[2]).toEqual(18193.75);
    });
    it("Tax on income  $0 to $89,350 + " + "28 percent
Tax Rate should be applied for the income between $89,351 and
$186,350", function(){
        expect(myTDS_TaxBracket[3]).toEqual(45353.75);
    });
    it("Tax on income  $0 to $186,350 + " + "33 percent
Tax Rate should be applied for the income between $186,351 and
$405,100", function(){
        expect(myTDS_TaxBracket[4]).toEqual(117541.25);
    });
    it("Tax on income  $0 to $405,100 + " + "35 percent
Tax Rate should be applied for the income between $405,101 and
$406,750", function(){
        expect(myTDS_TaxBracket[5]).toEqual(118118.75);
    });
    it("Tax on income  $0 to $406,750 + " + "39.6 percent
Tax Rate should be applied for the income more than $406,750",
function(){
```

```
                            expect(Number($("#myEstimatedTax").html())).
        toEqual(132790.55);
                });
        });
```

19. Finally, run the `US_Tax_Estimation_spec.js` spec file with Jasmine runner for both the scenarios. You should see the following screenshot, letting you know that all the specs are passing:

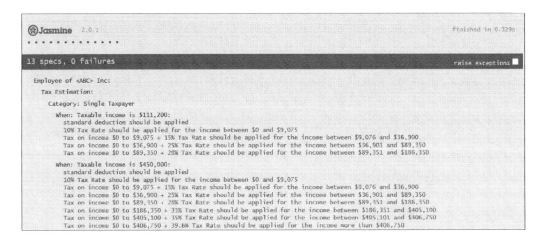

In the preceding screenshot, you can see that the Tax Calculator application/utility is able to estimate tax/TDS as per gross income and both the scenarios are passing for the **Single Taxpayer** category. I would recommend you prepare a few more scenarios with different gross incomes and tax categories (head of household, married-separately, married-jointly, and trust). For instance, you can prepare scenarios for the married-jointly category with a gross income of $550,000, $365,000, or anything that you want to check, and refactor and validate the JavaScript code by following the BDD process.

How it works...

Let's take a look at the steps of this recipe.

In step 1, we created the `US_Tax_Estimation_spec.js` spec file and got the empty specs from the `US_Tax_spec.js` spec file.

In step 2, we loaded a fixture `TaxCalculator.html`, using the `loadFixtures` function and made it available in DOM.

In step 3, we provided all the input values (tax filing status and gross income) that are required to run scenario 1, and then triggered the `click` event.

In steps 4 to 11, we implemented the first test condition ($6,200 standard deduction should be applied) for scenario 1. In step 5, we defined the getTaxDetails function. In step 8, we refactored the getTaxDetails function as guided by the failing spec. This function receives the input values from the web page. Here, we also declared a global variable myTDS_TaxBracket, to hold intermediate results.

In steps 12 to 16, we implemented the second test condition (a 10 percent tax rate should be applied for income between $0 and $9,075) for scenario 1. In step 13, we refactored the code for the getTaxDetails function and called a function calculateTDS, to calculate tax. The calculateTDS function accepts a myGrossIncome parameter. In step 15, we defined the calculateTDS function.

In steps 17 to 19, following the BDD process, we implemented the remaining specs of scenarios 1 and 2.

Implementing Jasmine tests with a Data-Driven approach

In the Data-Driven approach, Jasmine specs get input or expected values from the external data files (JSON, CSV, or TXT files, and so on) that are required to run the tests. In other words, we isolate test data and Jasmine specs so that we can prepare the test data (input or expected values) separately as per the need of the specs or scenarios. You can see the Data-Driven approach in the following diagram:

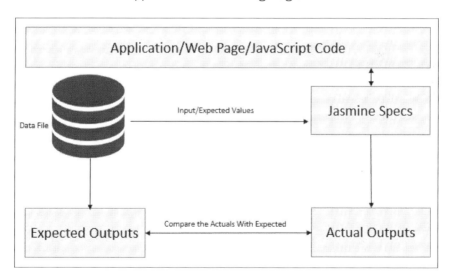

In this recipe, we will learn how to implement Jasmine specs for the scenarios described in the previous recipe, using the Data-Driven approach. For more details, refer to the previous recipe, *Implementing Jasmine specs with Web/HTML*.

How to do it...

You need to perform the following steps to implement Jasmine tests with the Data-Driven approach:

1. First, you need to create a `US_TaxEstimation_DataDriven_spec.js` spec file under the `/spec` folder and get the following code from the `US_Tax_Estimation_spec.js` spec file created in the previous recipe, *Implementing Jasmine specs with Web/HTML*:

```
describe("Employee of <ABC> Inc:",function(){
  describe("Tax Estimation:",function(){
    beforeEach(function() {
        loadFixtures('TaxCalculator.html');
    });
    describe("Category: Single Taxpayer",function(){
      //Scenario-1
      describe("When: Taxable income is $111,200: ",function(){
        beforeEach(function() {
            $("#taxFilingStatusID").val("S");
          $("#taxGrossIncomeID").val(111200);
          $('#mySubmitID').trigger("click");
        });
        it("standard deduction should be applied", function(){
            expect(Number($("#myTaxableIncome").html())).
toEqual(105000);
        });
        it("10 percent Tax Rate should be applied for the income
between $0 and $9,075", function(){
            expect(myTDS_TaxBracket[0]).toEqual(907.5);
        });
        it("Tax on income  $0 to $9,075 + " + "15 percent Tax Rate
should be applied for the income between $9,076 and $36,900",
function(){
            expect(myTDS_TaxBracket[1]).toEqual(5081.25);
        });
        it("Tax on income  $0 to $36,900 + " + "25 percent
Tax Rate should be applied for the income between $36,901 and
$89,350", function(){
            expect(myTDS_TaxBracket[2]).toEqual(18193.75);
        });
        it("Tax on income  $0 to $89,350 + " + "28 percent
Tax Rate should be applied for the income between $89,351 and
$186,350", function(){
```

```
                    expect(Number($("#myEstimatedTax").html())).
toEqual(22575.75);
                });
            });
        //Scenario-2
        describe("When: Taxable income is $450,000: ",function(){
            beforeEach(function() {
                $("#taxFilingStatusID").val("S");
                $("#taxGrossIncomeID").val(450000);
                $('#mySubmitID').trigger("click");
            });
            //Test Code to implement scenario 2.....
            it("standard deduction should be applied ", function(){
                expect(Number($("#myTaxableIncome").html())).
toEqual(443800);
            });
            it("10 percent Tax Rate should be applied for the income
between $0 and $9,075", function(){
                expect(myTDS_TaxBracket[0]).toEqual(907.5);
            });
            it("Tax on income  $0 to $9,075 + " + "15 percent Tax Rate
should be applied for the income between $9,076 and $36,900",
function(){
                expect(myTDS_TaxBracket[1]).toEqual(5081.25);
            });
            it("Tax on income  $0 to $36,900 + " + "25 percent
Tax Rate should be applied for the income between $36,901 and
$89,350", function(){
                expect(myTDS_TaxBracket[2]).toEqual(18193.75);
            });
            it("Tax on income  $0 to $89,350 + " + "28 percent
Tax Rate should be applied for the income between $89,351 and
$186,350", function(){
                expect(myTDS_TaxBracket[3]).toEqual(45353.75);
            });
            it("Tax on income  $0 to $186,350 + " + "33 percent
Tax Rate should be applied for the income between $186,351 and
$405,100", function(){
                expect(myTDS_TaxBracket[4]).toEqual(117541.25);
            });
            it("Tax on income  $0 to $405,100 + " + "35 percent
Tax Rate should be applied for the income between $405,101 and
$406,750", function(){
```

```
                    expect(myTDS_TaxBracket[5]).toEqual(118118.75);
                });
                it("Tax on income   $0 to $406,750 + " + "39.6 percent
    Tax Rate should be applied for the income more than $406,750",
    function(){
                    expect(Number($("#myEstimatedTax").html())).
    toEqual(132790.55);
                });
            });
        });
      });
    });
```

2. Now, let's create the `FixtureInputData.json` data file to provide input values for both the scenarios, using the following data in the JSON format:

```
[
{
"TaxFilingStatus": "S",
"GrossIncome": 111200,
"IRAContribution": 0,
"Exemptions": 0,
"Dependent": 0
},
{
"TaxFilingStatus": "S",
"GrossIncome": 450000,
"IRAContribution": 0,
"Exemptions": 0,
"Dependent": 0
}
]
```

   Here, you can see that we created input values/data for both the scenarios described in the previous recipe. We set the value a of gross income as $111200 and $450000 for scenario 1 and scenario 2, respectively.

3. To implement the Data-Driven approach, first let's refactor the test code for scenario 1, using the following code:

```
describe("Employee of <ABC> Inc:",function(){
  describe("Tax Estimation:",function(){
        var fixtureFile, fixtures, myResult;
    beforeEach(function() {
            loadFixtures('TaxCalculator.html');
```

```
        //Start - Load JSON Files to provide input data for all
the test scenarios
        fixtureFile = "FixtureInputData.json";
        fixtures = loadJSONFixtures(fixtureFile);
        myResult = fixtures[fixtureFile];
        //End - Load JSON Files to provide input data for all
the test scenarios
    });
    describe("Category: Single Taxpayer",function(){
      //Scenario-1
      describe("When: Taxable income is $111,200: ",function(){
        beforeEach(function() {
        $("#taxFilingStatusID").val(myResult[0].
TaxFilingStatus);
        $("#taxGrossIncomeID").val(myResult[0].GrossIncome);
        $('#mySubmitID').trigger("click");
        });
        it("standard deduction should be applied", function(){
        expect(Number($('#taxGrossIncomeID').val())).
toEqual(111200);
        expect(Number($("#myTaxableIncome").html())).
toEqual(105000);
        });
        it("10 percent Tax Rate should be applied for the income
between $0 and $9,075", function(){
        expect(myTDS_TaxBracket[0]).toEqual(907.5);
        });
        it("Tax on income  $0 to $9,075 + " + "15 percent Tax Rate
should be applied for the income between $9,076 and $36,900",
function(){
        expect(myTDS_TaxBracket[1]).toEqual(5081.25);
        });
        it("Tax on income  $0 to $36,900 + " + "25 percent
Tax Rate should be applied for the income between $36,901 and
$89,350", function(){
        expect(myTDS_TaxBracket[2]).toEqual(18193.75);
        });
        it("Tax on income  $0 to $89,350 + " + "28 percent
Tax Rate should be applied for the income between $89,351 and
$186,350", function(){
        expect(Number($("#myEstimatedTax").html())).
toEqual(22575.75);
        });
      });
    });
  });
});
```

In the preceding code snapshot, you can see that we provided the input data from the external JSON file (that is, `FixtureInputData.json`) using the `loadJSONFixtures` function and made it available at run time. To find out more about how to load JSON fixtures, refer to the *Designing Jasmine specs with HTML and JSON fixtures* recipe, in *Chapter 6, Jasmine with Ajax, jQuery, and Fixtures*.

Then, we set the values of the input parameters, tax filing status and gross income. Here, we also validated whether gross income is configured with HTML element (that is, `taxGrossIncomeID`) or not using custom matchers provided by jasmine-jquery. For more information on jQuery custom matchers, refer to the *Writing Jasmine tests using custom jQuery matchers* recipe, in *Chapter 6, Jasmine with Ajax, jQuery, and Fixtures*.

> If the test data (input or expected) is required during execution, it is recommended that you provide it from the external file.

Now we have covered how to provide input data from the external file. Next, I would recommend you create a separate `FixtureExpectedData.json` data file and implement the Data-Driven approach for the expected values (that is, estimated tax/ TDS for different tax brackets), which are currently hard-coded in both the scenarios. So, let's implement it and see how data can be provided from the external file.

4. To implement the Data-Driven approach for scenario 2, let's refactor the test code for it, using the following code:

```
//Scenario-2
describe("When: Taxable income is $450,000: ",function(){
  beforeEach(function() {
      $("#taxFilingStatusID").val(myResult[1].TaxFilingStatus);
      $("#taxGrossIncomeID").val(myResult[1].GrossIncome);
      $('#mySubmitID').trigger("click");
  });
  //Test Code to implement scenario 2.....
  it("standard deduction should be applied ", function(){
    expect(Number($('#taxGrossIncomeID').val())).toEqual(450000);
    expect(Number($("#myTaxableIncome").html())).toEqual(443800);
  });
    it("10 percent Tax Rate should be applied for the income between
$0 and $9,075", function(){
```

```
        expect(myTDS_TaxBracket[0]).toEqual(907.5);
    });
    it("Tax on income  $0 to $9,075 + " + "15 percent Tax Rate
should be applied for the income between $9,076 and $36,900",
function(){
        expect(myTDS_TaxBracket[1]).toEqual(5081.25);
    });
    it("Tax on income  $0 to $36,900 + " + "25 percent Tax Rate
should be applied for the income between $36,901 and $89,350",
function(){
        expect(myTDS_TaxBracket[2]).toEqual(18193.75);
    });
    it("Tax on income  $0 to $89,350 + " + "28 percent Tax Rate
should be applied for the income between $89,351 and $186,350",
function(){
        expect(myTDS_TaxBracket[3]).toEqual(45353.75);
    });
    it("Tax on income  $0 to $186,350 + " + "33 percent Tax Rate
should be applied for the income between $186,351 and $405,100",
function(){
        expect(myTDS_TaxBracket[4]).toEqual(117541.25);
    });
    it("Tax on income  $0 to $405,100 + " + "35 percent Tax Rate
should be applied for the income between $405,101 and $406,750",
function(){
        expect(myTDS_TaxBracket[5]).toEqual(118118.75);
    });
    it("Tax on income  $0 to $406,750 + " + "39.6 percent Tax Rate
should be applied for the income more than $406,750", function(){
        expect(Number($("#myEstimatedTax").html())).
toEqual(132790.55);
    });
});
```

In the preceding code snapshot, you can see that we set the values of input parameters and checking whether gross income is being configured with the HTML element `taxGrossIncomeID` or not.

5. Finally, run the `US_TaxEstimation_DataDriven_spec.js` spec file with Jasmine runner for both the scenarios. You should see the following screenshot, letting you know that all the specs are passing:

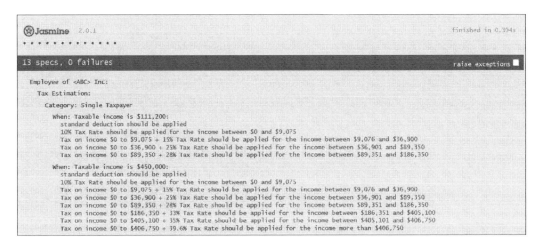

Creating Jasmine tests for a change request

A change request comes into the picture whenever there is a request from the client for an addition or alteration to the agreed deliverables. A change request can also originate from internal reviews. This could be delivered as a planned release or a patch release for hot fixes or hardware upgrades. Primarily, a change request originates from the following sources:

- ▶ Bugs identified during alpha or beta testing, or bugs/issues reported on the production environment by customers

- ▶ A system/feature enhancement request from users

- ▶ Changes in business rules

- ▶ Requests from product management or the owner

For more details on change requests, you can refer to the following websites:

- ▶ `http://en.wikipedia.org/wiki/Change_request`

- ▶ `https://msdn.microsoft.com/en-us/library/ee332482(v=vs.100).aspx`

Getting ready

In this recipe, we will create Jasmine tests corresponding to a change request using both the first and the previous recipes from this chapter. For more information, refer to the first recipe, *Defining Jasmine specs corresponding to user story*, and the previous recipe, *Implementing Jasmine tests with Data-Driven approach*.

Let's assume that there is a new rule introduced for all taxpayers. According to the new rule, taxpayers should get the benefit of the Individual Retirement Account (IRA) contribution and it should be deducted from their gross income before the tax/TDS calculation.

So, based on the preceding information, let's also add the following acceptance criteria to both the scenarios described in the first recipe:

- ▶ An IRA contribution of $5,500 should be applied for single taxpayers (the IRA contribution should be deducted from gross income before the tax/TDS calculation)

How to do it...

You need to perform the following steps to create Jasmine tests corresponding to this change request:

1. Create a US_TaxEstimation_WithChangeRequest_spec.js spec file under the /spec folder and get the following code from the US_TaxEstimation_DataDriven_spec.js spec file created in the previous recipe, *Implementing Jasmine tests with a Data-Driven approach*:

```
describe("Employee of <ABC> Inc:",function(){
  describe("Tax Estimation:",function(){
        var fixtureFile,fixtures, myResult;
    beforeEach(function() {
          loadFixtures('TaxCalculator.html');
          //Start - Load JSON Files to provide input data for all
    the test scenarios
          fixtureFile = "FixtureInputData.json";
          fixtures = loadJSONFixtures(fixtureFile);
          myResult = fixtures[fixtureFile];
          //End - Load JSON Files to provide input data for all
    the test scenarios
      });
      describe("Category: Single Taxpayer",function(){
        //Scenario-1
```

```
describe("When: Taxable income is $111,200: ",function(){
  beforeEach(function() {
    $("#taxFilingStatusID").val(myResult[0].
TaxFilingStatus);
    $("#taxGrossIncomeID").val(myResult[0].GrossIncome);
    $('#mySubmitID').trigger("click");
  });
  it("standard deduction should be applied", function(){
    expect(Number($('#taxGrossIncomeID').val())).
toEqual(111200);
    expect(Number($("#myTaxableIncome").html())).
toEqual(105000);
  });
  it("10 percent Tax Rate should be applied for the income
between $0 and $9,075", function(){
    expect(myTDS_TaxBracket[0]).toEqual(907.5);
  });
  it("Tax on income  $0 to $9,075 + " + "15 percent Tax Rate
should be applied for the income between $9,076 and $36,900",
function(){
    expect(myTDS_TaxBracket[1]).toEqual(5081.25);
  });
  it("Tax on income  $0 to $36,900 + " + "25 percent
Tax Rate should be applied for the income between $36,901 and
$89,350", function(){
    expect(myTDS_TaxBracket[2]).toEqual(18193.75);
  });
  it("Tax on income  $0 to $89,350 + " + "28 percent
Tax Rate should be applied for the income between $89,351 and
$186,350", function(){
    expect(Number($("#myEstimatedTax").html())).
toEqual(22575.75);
  });
});
//Scenario-2
describe("When: Taxable income is $450,000: ",function(){
  beforeEach(function() {
    $("#taxFilingStatusID").val(myResult[1].
TaxFilingStatus);
    $("#taxGrossIncomeID").val(myResult[1].GrossIncome);
    $('#mySubmitID').trigger("click");
  });
  //Test Code to implement scenario 2.....
```

```
            it("standard deduction should be applied ", function(){
                expect(Number($('#taxGrossIncomeID').val())).
toEqual(450000);
                expect(Number($("#myTaxableIncome").html())).
toEqual(443800);
            });
            it("10 percent Tax Rate should be applied for the income
between $0 and $9,075", function(){
                expect(myTDS_TaxBracket[0]).toEqual(907.5);
            });
            it("Tax on income  $0 to $9,075 + " + "15 percent Tax Rate
should be applied for the income between $9,076 and $36,900",
function(){
                expect(myTDS_TaxBracket[1]).toEqual(5081.25);
            });
            it("Tax on income  $0 to $36,900 + " + "25 percent
Tax Rate should be applied for the income between $36,901 and
$89,350", function(){
                expect(myTDS_TaxBracket[2]).toEqual(18193.75);
            });
            it("Tax on income  $0 to $89,350 + " + "28 percent
Tax Rate should be applied for the income between $89,351 and
$186,350", function(){
                expect(myTDS_TaxBracket[3]).toEqual(45353.75);
            });
            it("Tax on income  $0 to $186,350 + " + "33 percent
Tax Rate should be applied for the income between $186,351 and
$405,100", function(){
                expect(myTDS_TaxBracket[4]).toEqual(117541.25);
            });
            it("Tax on income  $0 to $405,100 + " + "35 percent
Tax Rate should be applied for the income between $405,101 and
$406,750", function(){
                expect(myTDS_TaxBracket[5]).toEqual(118118.75);
            });
            it("Tax on income  $0 to $406,750 + " + "39.6 percent
Tax Rate should be applied for the income more than $406,750",
function(){
                expect(Number($("#myEstimatedTax").html())).
toEqual(132790.55);
            });
        });
      });
    });
});
```

For learning purposes, we have created a separate spec file `US_TaxEstimation_WithChangeRequest_spec.js`. However, in real time, it is recommend you refactor the existing test code in the same spec file `US_TaxEstimation_DataDriven_spec.js`, instead of creating a new one.

2. Now, as per the acceptance criteria, let's update the test data in the external file `FixtureInputData.json`, created in the previous recipe, using the following data:

```
[
{
"TaxFilingStatus": "S",
"GrossIncome": 111200,
"IRAContribution": 5500,
"Exemptions": 0,
"Dependent": 0
},
{
"TaxFilingStatus": "S",
"GrossIncome": 450000,
"IRAContribution": 5500,
"Exemptions": 0,
"Dependent": 0
}
]
```

Here, you can see that we set the value of `IRAContribution` as $5,500 as per the new acceptance criteria.

3. Let's refactor the test code for scenario 1 only and add the spec for a new acceptance criteria for scenario 1, using the following code:

```
//Scenario-1
describe("When: Taxable income is $111,200: ",function(){
  beforeEach(function() {
     $("#taxFilingStatusID").val(myResult[0].TaxFilingStatus);
     $("#taxGrossIncomeID").val(myResult[0].GrossIncome);
     $("#taxIRAID").val(myResult[0].IRAContribution);
     $('#mySubmitID').trigger("click");
  });
  it("IRA Contribution should be adjusted from Gross Income",
function(){
     expect(Number($("#myAdjustedGrossIncome").html())).
toEqual(105700);
  });
  it("standard deduction should be applied", function(){
     expect(Number($('#taxGrossIncomeID').val())).toEqual(111200);
     expect(Number($("#myTaxableIncome").html())).toEqual(99500);
  });
```

```
    it("10 percent Tax Rate should be applied for the income between
$0 and $9,075", function(){
        expect(myTDS_TaxBracket[0]).toEqual(907.5);
    });
    it("Tax on income  $0 to $9,075 + " + "15 percent Tax Rate
should be applied for the income between $9,076 and $36,900",
function(){
        expect(myTDS_TaxBracket[1]).toEqual(5081.25);
    });
    it("Tax on income  $0 to $36,900 + " + "25 percent Tax Rate
should be applied for the income between $36,901 and $89,350",
function(){
        expect(myTDS_TaxBracket[2]).toEqual(18193.75);
    });
    it("Tax on income  $0 to $89,350 + " + "28 percent Tax Rate
should be applied for the income between $89,351 and $186,350",
function(){
        expect(Number($("#myEstimatedTax").html())).toEqual(21035.75);
    });
});
```

In the preceding code snapshot, you can see that we configured the value of
IRAContribution to be $5,500, as per the new rule, and created a new spec to
validate it. Furthermore, to nullify the impact of the new changes, we also updated
the expected value corresponding to the impacted specs.

4. Run the US_TaxEstimation_WithChangeRequest_spec.js spec file with
   Jasmine runner for both the scenarios. You should see the following screenshot,
   letting you know that three specs are failing for scenario 1:

5. Now we need to refactor and implement the code corresponding to the new rule. Let's enhance and refactor the JavaScript code for the `getTaxDetails` function created under the `US_Tax_Estimation.js` file. Use the following updated code for the `getTaxDetails` function:

```javascript
function getTaxDetails(){
  //Define variables to collects details
  var myTaxFilingStatus, myGrossIncome, myIRAContribution,
myStandardDeduction, myExemptions, myDependent;
  var myTax=0; //Variable to hold the value of estimated tax
  myTaxFilingStatus = $("#taxFilingStatusID").val();
  if ($("#taxGrossIncomeID").val() > 0) {
    myGrossIncome = $("#taxGrossIncomeID").val();
  }
  else {
    myGrossIncome = 0;
  }
  //Get IRA Contribution
  if ($("#taxIRAID").val() > 0) {
    myIRAContribution = $("#taxIRAID").val();
    myGrossIncome = myGrossIncome - Number(myIRAContribution);
    $("#myAdjustedGrossIncome").html(myGrossIncome);
  }
  else {
    myIRAContribution = 0;
  }
  if (myTaxFilingStatus != null) {
    myStandardDeduction= getStandardDeduction(myTaxFilingStatus);
    myGrossIncome = myGrossIncome - myStandardDeduction;
  }
  else {
    myStandardDeduction= 0;
  }
  $("#myTaxableIncome").html(myGrossIncome);
  myTax= calculateTDS(myGrossIncome);
  $("#myEstimatedTax").html(myTax);
};
```

In the preceding code snapshot, you can see that we introduced a new `if-else` block and implemented the code corresponding to the new spec (that the IRA contribution should be adjusted to the gross income). Here, we simply checked that if the IRA contribution is greater than zero, the adjusted gross income should be considered as gross income minus the IRA contribution.

The `US_Tax_Estimation.js` file was created in the second recipe of this chapter, *Implementing Jasmine specs with Web/HTML*.

6. Now following the same pattern, refactor the test code for scenario 2 and run the `US_TaxEstimation_WithChangeRequest_spec.js` spec file with Jasmine runner for both the scenarios. You should see the following screenshot, letting you know that all the specs are passing:

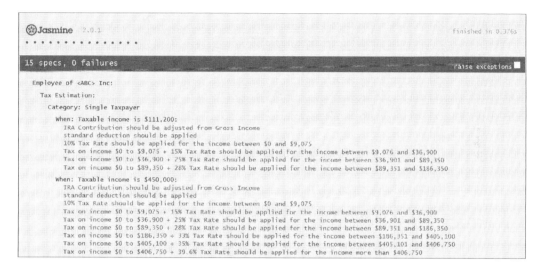

In the preceding screenshot, you can see that the Tax Calculator application/utility is able to estimate tax/TDS as per the new change request for the **Single Taxpayer** category.

So far in this book, we have learned how to develop an application with Jasmine using the Behavior-Driven Development approach. We also looked at how Jasmine spies and custom matchers play an important role in testing applications from an E2E perspective. We learned how to implement Jasmine specs for jQuery/Ajax and fixtures along with code coverage analysis. Finally, we implemented Jasmine specs with Web/HTML using the BDD process and the Data-Driven approach.

I would recommend practicing what you have learned by implementing more scenarios and completing development of the tax/TDS application. For instance, you can make a provision in your application for evaluating tax/TDS for other tax categories (head of household, married-separately, married-jointly, and trust) along with various tax exemption options (itemized deductions, earned income, tax credit, child tax credit, personal exemption, and so on).

Index

E

Esprima
 about 183
 URL 183
exceptions
 Jasmine test, writing for 77-84
expect function
 about 4
 actual value 11
 expected value 11
expectation
 about 4
 adding, to test 11-15

G

groups
 specs, organizing into 103-107

H

HTML fixtures
 Jasmine specs, designing 146-153

I

inject function
 about 199
 URL 199
istanbul
 about 174
 URL 174
 used, for generating code coverage 180-185

J

Jasmine 2
jasmine-ajax plugin
 about 143
 URL 143
jasmine.any function
 used, for designing Jasmine tests 132-136
jasmine-jquery plugin
 about 147
 URL 147

jasmine-node package
 about 216
 URL 216
jasmine.objectContaining function
 used, for designing Jasmine tests 132-136
Jasmine Standalone release
 URL, for downloading 2
Jasmine test
 Acceptance Criteria,
  implementing to 100-103
 creating, for change request 246-253
 designing, jasmine.any function
  used 132-136
 designing, jasmine.objectContaining function
  used 132-136
 expectation, adding to 11-15
 implementing, corresponding to specs 93-99
 implementing, with Data-Driven
  approach 239-246
 matchers, adding to 11-15
 matchers, applying to 16-26
 pending specs, declaring with 84-87
 setup function, applying to 26-30
 specs, adding to 6-10
 teardown function, applying to 26-30
 writing 2-5
 writing, BDD process used 36-46
 writing, custom equality tester function
  used 66-68
 writing, for AngularJS 195-201
 writing, for CoffeeScript 202-210
 writing, for exceptions 77-84
 writing, for mocking JavaScript timeout
  functions 136-138
 writing, for Node.js 211-216
 writing, spies used 110-117
 writing, spyOn() method used 110-117
 writing, TDD process used 36-46
 writing, tracking properties used 118-126
 writing, with custom matchers 68-77
 writing, with custom spy method 126-132
JavaScript timeout functions
 mocking 136-138
jQuery
 Jasmine specs, writing 153-159
JSON fixtures
 Jasmine specs, designing 146-152

K

karma
about 174
URL 174
used, for generating code coverage 180-185

M

matchers
about 65
adding, to test 11-15
applying, to Jasmine test 16-26
toBe 16
toBcCloseTo 16
toBeContain 16
toBeDefined 16
toBeFalsy 16
toBeGreaterThan 16
toBeLessThan 16
toBeNull 16
toBeTruthy 16
toBeUndefined 16
toEqual 16
toMatch 16
mocks 109

N

nested suites
defining, for meaningful specs 56-64
Node.js
about 174, 211
Jasmine tests, writing 211-216
URL 174, 211
npm
about 174
URL 175
used, for configuring code coverage
tools 174-180

P

pending specs
about 58
declaring, with Jasmine test 84-87
Product Requirement Document (PRD) 89

R

regular expression
about 17
URL 17

S

scrum (software development)
reference link 90
setup function
applying, to Jasmine test 26-30
Software Requirement Specification (SRS) 89
SpecRunner.html file 5
specs
adding, to Jasmine test 6-10
defining, for user story 218-223
designing, with HTML fixtures 146-153
designing, with JSON fixtures 146-153
implementing, with Web/HTML 223-238
Jasmine test, implementing 93-99
organizing, into groups 103-107
organizing, into subgroups 103-107
writing, by analyzing test
    requirements 90-93
writing, custom jQuery matchers
    used 160-170
writing, done() function used 170-172
writing, for AJAX 141-146
writing, for jQuery 153-159
writing, for uncovered
    branches/code 185-190
writing, with nested suites 56-64
spies
about 110
used, for writing Jasmine tests 110-117
spyOn() method
used, for writing Jasmine tests 110-117
subgroups
specs, organizing into 103-107

T

teardown function
applying, to Jasmine test 26-30
test requirements
analyzing, by writing useful specs 90-93

Thank you for buying
Jasmine Cookbook

About Packt Publishing

Packt, pronounced 'packed', published its first book, *Mastering phpMyAdmin for Effective MySQI Management*, in April 2004, and subsequently continued to specialize in publishing highly focused books on specific technologies and solutions.

Our books and publications share the experiences of your fellow IT professionals in adapting and customizing today's systems, applications, and frameworks. Our solution-based books give you the knowledge and power to customize the software and technologies you're using to get the job done. Packt books are more specific and less general than the IT books you have seen in the past. Our unique business model allows us to bring you more focused information, giving you more of what you need to know, and less of what you don't.

Packt is a modern yet unique publishing company that focuses on producing quality, cutting-edge books for communities of developers, administrators, and newbies alike. For more information, please visit our website at www.packtpub.com.

About Packt Open Source

In 2010, Packt launched two new brands, Packt Open Source and Packt Enterprise, in order to continue its focus on specialization. This book is part of the Packt open source brand, home to books published on software built around open source licenses, and offering information to anybody from advanced developers to budding web designers. The Open Source brand also runs Packt's open source Royalty Scheme, by which Packt gives a royalty to each open source project about whose software a book is sold.

Writing for Packt

We welcome all inquiries from people who are interested in authoring. Book proposals should be sent to author@packtpub.com. If your book idea is still at an early stage and you would like to discuss it first before writing a formal book proposal, then please contact us; one of our commissioning editors will get in touch with you.

We're not just looking for published authors; if you have strong technical skills but no writing experience, our experienced editors can help you develop a writing career, or simply get some additional reward for your expertise.

Web App Testing Using Knockout.JS

ISBN: 978-1-78398-284-4   Paperback: 154 pages

Design, implement, and maintain a fully tested JavaScript web application using Knockout.JS

1. Test JavaScript web applications using one of the most known unit testing libraries—Jasmine.js.

2. Leverage the two way bindings and dependency tracking mechanism to test web applications using Knockout.js.

3. The book covers different JavaScript application testing strategies supported by real-world examples.

JavaScript Mobile Application Development

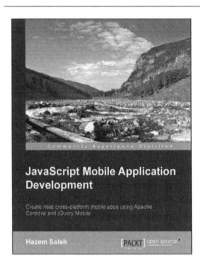

ISBN: 978-1-78355-417-1   Paperback: 332 pages

Create neat cross-platform mobile apps using Apache Cordova and jQuery Mobile

1. Configure your Android, iOS, and Window Phone 8 development environments.

2. Extend the power of Apache Cordova by creating your own Apache Cordova cross-platform mobile plugins.

3. Enhance the quality and the robustness of your Apache Cordova mobile application by unit testing its logic using Jasmine.

Please check **www.PacktPub.com** for information on our titles

Jasmine JavaScript Testing

ISBN: 978-1-78216-720-4   Paperback: 146 pages

Leverage the power of unit testing to create bigger and better JavaScript applications

1. Learn the power of test-driven development while creating a fully-featured web application.

2. Understand the best practices for modularization and code organization while putting your application to scale.

3. Leverage the power of frameworks such as BackboneJS and jQuery while maintaining the code quality.

JavaScript Unit Testing

ISBN: 978-1-78216-062-5   Paperback: 190 pages

Your comprehensive and practical guide to efficiently performing and automating JavaScript unit testing

1. Learn and understand, using practical examples, synchronous and asynchronous JavaScript unit testing.

2. Cover the most popular JavaScript Unit Testing Frameworks including Jasmine, YUITest, QUnit, and JsTestDriver.

3. Automate and integrate your JavaScript Unit Testing for ease and efficiency.

Please check **www.PacktPub.com** for information on our titles

Made in the USA
Lexington, KY
07 November 2015